Experimental Philosophy

EXPERIMENTAL PHILOSOPHY

Edited by
Joshua Knobe
Shaun Nichols

OXFORD
UNIVERSITY PRESS

2008

OXFORD
UNIVERSITY PRESS

Oxford University Press, Inc., publishes works that further
Oxford University's objective of excellence
in research, scholarship, and education.

Oxford   New York
Auckland   Cape Town   Dar es Salaam   Hong Kong   Karachi
Kuala Lumpur   Madrid   Melbourne   Mexico City   Nairobi
New Delhi   Shanghai   Taipei   Toronto

With offices in
Argentina   Austria   Brazil   Chile   Czech Republic   France   Greece
Guatemala   Hungary   Italy   Japan   Poland   Portugal   Singapore
South Korea   Switzerland   Thailand   Turkey   Ukraine   Vietnam

Copyright © 2008 by Oxford University Press, Inc.

Published by Oxford University Press, Inc.
198 Madison Avenue, New York, New York 10016

www.oup.com

Oxford is a registered trademark of Oxford University Press

Library of Congress Cataloging-in-Publication Data
Experimental philosophy / edited by
Joshua Knobe and Shaun Nichols.
    p. cm.
ISBN 978-0-19-532325-2; 978-0-19-532326-9 (pbk.)
1. Philosophy—Research. 2. Psychology—Research. I. Knobe, Joshua Michael, 1974–
II. Nichols, Shaun.
B52.E97 2008
107.2—dc22   2007031136

9 8 7 6 5 4 3 2 1
Printed in the United States of America
on acid-free paper

Preface

This volume is intended as an introduction to the new field of experimental philosophy. Reprinted here are seven influential papers that apply experimental methods to a variety of different philosophical issues. These papers should offer a sense of the methods and scope of the work that has been done in experimental philosophy thus far and, we hope, inspire future researchers to apply experimental approaches in areas that still remain unexplored. We have also included an introductory chapter that takes up more general metaphilosophical questions concerning the methods and aims of experimental philosophy, as well as four papers offering theoretical reflections on specific issues arising out of existing experimental work.

We would like to thank Michael Gill, Ron Mallon, Jesse Prinz, and Walter Sinnott-Armstrong for excellent advice on various aspects of the volume. We would also like to thank Peter Ohlin of Oxford University Press, not only for his help in preparing the manuscript, but also for suggesting the volume to us in the first place.

On a broader level, we are deeply grateful to Steve Stich, who has been generous to us in so many ways—intellectually, personally, and professionally.

Finally and especially, we'd like to thank our spouses, Alina and Heather. When the experimental philosophy movement first began, it was regarded as pretty far outside the mainstream of academic philosophy, and we have often felt a great deal of anxiety about our work. Alina and Heather, however, have never doubted us. It's hard to imagine how we could have carried on without them.

Credits

We would like to thank the publishers for permission to reprint eight of the essays that appear in this volume. The original publication details are as follows:

Joshua Knobe. 2006. "The Concept of Intentional Action: A Case Study in the Uses of Folk Psychology." *Philosophical Studies* 130: 203–231. Used with kind permission of Springer Science and Business Media.

Edouard Machery, Ron Mallon, Shaun Nichols, and Stephen Stich. 2004. "Semantics Cross-Cultural Style." *Cognition* 92: B1–B12. Used with permission of Elsevier.

Thomas Nadelhoffer. 2006. "Bad Acts, Blameworthy Agents, and Intentional Actions: Some Problems for Jury Impartiality." *Philosophical Explorations* 9: 203–220. Used with permission of Taylor & Francis Ltd., http://www.tandf.co.uk/journals

Eddy Nahmias, Stephen Morris, Thomas Nadelhoffer, and Jason Turner. 2006. "Is Incompatibilism Intuitive?" *Philosophy and Phenomenological Research* 73: 28–53. Used with permission of *Philosophy and Phenomenological Research*.

Shaun Nichols and Joshua Knobe. 2007. "Moral Responsibility and Determinism: The Cognitive Science of Folk Intuitions". *Noûs.* Used with the permission of Blackwell Publishing.

Ernest Sosa. 2007. "Experimental Philosophy and Philosophical Intuition." *Philosophical Studies* 132: 99–107. Used with kind permission of Springer Science and Business Media.

Jonathan M. Weinberg, Shaun Nichols, and Stephen Stich. 2001. "Normativity and Epistemic Intuitions." *Philosophical Topics* 29: 429–460. Used with permission of Arkansas Press, www.uapress.com

Rob Woolfolk, John Doris, and John Darley. 2006. "Identification, Situational Constraint, and Social Cognition: Studies in the Attribution of Moral Responsibility." *Cognition* 100: 283–301. Used with permission of Elsevier.

Contents

Contributors

FIERY CUSHMAN, Harvard University

JOHN M. DARLEY, Princeton University

JOHN M. DORIS, Washington University

JOSHUA KNOBE, University of North Carolina

EDOUARD MACHERY, University of Pittsburgh

RON MALLON, University of Utah

ALFRED MELE, Florida State University

STEPHEN G. MORRIS, Missouri Western State University

THOMAS NADELHOFFER, Dickinson College

EDDY NAHMIAS, Georgia State University

SHAUN NICHOLS, University of Arizona

JESSE J. PRINZ, University of North Carolina

WALTER SINNOTT-ARMSTRONG, Dartmouth College

ERNEST SOSA, Rutgers University

STEPHEN P. STICH, Rutgers University

JASON TURNER, Rutgers University

JONATHAN M. WEINBERG, Indiana University

ROBERT L. WOOLFOLK, Rutgers University

Experimental Philosophy

1

An Experimental Philosophy Manifesto

Joshua Knobe & Shaun Nichols

It used to be a commonplace that the discipline of philosophy was deeply concerned with questions about the human condition. Philosophers thought about human beings and how their minds worked. They took an interest in reason and passion, culture and innate ideas, the origins of people's moral and religious beliefs. On this traditional conception, it wasn't particularly important to keep philosophy clearly distinct from psychology, history, or political science. Philosophers were concerned, in a very general way, with questions about how everything fit together.

The new movement of *experimental philosophy* seeks a return to this traditional vision. Like philosophers of centuries past, we are concerned with questions about how human beings actually happen to be. We recognize that such an inquiry will involve us in the study of phenomena that are messy, contingent, and highly variable across times and places, but we do not see how that fact is supposed to make the inquiry any less genuinely philosophical. On the contrary, we think that many of the deepest questions of philosophy can only be properly addressed by immersing oneself in the messy, contingent, highly variable truths about how human beings really are.

But there is also an important respect in which experimental philosophers depart from this earlier tradition. Unlike the philosophers of centuries past, we think that a critical method for figuring out how human beings think is to go out and actually run systematic empirical studies. Hence, experimental philosophers proceed by conducting experimental investigations of the psychological processes underlying people's intuitions about central philosophical issues. Again and again, these investigations have challenged familiar assumptions, showing that people do not actually think about these issues in anything like the way philosophers had assumed.

Reactions to this movement have been largely polarized. Many find it an exciting new way to approach the basic philosophical concerns that attracted them to philosophy in the first place. But many others regard the movement as insidious—a specter haunting contemporary philosophy. We suspect that the subsequent cries for exorcism are often based on an incomplete understanding of the diverse ambitions of experimental philosophy. In this brief manifesto, we aim to make clear the nature of experimental philosophy, as well as its continuity with traditional philosophy.

1. EXPERIMENTAL PHILOSOPHY AND CONCEPTUAL ANALYSIS

Experimental philosophers are certainly not the first to think that important philosophical lessons can be learned by looking carefully at ordinary people's intuitions about cases. This methodological approach has a long history within the research program sometimes known as 'conceptual analysis.' It may be helpful, then, to begin by discussing the ways in which experimental philosophy departs from this earlier program.

Of course, the most salient difference is just the fact that experimental philosophers conduct experiments and conceptual analysts do not. Thus, the conceptual analyst might write, "In this case, one would surely say...," while the experimental philosopher would write, "In this case, 79% of subjects said..." But this is only the most superficial difference. Over time, experimental philosophers have developed a way of thinking about these issues that departs in truly substantial respects from the approaches familiar from conceptual analysis.

There is no single method of conceptual analysis, but typically a conceptual analysis attempts to identify precisely the meaning of a concept by breaking the concept into its essential components, components which themselves typically involve further concepts. In an attempt to determine the meaning of a philosophically important concept, one often considers whether the concept applies in various possible cases.

The aim of this project is to achieve ever greater levels of precision. Typically, one starts out with a nebulous sense of how to pick out the property in question. Perhaps something like this:

> Knowledge seems to involve some kind of counterfactual relation between people's beliefs and actual facts.

But, over time, one hopes to arrive at a more precise analysis. For example:

S knows that p if and only if
1. p
2. S believes that p
3. Not-$p \rightarrow$ S does not believe p
4. $p \rightarrow$ S believes that p

This research program is, by all accounts, exceedingly difficult. The philosopher toils to put together his set of necessary and sufficient conditions for the concept of interest, let's say PENCIL. But then, when he presents his results, it inevitably happens that some guy in the back of the room gives an example of an object that meets all the conditions but isn't a pencil. This sends the philosopher back to his study to make some adjustments in his definition.

The program of conceptual analysis is a highly controversial one. Some believe that it is making considerable progress and will eventually converge on correct analyses of certain important concepts; others feel that we have never succeeded in analyzing anything in terms of anything else and that this failure points to some intrinsic flaw in the assumptions that underlie the program itself. Regardless of how one feels about this controversy, it is important to understand how the aim of experimental philosophy differs from that of conceptual analysis.

As far as we know, no experimental philosopher has ever offered an analysis of one concept in terms of another. Instead, the aim is usually to provide an account of the factors that influence applications of a concept, and in particular, the *internal psychological processes* that underlie such applications. Progress here is measured not in terms of the precision with which one can characterize the actual patterns of people's intuitions but in terms of the degree to which one can achieve explanatory depth. Typically, one starts out with a fairly superficial characterization of certain patterns in people's intuitions. Maybe something like this:

> People are more inclined to regard an agent as morally
> responsible when the case is described in vivid and concrete
> detail than they are when the case is described more abstractly.

The goal, however, is to provide some deeper explanation of why the intuitions come out this way. For example:

> People are more inclined to regard an agent as morally
> responsible when they have a strong affective reaction to
> his or her transgression.

And ultimately, the hope is that one will be able to arrive at a more fundamental understanding of people's thinking in the relevant domain. Maybe something like this:

> People's intuitions about moral responsibility are shaped by the
> interaction of two different systems—one that employs an abstract
> theory, another that relies more on immediate affective reactions.

But note that, even if we are able to construct a theory of this sort, we still may not be able to predict people's intuitions in all possible cases. Indeed, if our theory is that people's intuitions are shaped by their affective reactions to the case at hand, we would not be able to perfectly characterize the pattern of people's intuitions unless we could develop a complete theory of the nature of people's affective reactions.

In one sense, then, it seems that the task of experimental philosophy is considerably less demanding than that of conceptual analysis. As long as we can offer an account of the internal psychological processes that underlie our judgments, we do not also need to find necessary and sufficient conditions for the application of the concept in particular cases. Some philosophers think that this fact gives us reason for optimism. They think it amounts to trading an impossible task for one in which researchers are actually making substantial progress.

In another sense, though, the task of experimental philosophy is quite a bit more demanding than that of conceptual analysis as traditionally practiced. Experimental philosophers would not be content just to have an understanding of the patterns of intuition one finds on the surface. Indeed, even if we had a complete and perfectly accurate characterization of those patterns, we might feel that all of the truly deep questions still remained to be answered. What we really want to know is *why* people have the intuitions they do.

2. EXPERIMENTAL PHILOSOPHY AND PHILOSOPHICAL SIGNIFICANCE

With these considerations in the background, we can turn to an issue that might at first seem rather puzzling. The puzzle arises from a kind of gulf between the *evidence* that experimental philosophers are actually gathering and the *theories* that this evidence is alleged to support. In a typical experimental philosophy paper, the evidence being gathered is about the percentages of people who hold various sorts of intuitions, but the theories under discussion are not about people's intuitions but about substantive philosophical questions in epistemology, metaphysics, or ethics. It may appear, at least on first glance, that there must be some sleight of hand involved here. How on earth could information about the statistical distribution of intuitions ever give us reason to accept or reject a particular philosophical view?

The problem only becomes more acute when one thinks about how the approach could actually be applied in practice. Suppose, for example, that a philosopher has thought deeply about a particular case and, after sustained reflection, concluded that the agent in this case is morally responsible. And now suppose that experimental studies reveal that a majority of subjects (say, 63%) hold the opposite opinion. How could such a result possibly have any impact on her philosophical work? Is she supposed to change her mind just because she finds herself in the minority?

Of course she isn't. Philosophical inquiry has never been a popularity contest, and experimental philosophy is not about to turn it into one. If the experimental results are to have any meaningful impact here, it must be in some more indirect way. The mere fact that a certain percentage of subjects hold a particular view cannot on its own have a significant impact on our philosophical work. Instead, it must be that the statistical information is somehow helping us to gain access to some other fact and that this other fact—whatever it turns out to be—is what is really playing a role in philosophical inquiry.

Our aim in this section is to explain how this trick is supposed to work. The exposition here is somewhat complicated by the fact that different projects within experimental philosophy have used fundamentally different approaches. Hence, it is not possible to point to a single basic viewpoint and say: "This viewpoint lies at the heart of all contemporary work in experimental philosophy." The only way to present this material is to look separately at a number of different strands within the movement. Although experimental philosophy is a young movement, there are already more strands than we can adequately cover.

For instance, there has been interesting work on the meanings of words and on cultural universals that we will not be able to treat here. Instead, our focus will be on three strands that have proven especially influential.

2.1. Sources and Warrant

It is a commonplace that sometimes people acquire beliefs from untrustworthy sources. Some cultural sources—some books, some news media, some people— are manifestly unreliable. If the source of your belief that there is extraterrestrial life is the *National Enquirer,* then your belief lacks adequate justification.

But concerns about the sources of our beliefs are not limited to processes that take place outside of us; they can extend to processes inside the human psyche. Just as we might learn that a belief comes from an unreliable *external* source (e.g., an unreliable newspaper), we might learn that a belief is the result of an unreliable or distorting *internal* source (e.g., an unreliable cognitive process). This leads us to the first major goal of experimental philosophy. The goal is to determine what leads us to have the intuitions we do about free will, moral responsibility, the afterlife. The ultimate hope is that we can use this information to help determine whether the psychological sources of the beliefs undercut the warrant for the beliefs.

The basic approach here should be familiar from the history of philosophy. Just take a look at nineteenth-century philosophy of religion. At the time, there was a raging debate about whether people's religious beliefs were warranted, and a number of philosophers (Marx, Nietzsche, Feuerbach, etc.) contributed to this debate by offering specific hypotheses about the psychological sources of religious faith. These hypotheses led to an explosion of further discussion that proved enormously valuable for a broad variety of philosophical issues.

But then something strange happened. Although arguments of this basic type had traditionally been regarded as extremely important, they came to occupy a far less significant role in the distinctive form of philosophy that rose to prominence in the twentieth century. The rise of analytic philosophy led to a diminished interest in questions about, for example, the fundamental sources of religious faith and a heightened interest in more technical questions that could be addressed from the armchair. The shift here is a somewhat peculiar one. It is not that anyone actually offered arguments against the idea that it was worthwhile to understand the underlying sources of our beliefs; rather, this traditional form of inquiry seems simply to have fallen out of fashion. We regard this as a highly regrettable development. It seems to us that questions about the sources of our religious, moral, and metaphysical beliefs are deeply important questions and that there was never any good reason to stop pursuing them. Our aim now is to return to these questions, this time armed with the methods of contemporary cognitive science.

When experimental research is understood in this broader context, one can easily see how it might have important philosophical implications. It is not that the actual percentages themselves are supposed to directly impact our philosophical inquiries. Rather, the idea is that these experimental results can have a kind of indirect impact. First we use the experimental results to develop a theory about the underlying psychological processes that generate people's intuitions; then we use our theory about the psychological processes to determine whether or not those intuitions are warranted.

Of course, this sort of question becomes especially pressing in cases where the intuitions are actually serving as evidence for a particular philosophical view. Thus, suppose we return to our hypothetical philosopher and her question about the nature of moral responsibility. She considers a particular case and finds herself inclined to think that the agent described in this case is morally responsible. But now there is often an additional question—can the intuition be *trusted?* Clearly, an intuition developed in a jealous rage is less trustworthy than one developed after calm and careful consideration. Thus, if our hypothetical philosopher discovers that her intuition about a case is driven by such distorting emotional reactions, this will and should affect how much she trusts the intuition.

Not only does it seem to us that empirical considerations can be relevant here; it seems to us just *obvious* that empirical considerations are relevant. Surely, the degree to which an intuition is warranted depends in part on the process that generated it, and surely the best way to figure out which processes generate which intuitions is to go out and gather empirical data. How else is one supposed to proceed?

But, unfortunately, what seems obvious to one philosopher often seems obviously mistaken to another. Instead of greeting these methodological remarks as simple truisms (which, we continue to think, is what they really are), many philosophers have reacted by offering various sorts of objections. We focus here on four of the most prominent.

The Expertise Objection, Version 1

"Throughout the academy, we rely on experts to advance inquiry. It would be absurd for physicists or biologists to conduct surveys on folk intuitions about physics or biology. Rather, physicists and biologists specialize in their domains and advance the field by exploiting their specialized knowledge. The same is true of philosophy. Just as physicists don't consult folk physics, so philosophers needn't consult folk philosophy."

Reply: This view of academic specialization strikes us as entirely apt for some philosophical concerns. In some areas of philosophy, the disputes float free of commonsense intuitions. If we want to know whether the representational theory of mind is superior to connectionist alternatives, it would be ridiculous to think that we should invest our resources mulling over what the folk think about connectionism. That debate turns on facts about cognitive architecture, not facts about what people think about cognitive architecture. But in many other areas of philosophy, it's much harder to maintain that the disputes are so disconnected from commonsense intuitions. Indeed, for many standard philosophical problems—for example, problems concerning free will, personal identity, knowledge, and morality—if it weren't for commonsense intuitions, there wouldn't *be* a felt philosophical problem. The problem of moral responsibility, for instance, can't be read off of the biological or psychological facts. It arises because people think of themselves as morally responsible, and this seems at odds with other important and plausible world views. Consider how marginalizing it would be to say, "We philosophers have written a lot about something we call 'moral responsibility,' though our notion is completely unrelated to anything ordinary people mean by their homonymous term 'moral responsibility.'" Philosophical discussions of moral responsibility are captivating precisely because they engage our everyday views of ourselves, by threatening, supporting, or exposing problems in those views. Like many other central philosophical notions, *moral responsibility* is not reserved for specialists.

The Expertise Objection, Version 2

"It's true that we are concerned with questions about commonsense concepts. The point is just that philosophers can use those very concepts—the ordinary commonsense concepts that people employ every day—with a precision and subtlety that ordinary people can't quite achieve. For the philosophers are specially trained to draw fine distinctions and to think carefully; and philosophers bring these skills to bear on uncovering the true nature of our commonsense intuitions. As a result, philosophers have a much more tightly honed ability to arrive at unsullied intuitions about cases than the folk."

Reply: This version of the expertise objection argument brings up a number of fascinating issues, but we don't see how it even begins to serve as an objection to the practice of experimental philosophy. On the contrary, we would love to know more about the ways in which philosophers differ from ordinary folks, and it seems to us that the best way to find out would be to run some experiments. One could devise a series of questions and then give those questions both to philosophers and non-philosophers, checking to see how intuitions differed between the two groups. Although these experiments have not yet been conducted, we have a tentative guess about how the results would turn out. Specifically, our guess is that the overall pattern will be far more complex—and far more interesting—than anyone could have predicted from the armchair.

Furthermore, even if we discover important differences between the philosophers and the folk, it would hardly follow that data from the folk are irrelevant. Rather, the whole pattern of the data might tell us something important about the ultimate source of the philosophical problems. Philosophers are less prone to certain mistakes when processing thought experiments. On the other hand, the folk are less likely to have their intuitions biased by extensive philosophical training and theoretical affiliations. As a result, if problems like free will, moral responsibility, and personal identity flow from commonsense, then to understand these problems, it would be myopic to look only at the responses of philosophers. Rather, to understand the intuitions that are at the core of philosophical problems, one would surely want to look at different groups to see whether interesting patterns of similarity and difference emerge. The extant work in experimental philosophy already suggests that such an investigation will reveal some very interesting patterns indeed.

The That's-Not-All-There-Is Objection

"You are simply missing the whole point of philosophy. Philosophy isn't just a matter of looking at people's intuitions and trying to understand how people think. Rather, when we are truly philosophizing, we need to subject people's intuitions to criticism, looking at arguments that might show that people's intuitions are actually mistaken in certain cases."

Reply: Here again, we think the point is well taken, but we can't see how it is supposed to be an objection to experimental philosophy. No one is suggesting that we boot out all of the moral philosophers and replace them with experimentalists, nor is anyone suggesting that we do away with any of the methods that have traditionally been used for figuring out whether people's intuitions truly are right or wrong. What we are proposing is just to add another tool to the philosopher's toolbox. That is, we are proposing another method (on top of all of the ones that already exist) for pursuing certain philosophical inquiries. Clearly, nothing in this proposal commits us to the preposterous idea that we should stop subjecting people's intuitions to philosophical scrutiny.

The You-Can't-Get-Something-for-Nothing Objection

"You'll never get anywhere if you just run a lot of experiments. Thus, suppose you are wondering about certain questions in moral philosophy. You might find that a particular psychological process tends to yield a particular type of intuition about those questions, but that knowledge won't do you any good unless you *already* have some information about either whether the process is reliable or whether the intuitions are correct. And how are you going to figure that out? Surely not just by running more experiments!"

Reply: We think that the key claim being made in this objection is right on target. If philosophers gave up all other forms of thought and just spent all of their time running experiments, it really is true that they would never get anywhere. But what we don't understand is how this claim is supposed to be an objection to the practice of experimental philosophy. After all, we are *not* going to give up all other forms of thought, and we therefore *do* have independent reasons to adopt certain beliefs. Once experimental philosophy is understood in this way as part of a broader philosophical inquiry, it shouldn't be hard to see how it could prove helpful.

The basic idea here is a straightforward one. Before we begin experimental work, we have certain beliefs both about which processes are reliable and about which answers are correct. We can then update these beliefs in light of the experimental data. Hence, when we learn that a particular process tends to generate certain types of answers, we can adjust our assessment of the process using our prior assessments of the answers. But the inference also goes in the other direction. We can use our prior beliefs about whether a given process is reliable to adjust our assessments of the answers it generates. Working back and forth in this way, we gradually arrive at better assessments both of the processes and of the answers.

2.2. Diversity

People in different cultures have different beliefs about absolutely fundamental issues, and the recognition of this can be powerfully transforming. When Christian children learn that many people have very different religious beliefs, this can provoke a deep and disorienting existential crisis. For the discovery of religious diversity can prompt the thought that it's in some sense accidental that one happens to be raised in a Christian household rather than a Hindu household. This kind of arbitrariness can make the child wonder whether there's any reason to think that his religious beliefs are more likely to be right than those of the Hindu child. These matters are not peripheral—they strike to the heart of issues we care about most deeply.

The philosophical import of doxastic diversity is hardly restricted to childhood. At the turn of the century, anthropologists provided a catalog of the striking cultural diversity in moral views. Some cultures, it turned out, thought that one is morally obligated to eat parts of one's deceased parents; other cultures thought it was permissible to rape women from an enemy tribe. Such diversity in moral norms was an important catalyst to philosophical reflections about the status of our moral norms, and this led to deep discussions in metaethics and normative ethics that persist to this day.

Experimental philosophy promises to make significant new contributions in this arena. Work in experimental philosophy suggests that there is diversity even in the most basic concepts we deploy in Western philosophy. For instance, basic ideas about what is required for knowledge are apparently different across cultures. This can generate a crisis akin to that of the child confronted with religious diversity. If I find out that my philosophical intuitions are a product of my cultural upbringing, then, since it's in some sense an accident that I had the cultural upbringing that I did, I am forced to wonder whether my intuitions are superior at tracking the nature of the world, the mind, and the good. These are manifestly philosophical questions. And to determine the answers, we need to know a great deal more about both our own intuitions and those of other cultures. In some cases, we might find that there are large swathes of universality in intuitions about philosophical cases. Where we do find diversity, then, we can ask more informed questions about the relative merits of these different ways of thinking about the world. And just as some Christian children come to think that there's no rational basis for preferring Christian to Hindu beliefs, we too might come to think that there's no rational basis for preferring Western philosophical notions to Eastern ones.

2.3. The Mind and Its Workings

Analytic philosophers have long been concerned with patterns in people's intuitions about cases, but the study of these patterns has been regarded merely as a means to an end. Hence, the philosopher might look at people's ordinary intuitions about causation, but the true goal would not be to learn something about people and their intuitions. Instead, the goal would be to reach a better understanding of the true nature of causation, and people's intuitions would be considered relevant only insofar as they shed light on this other topic.

With the advent of experimental philosophy, this familiar approach is being turned on its head. More and more, philosophers are coming to feel that questions about how people ordinarily think have great philosophical significance in their own right. So, for example, it seems to us that there are important philosophical lessons to be gleaned from the study of people's intuitions about causation, but we do not think that the significance of these intuitions is exhausted by the evidence they might provide for one or another metaphysical theory. On the contrary, we think that the patterns to be found in people's intuitions point to important truths about how the mind works, and these truths—truths about people's minds, not about metaphysics—have great significance for traditional philosophical questions.

We are well aware that this approach is a controversial one, but we find it hard to say precisely where the controversy might lie. It seems unlikely that anyone would literally say, for example, "I know that some researchers are trying to investigate the most fundamental concepts that people use to understand their world, but that whole research program strikes me as a big mistake. In my view, these issues just aren't all that interesting or important." Nor does it seem plausible for a person to say, "I agree that we ought to be studying people's concepts and the way they think, but I don't think there is any need for experimental research here. These are the sorts of problems one can resolve entirely from the armchair." But if no one would make either of these claims, how exactly can the approach be controversial?

One complaint we sometimes hear is that philosophers should not be content merely to understand how people think, that they should also be engaged in an effort to figure out whether people's ordinary views are actually right or wrong. The thought here seems to be that, for instance, philosophers should be concerned not just with people's ordinary intuitions about causation but also with questions about what truly causes what. Clearly, this complaint rests on a confusion. No one is suggesting that philosophers should stop thinking about what really causes what. The suggestion is just that, whatever else we do, we should *also* be looking at people's intuitions about causation as a way of coming to a deeper understanding of how the human mind works. In other words, experimental philosophers are calling for a more pluralistic approach to philosophy. The philosopher on one end of the hall can be developing complex mathematical theories about the relevance of Bayesian inference to causal modeling, while the philosopher at the other end of the hall can be developing complex theories about how people's causal intuitions reveal some fundamental truth about human nature. If all goes well, the two philosophers will actually be able to help each other's projects advance.

As far as we can tell, the only legitimate controversy here is about whether this sort of inquiry can legitimately be considered philosophy. That is, someone might think that it is all well and good to launch an inquiry into basic questions about human nature but that such an inquiry should not take place in a philosophy department, should not be discussed in philosophy journals, should not be featured in the philosophy section of the bookstore, and so forth.

To this objection, we respond with what we have come to call the *quizzical stare*. The questions addressed in this research program strike us as so obviously philosophical that we find it a little bit difficult to know how to respond. To understand our confusion here, perhaps it would be helpful to think about the questions we ourselves have actually been investigating. One of us has been trying to figure out whether people's moral judgments are derived from reasoning, from emotion, or from some mixture of the two. The other has been trying to figure out whether the basic concepts people use to understand their world are similar to scientific concepts or whether science should be regarded as a radical departure from people's ordinary mode of understanding. To us at least, these questions seem to lie at the core of what is ordinarily regarded as philosophy.

Now, it is true that some philosophers have thought that questions about how the mind works lie outside the proper domain of philosophy, but this is a relatively recent development. Throughout almost all of the history of philosophy, questions about the workings of the mind were regarded as absolutely central. Philosophers wanted to know whether the mind was composed of distinct parts (reason, the passions, etc.) and how these parts might interact with each other. They wanted to know whether all knowledge came from experience or whether we were endowed by God with certain innate ideas. They wanted to know how exactly people come to make the moral judgments they do. The view that questions like these lie at the core of our discipline prevailed throughout most of the history of philosophy, and we therefore refer to it as the *traditional conception*.

In the early twentieth century, the rise of analytic philosophy led to a diminished interest in questions about how the mind works and a greater interest in more technical questions involving language and logic. Some of the more radical adherents of this new approach developed a particularly extreme view about how the discipline should proceed. They suggested that philosophers should not only begin to think more seriously about the new sorts of questions they had recently introduced but also stop thinking at all about more traditional questions regarding the workings of the mind. In other words, the suggestion was that the questions that had traditionally been taken to lie at the core of philosophy should now be regarded as falling outside the discipline altogether.

The result is a curious approach to undergraduate education. When students first enter the program, we tell them in reverential tones about how Plato posited a number of different parts of the mind and explained various phenomena in terms of conflict and cooperation between them. The most thoughtful and motivated students then find themselves thinking: "What an interesting idea! I wonder whether it's actually true. Let's see; I wonder what sorts of evidence might be relevant here…" But then we are immediately supposed to put a stop to such thoughts: "No, no, you've got it all wrong. If you actually start trying to figure out whether the mind has different parts, you aren't doing philosophy at all. To truly be a philosopher, you've got to learn to leave those questions to someone else."

In our view, this is all a big mistake. There simply wasn't anything wrong with the traditional conception of philosophy. The traditional questions of philosophy—the questions that animated Plato, Aristotle, Spinoza, Hume, Nietzsche, and so many others—are just as profound and important today as they were when they were first posed. If experimental philosophy helps to bring our discipline back to these issues, we think that is cause for celebration.

3. CONCLUSION

We hope we've said enough to justify the initiation of the enterprise of experimental philosophy. But we don't think that such general considerations can provide any ultimate justification to sustain experimental philosophy. The real measure of a research program depends on whether the program generates exciting new discoveries. We invite you to read the papers and decide for yourself. For our part, we think that experimental philosophy has already begun to produce surprising and illuminating results. The thing to do now is just to cast off our methodological chains and go after the important questions with everything we've got.

PART I

CROSS-CULTURAL DIFFERENCES
IN INTUITIONS

In much of everyday life, we assume that other people think the way that we do. Similarly, much work in analytic philosophy seems to presuppose that when it comes to philosophical topics like knowledge, freedom, and reference, everyone will have the same intuitions. However, recent work in cultural psychology shows systematic cognitive differences between East Asians and Westerners. This has led experimental philosophers to wonder whether something similar might be true for intuitions about philosophical topics.

Weinberg, Nichols, and Stich explore attributions of knowledge. They used standard thought experiments from analytic epistemology, and they found significant differences between the responses of East Asians and Westerners. They also found differences between participants of different socioeconomic status. The authors argue that these results present analytic epistemology with a challenge. Either the epistemologists must explain away the results, or they must show how their projects can be rendered consistent with cultural diversity in epistemic intuitions.

Machery, Mallon, Nichols, and Stich explore cultural differences in another central area of philosophy—the theory of reference. An adequate theory of reference is supposed to tell us, among other things, what determines the reference of a proper name. Two views have predominated in analytic philosophy. According to the *descriptivist* view, the reference of a name is determined by a description associated with the name. On the *causal-historical* view, the reference is determined by a causal chain stretching back to the naming of the individual. Analytic philosophers have relied on intuitions about various thought experiments to decide between these theories. The researchers predicted that Westerners would be more likely than Easterners to respond in line with the causal-historical view. And this is exactly what they found. This, according to the researchers, raises important questions about philosophical attempts to determine the right theory of reference.

SUGGESTED READINGS

Doris, J. M., and Plakias, A. 2008. "How to Argue about Disagreement: Evaluative Diversity and Moral Realism." In W. Sinnott-Armstrong (ed.), *The Biology and Psychology of Morality*. New York: Oxford University Press.

Jackson, F. 2001. "Précis of 'From Metaphysics to Ethics' and 'Responses.'" *Philosophy and Phenomenological Research* 62(3): 617–624, 653–664.

Liao, S. Forthcoming. "A Defense of Intuitions." *Philosophical Studies*.

Nichols, S., Stich, S., and Weinberg, J. 2003. "Metaskepticism: Meditations in Ethno-Epistemology." In S. Luper (ed.), *The Skeptics*. Burlington, VT: Ashgate.

Reimer, M. Forthcoming. "Jonah Cases: What They Tell Us about the Nature of Reference." In A. Everett and H. Deutsch (eds.), *Empty Names*. Oxford: Oxford University Press.

Sosa, E. 2005. "A Defense of the Use of Intuitions in Philosophy." In M. Bishop and D. Murphy (eds.), *Stich and His Critics*. Oxford: Blackwell Publishers.

Swain, S., Alexander, J., and Weinberg, J. 2008. "The Instability of Philosophical Intuitions: Running Hot and Cold on Truetemp." *Philosophy and Phenomenological Research*.

2

Normativity and Epistemic Intuitions

Jonathan M. Weinberg, Shaun Nichols, & Stephen P. Stich

I. INTRODUCTION

In this essay we propose to argue for two claims. The first is that a sizable group of epistemological projects—a group which includes much of what has been done in epistemology in the analytic tradition—would be seriously undermined if one or more of a cluster of empirical hypotheses about epistemic intuitions turns out to be true. The basis for this claim will be set out in section 2. The second claim is that, while the jury is still out, there is now a substantial body of evidence suggesting that some of those empirical hypotheses *are* true. Much of this evidence derives from an ongoing series of experimental studies of epistemic intuitions that we have been conducting. A preliminary report on these studies will be presented in section 3. In light of these studies, we think it is incumbent on those who pursue the epistemological projects in question to either explain why the truth of the hypotheses does not undermine their projects, or to say why, in light of the evidence we will present, they nonetheless assume that the hypotheses are false. In section 4, which is devoted to Objections and Replies, we'll consider some of the ways in which defenders of the projects we are criticizing might reply to our challenge. Our goal is not to offer a conclusive argument demonstrating that the epistemological projects we will be criticizing are untenable. Rather, our aim is to shift the burden of argument. For far too long, epistemologists who rely heavily on epistemic intuitions have proceeded as though they could simply ignore the empirical hypotheses we will set out. We will be well satisfied if we succeed in making a plausible case for the claim that this approach is no longer acceptable.

To start, it will be useful to sketch a brief—and perhaps somewhat idiosyncratic—taxonomy of epistemological projects. With the aid of this taxonomy we will try to "locate in philosophical space" (as Wilfrid Sellars used to say) those epistemological projects which, we maintain, are threatened by the evidence we will present. There are at least four distinct, though related, projects that have occupied the attention of epistemologists. Following Richard Samuels,[1] we'll call them the Normative Project, the Descriptive Project, the Evaluative Project, and the Ameliorative Project.

The Normative Project, which we're inclined to think is the most philosophically central of the four, attempts to establish norms to guide our epistemic efforts. Some of these norms may be explicitly regulative, specifying which ways of going about the quest for knowledge should be pursued and which should not. This articulation of regulative norms is one of the more venerable of philosophical undertakings, going back at least to Descartes's *Regulae* and evident in the work of Mill, Popper, and many other important figures in the history of philosophy, and it continues in philosophy today. For example, when Alvin Goldman chastises internalism for being unable to provide us with "Doxastic Decision Principles," he is challenging the ability of internalism to pull its weight in this aspect of the Normative Project.[2] The Normative Project also aims to articulate what might be called *valuational* norms, which attempt to answer questions like: What is our epistemic good? and how should we prefer to structure our doxastic lives? One may not be able to generate regulative principles from the answers provided; rather, the answers tell us at what target the regulative principles should aim.

The Descriptive Project can have a variety of targets, the two most common being epistemic concepts and epistemic language. When concepts are the target, the goal is to describe (or "analyze") the epistemic concepts that some group of people actually invoke. When pursued by epistemologists (rather than linguists or anthropologists), the group in question is typically characterized rather vaguely by using the first-person plural. They are "our" concepts, the ones that "we" use. Work in this tradition has led to a large literature attempting to analyze concepts like knowledge, justification, warrant, and rationality.[3] When language is the focus of the Descriptive Project, the goal is to describe the way some group of people use epistemic language or to analyze the meaning of their epistemic terms. Here again, the group is almost invariably "us."

Many epistemologists think that there are important links between the Normative and Descriptive Projects. Indeed, we suspect that these (putative) links go a long way toward explaining why philosophers think the Descriptive Project is so important. In epistemology, knowledge is "the good stuff" and to call a belief an instance of knowledge is to pay it one of the highest compliments an epistemologist can bestow.[4] Thus, terms like "knowledge," "justification," "warrant," etc., and the concepts they express are themselves plausibly regarded as implicitly normative. Moreover, many philosophers hold that sentences invoking epistemic terms have explicitly normative consequences. So, for example, "S's belief that p is an instance of knowledge" might plausibly be taken to entail "*Ceteris paribus*, S ought to believe that p" or perhaps "*Ceteris paribus*, it is a good thing for S to believe that p."[5] For reasons that will emerge, we are more than a bit skeptical about the alleged links between the Descriptive and Normative Projects. For the time being, however, we will leave the claim that the two projects are connected unchallenged.

The Evaluative Project tries to assess how well or poorly people's actual belief-forming practices accord with the norms specified in the Normative Project. To do this, of course, another sort of descriptive effort is required. Before we can say how well or poorly people are doing at the business of belief formation and revision, we have to say in some detail how they actually go about the process of belief formation and revision.[6] The Ameliorative Project presupposes that we don't all come out with the highest possible score in the assessment produced by the Evaluative Project and asks how we can improve the way we go about the business of belief formation. In this chapter our primary focus will be on the Normative Project and on versions of the Descriptive Project which assume that the Descriptive and Normative Projects are linked in something like the way sketched above.

II. INTUITION-DRIVEN ROMANTICISM
AND THE NORMATIVITY PROBLEM

A. Epistemic Romanticism and Intuition-Driven Romanticism

A central question that the Normative Project tries to answer is: *How ought we to go about the business of belief formation and revision?* How are we to go about finding an answer to this question? And once an answer has been proposed, how are we to assess it? If two theorists offer different answers, how can we determine which one is better? Philosophers who have pursued the Normative Project have used a variety of methods or strategies. In this section we want to begin by describing one very influential family of strategies.

The family we have in mind belongs to a larger group of strategies which (just to be provocative) we propose to call *Epistemic Romanticism*. One central idea of nineteenth-century Romanticism was that our real selves, the essence of our identity, is implanted within us, and that to discover who we really are we need but let that real identity emerge. Epistemic Romanticism assumes something rather similar about epistemic norms. According to Epistemic Romanticism, knowledge of the correct epistemic norms (or information that can lead to knowledge of the correct norms) is implanted within us in some way, and with the proper process of self-exploration we can discover them. As we read him, Plato was an early exponent of this kind of Romanticism about matters norma-tive (and about much else besides). So *Epistemic Platonism* might be another (perhaps equally provocative) label for this group of strategies for discovering or testing epistemic norms.

There are various ways in which the basic idea of Epistemic Romanticism can be elaborated. The family of strategies that we want to focus on all accord a central role to what we will call *epistemic intuitions*. Thus, we will call this fam-ily of strategies *Intuition-Driven Romanticism* (or IDR). As we use the notion, an epistemic intuition is simply a spontaneous judgment about the epistemic properties of some specific case—a judgment for which the person making the judgment may be able to offer no plausible justification. To count as an

Intuition-Driven Romantic strategy for discovering or testing epistemic norms, the following three conditions must be satisfied:

(i) The strategy must take epistemic intuitions as data or input. (It can also exploit various other sorts of data.)

(ii) It must produce, as output, explicitly or implicitly normative claims or principles about matters epistemic. Explicitly normative claims include regulative claims about how we ought to go about the business of belief formation, claims about the relative merits of various strategies for belief formation, and evaluative claims about the merits of various epistemic situations. Implicitly normative claims include claims to the effect that one or another process of belief formation leads to justified beliefs or to real knowledge or that a doxastic structure of a certain kind amounts to real knowledge.

(iii) The output of the strategy must depend, in part, on the epistemic intuitions it takes as input. If provided with significantly different intuitions, the strategy must yield significantly different output.[7]

Perhaps the most familiar examples of Intuition-Driven Romanticism are various versions of the reflective equilibrium strategy in which (to paraphrase Goodman slightly) "a [normative] rule is amended if it yields an inference we are [intuitively] unwilling to accept [and] an inference is rejected if it violates a [normative] rule we are [intuitively] unwilling to amend."[8] In a much discussed paper called "Can Human Irrationality Be Experimentally Demonstrated," L. J. Cohen proposes a variation on Goodman's strategy as a way of determining what counts as rational or normatively appropriate reasoning.[9] It is of some importance to note that there are many ways in which the general idea of a reflective equilibrium process can be spelled out. Some philosophers, including Cohen, advocate a "narrow" reflective equilibrium strategy. Others advocate a "wide" reflective equilibrium strategy. And both of these alternatives can be elaborated in various ways.[10] Moreover, the details are often quite important since different versions of the reflective equilibrium strategy may yield different outputs, even when provided with exactly the same input.

Another example of the IDR strategy can be found in Alvin Goldman's important and influential book *Epistemology and Cognition* (1986). A central goal of epistemology, Goldman argues, is to develop a theory that will specify which of our beliefs are epistemically justified and which are not, and a fundamental step in constructing such a theory will be to articulate a system of rules or principles evaluating the justificatory status of beliefs. These rules, which Goldman calls *J-rules*, will specify permissible ways in which cognitive agents may go about the business of forming or updating their beliefs. They "permit or prohibit beliefs, directly or indirectly, as a function of some states, relations, or processes of the cognizer."[11] But, of course, different theorists may urge different and incompatible sets of J-rules. So in order to decide whether a proposed system of J-rules is correct, we must appeal to a higher criterion—Goldman calls it "a criterion of rightness"—which will specify a "set of conditions that are necessary and sufficient for a set of J-rules to be right."[12] But now the theoretical disputes emerge at a higher level, for different theorists have suggested very different criteria of rightness. Indeed, as Goldman notes, an illuminating taxonomy of epistemological theories can be generated by classifying them on the basis of the sort of criterion of rightness they endorse. So how are we to go about deciding among these various criteria of rightness? The answer, Goldman maintains, is that the correct criterion of rightness is the one that comports with the conception of justification that is "embraced by everyday thought and language."[13] To test a criterion, we consider the judgments it would entail about specific cases, and we test these judgments against our "pretheoretic intuition." "A criterion is supported to the extent that implied judgments accord with such intuitions and weakened to the extent that they do not."[14]

The examples we have mentioned so far are hardly the only examples of Intuition-Driven Romanticism. Indeed, we think a plausible case can be made that a fair amount of what goes on in normative epistemology can be classified as Intuition-Driven Romanticism. Moreover, to the extent that it is assumed to have normative implications, much of what has been written in descriptive epistemology in recent decades also counts as Intuition-Driven Romanticism. For example, just about all of the vast literature that arose in response to Gettier's classic paper uses intuitions about specific cases to test proposed analyses of the concept of knowledge.[15]

For many purposes, the details of an IDR strategy—the specific ways in which it draws inferences from intuitions and other data—will be of enormous importance. But since our goal is to raise a problem for all IDR strategies, the exact details of how they work will play no role in our argument. Thus, for our purposes, an IDR strategy can be viewed as a "black box" which takes intuitions (and perhaps other data) as input and produces implicitly or explicitly normative claims as output. The challenge we are about to raise is, we claim, a problem for IDR accounts no matter what goes on within the black box.

B. The Normativity Problem

Reflective equilibrium strategies and other Intuition-Driven Romantic strategies all yield as outputs claims that putatively have normative force. These outputs tell us how people ought to go about forming and revising their beliefs, which belief-forming strategies yield genuinely justified beliefs, which beliefs are warranted, which count as real knowledge rather than mere opinion, etc. But there is a problem lurking here—we'll call it the *Normativity Problem*: What reason is there to think that the output of one or another of these Intuition-Driven Romantic strategies has real (as opposed to putative) normative force? Why should we care about the normative pronouncements produced by these strategies? Why should we try to do what these outputs claim we ought to do in matters epistemic? Why, in short, should we take any of this stuff seriously?

We don't think that there is any good solution to the Normativity Problem for Intuition-Driven Romanticism or indeed for any other version of Romanticism in epistemology. And because there is no solution to the Normativity Problem, we think that the entire tradition of Epistemic Romanticism has been a very bad idea. These, obviously, are very big claims, and this is not the place to mount a detailed argument for all of them. We do, however, want to rehearse one consideration, first raised in Stich's book, *The Fragmentation of Reason*.[16] We think it lends some plausibility to the claim that satisfying solutions to the Normativity Problem for Intuition-Driven Romanticism are going to be hard to find. It will also help to motivate the empirical studies we will recount in the section to follow.

What Stich noted is that the following situation seems perfectly possible. There might be a group of people who reason and form beliefs in ways that are significantly different from the way we do. Moreover, these people might also have epistemic intuitions that are significantly different from ours. More specifically, they might have epistemic intuitions which, when plugged into your favorite Intuition-Driven Romantic black box, yield the conclusion that *their* strategies of reasoning and belief formation lead to epistemic states that are rational (or justified, or of the sort that yield genuine knowledge—pick your favorite normative epistemic notion here). If this is right, then it looks like the IDR strategy for answering normative epistemic questions might sanction any of a wide variety of regulative and valuational norms. And that sounds like bad news for an advocate of the IDR strategy, since the strategy doesn't tell us what we really want to know. It doesn't tell us how we should go about the business of forming and revising our beliefs. One might, of course, insist that the normative principles that should be followed are the ones that are generated when we put *our* intuitions into the IDR black box. But it is less than obvious (to put it mildly) how this move could be defended. Why should we privilege our intuitions rather than the intuitions of some other group?

One objection that was occasionally raised in response to this challenge focused on the fact that the groups conjured in Stich's argument are just philosophical fictions.[17] While it may well be logically possible that there are groups of people whose reasoning patterns and epistemic intuitions differ systematically from our own, there is no reason to suppose that it is nomologically or psychologically possible. And without some reason to think that such people are psychologically possible, the objection continued, the thought experiment does not pose a problem that the defender of the IDR strategy needs to take seriously. We are far from convinced by this objection, though we are prepared to concede that the use of nomologically or psychologically impossible cases in normative epistemology raises some deep and difficult issues. Thus, for argument's sake, we are prepared to concede that a plausible case might be made for privileging normative claims based on actual intuitions over normative claims based on intuitions that are merely logically possible. But what if the people imagined in the thought experiment are not just logically possible, but psychologically possible? Indeed, what if they are not merely psychologically possible but real—and to all appearances normal and flourishing? Under those circumstances, we maintain, it is hard to see how advocates of an IDR strategy can maintain that their intuitions have any special standing or that the normative principles these intuitions generate when plugged into their favorite IDR black box should be privileged over the normative principles that would be generated if we plugged the other people's intuitions into the same IDR black box. In the section to follow we will argue that these "what ifs" are not *just* "what ifs." There really are people—normal, flourishing people—whose epistemic intuitions are systematically different from "ours."

III. CULTURAL VARIATION IN EPISTEMIC INTUITIONS

A. Nisbett and Haidt: Some Suggestive Evidence

Our suspicion that people like those imagined in Stich's thought experiment might actually exist was first provoked by the results of two recent research programs in psychology. In one of these, Richard Nisbett and his collaborators have shown that there are large and systematic differences between East Asians and Westerners[18] on a long list of basic cognitive processes, including perception, attention, and memory. These groups also differ in the way they go about describing, predicting, and explaining events; in the way they categorize objects; and in the way they revise beliefs in the face of new arguments and evidence. This work makes it very plausible that the first part of Stich's thought-experiment is more than just a logical possibility. There really are people whose reasoning and belief-forming strategies are very different from ours. Indeed, there are over a billion of them!

Though space does not permit us to offer a detailed account of the differences that Nisbett and his colleagues found, a few brief notes will be useful in motivating the studies we will describe later is this section. According to Nisbett and his colleagues, the differences "can be loosely grouped together under the heading of holistic vs. analytic thought." Holistic thought, which predominates among East Asians, is characterized as "involving an orientation to the context or field as a whole, including attention to relationships between a focal object and the field, and a preference for explaining and predicting events on the basis of such relationships." Analytic thought, the prevailing pattern among Westerners, is characterized as "involving detachment of the object from its context, a tendency to focus on attributes of the object in order to assign it to categories, and a preference for using rules about the categories to explain and predict the object's behavior."[19] One concomitant of East Asian holistic thought is the tendency to focus on chronological rather than causal patterns in describing and recalling events. Westerners, by contrast, focus on causal patterns in these tasks.[20] Westerners also have a stronger sense of agency and independence, while East Asians have a much stronger commitment to social harmony. In East Asian society, the individual feels very much a part of a large and complex social organism where behavioral prescriptions must be followed and role obligations adhered to scrupulously.[21]

The second research program that led us to suspect there might actually be people like those in Stich's thought experiment was the work of Jonathan Haidt and his collaborators.[22] These investigators were interested in exploring the extent to which moral intuitions about events in which no one is harmed track judgments about disgust in people from different cultural and socioeconomic groups. For their study they constructed a set of brief stories about victimless activities that were intended to trigger the emotion of disgust. They presented these stories to subjects using a structured interview technique designed to determine whether the subjects found the activities described to be disgusting and also to elicit the subjects' moral intuitions about the activities. As an illustration, here is a story describing actions which people in all the groups studied found (not surprisingly) to be quite disgusting:

> A man goes to the supermarket once a week and buys a dead chicken. But before cooking the chicken, he has sexual intercourse with it. Then he cooks it and eats it.

The interviews were administered to both high and low socioeconomic status (SES) subjects in Philadelphia (USA) and in two cities in Brazil. Perhaps the most surprising finding in this study was that there are large differences in moral intuitions between social classes. Indeed, in most cases the difference between social classes was significantly greater than the difference between Brazilian and American subjects of the same SES. Of course we haven't yet told you what the differences in moral intuitions were, though you should be able to predict them by noting your own moral intuitions. (Hint: If you are reading this article, you count as high SES.) Not to keep you in suspense, low SES subjects tend to think that the man who has sex with the chicken is doing something that is seriously morally wrong; high SES subjects don't. Much the same pattern was found with the other scenarios used in the study.

B. Four Hypotheses

For our purposes, Haidt's work, like Nisbett's, is only suggestive. Nisbett gives us reason to think that people in different cultural groups exploit very different belief-forming strategies. Haidt's work demonstrates that people in different SES groups have systematically different moral intuitions. Neither investigator explored the possibility that there might be differences in *epistemic* intuitions in different groups. However, the results they reported were enough to convince us that the following pair of hypotheses *might* be true, and that it was worth the effort to find out:

> *Hypothesis 1:*   Epistemic intuitions vary from culture to culture.
> *Hypothesis 2:*   Epistemic intuitions vary from one socioeconomic group to another.

To these two experimentally inspired hypotheses we added two more that were suggested by anecdotal rather than experimental evidence. It has often seemed to us that students' epistemic intuitions change as they take more philosophy courses, and we have often suspected that we and our colleagues were, in effect, teaching neophyte philosophers to have intuitions that are in line with those of more senior members of the profession. Or perhaps we are not modifying intuitions at all but simply weeding out students whose intuitions are not mainstream. If either of these is the case, then the intuitions that "we" use in our philosophical work are not those of the man and woman in the street, but those of a highly trained and self-selecting community. These speculations led to:

Hypothesis 3:   Epistemic intuitions vary as a function of how many philosophy courses a person has had.

It also sometimes seems that the order in which cases are presented to people can have substantial effects on people's epistemic intuitions. This hunch is reinforced by some intriguing work on neural networks suggesting that a variety of learning strategies may be "path dependent."[23] If this hunch is correct, the pattern of intuitions that people offer on a series of cases might well differ systematically as a function of the order in which the cases are presented. This suggested our fourth hypothesis:

Hypothesis 4:   Epistemic intuitions depend, in part, on the order in which cases are presented.

Moreover, it might well be the case that some of the results of order effects are very hard to modify.[24]

    If any one of these four hypotheses turns out to be true, then, we maintain, it will pose a serious problem for the advocate of Intuition-Driven Romanticism. If all of them are true, then it is hard to believe that any plausible case can be made for the claim that the normative pronouncements of Intuition-Driven Romanticism have real normative force—that they are norms that we (or anyone else) should take seriously.

C. Some Experiments Exploring Cultural Variation in Epistemic Intuitions

Are any of these hypotheses true? To try to find out we have been conducting a series of experiments designed to test Hypotheses 1 and 2. While the results we have so far are preliminary, they are sufficient, we think, to at least shift the burden of argument well over in the direction of the defender of IDR strategies. What our results show, we believe, is that the advocates of IDR can no longer simply ignore these hypotheses or dismiss them as implausible, for there is a growing body of evidence which suggests that they might well be true.

    In designing our experiments, we were guided by three rather different considerations. First, we wanted our intuition probes—the cases that we would ask subjects to judge—to be similar to cases that have actually been used in the recent literature in epistemology. Second, since the findings reported by Nisbett and his colleagues all focused on differences between East Asians (henceforth, EAs) and European Americans (henceforth, Ws, for

"Westerners"), we decided that would be the obvious place to look first for differences in epistemic intuitions. Third, since Nisbett and his colleagues argue that Ws are significantly more individualistic than EAs, who tend to be much more interdependent and "collectivist" and thus much more concerned about community harmony and consensus, we tried to construct some intuition probes that would tap into this difference. Would individualistic Ws, perhaps, be more inclined to attribute knowledge to people whose beliefs are reliably formed by processes that no one else in their community shares? The answer, it seems, is yes.

Truetemp Cases

An issue of great moment in recent analytic epistemology is the internalism/externalism debate. Internalism, with respect to some epistemically evaluative property, is the view that *only* factors within an agent's introspective grasp can be relevant to whether the agent's beliefs have that property. Components of an agent's doxastic situation available to introspection are internalistically kosher; other factors beyond the scope of introspection, such as the reliability of the psychological mechanisms that actually produced the belief, are epistemically external to the agent. Inspired by Lehrer,[25] we included in our surveys a number of cases designed to explore externalist/internalist dimensions of our subjects' intuitions. Here is one of the questions we presented to our subjects, all of whom were undergraduates at Rutgers University.[26]

> One day Charles is suddenly knocked out by a falling rock, and his brain becomes re-wired so that he is always absolutely right whenever he estimates the temperature where he is. Charles is completely unaware that his brain has been altered in this way. A few weeks later, this brain re-wiring leads him to believe that it is 71 degrees in his room. Apart from his estimation, he has no other reasons to think that it is 71 degrees. In fact, it is at that time 71 degrees in his room. Does Charles really know that it is 71 degrees in the room, or does he only believe it?
>
> REALLY KNOWS   ONLY BELIEVES

Although Charles's belief is produced by a reliable mechanism, it is stipulated that he is completely unaware of this reliability. So his reliability is epistemically external. Therefore, to the extent that a subject population is unwilling to attribute knowledge in this case, we have evidence that the group's "folk epistemology" may be internalist. We found that while both groups were more likely to deny knowledge, EA subjects were much more likely to deny knowledge than were their W classmates. The results are shown in figure 2.1.[27]

After finding this highly significant difference, we began tinkering with the text to see if we could construct other "Truetemp" cases in which the difference between the two groups would disappear. Our first thought was to

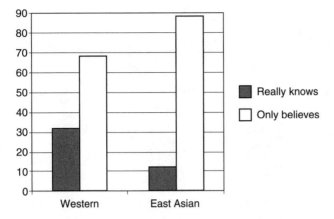

Figure 2.1. Individualistic Truetemp Case.

replace the rock with some socially sanctioned intervention. The text we used was as follows:

One day John is suddenly knocked out by a team of well-meaning scientists sent by the elders of his community, and his brain is re-wired so that he is always absolutely right whenever he estimates the temperature where he is. John is completely unaware that his brain has been altered in this way. A few weeks later, this brain re-wiring leads him to believe that it is 71 degrees in his room. Apart from his estimation, he has no other reasons to think that it is 71 degrees. In fact, it is at that time 71 degrees in his room. Does John really know that it was 71 degrees in the room, or does he only believe it?

REALLY KNOWS   ONLY BELIEVES

As we had predicted, the highly significant difference between the two groups disappeared. The results are shown in figure 2.2.

Encouraged by this finding we constructed yet another version of the "Truetemp" case in which the mechanism that reliably leads to a true belief is not unique to a single individual, but rather is shared by everyone else in the community. The intuition probe read as follows:

The Faluki are a large but tight-knit community living on a remote island. One day, a radioactive meteor strikes the island and has one significant effect on the Faluki—it changes the chemical make-up of their brains so that they are always absolutely right whenever they estimate the temperature. The Faluki are completely unaware that their brains have been altered in this way. Kal is a member of the Faluki community. A few weeks after the meteor strike, while Kal is walking along the beach, the changes in his brain lead him to believe that it is 71 degrees where he is. Apart

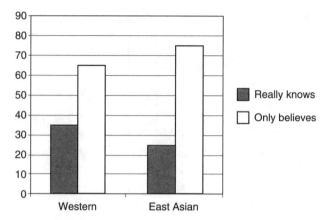

Figure 2.2. The Elders Version.

from his estimation, he has no other reasons to think that it is 71 degrees. In fact, it is at that time exactly 71 degrees where Kal is. Does Kal really know that it is 71 degrees, or does he only believe it?

REALLY KNOWS   ONLY BELIEVES

As predicted, on this case too there was no significant difference between Ws and EAs (see fig. 2.3).

Intriguingly, though the difference is not statistically significant, the percentage of EAs who answered "Really Knows" in this case was *greater* than the percentage of Ws who gave that answer, reversing the pattern in the individualistic "hit by a rock" case. Figure 2.4, which is a comparison of the three Truetemp cases, illustrates the way in which the large difference between Ws and EAs in the Individualistic version disappears in the Elders version and looks to be reversing direction in the Faluki version.

Gettier Cases

A category of examples that has loomed large in the recent epistemology literature are "Gettier cases," in which a person has good (though, as it happens, false, or only accidentally true, or in some other way warrant deprived) evidence for a belief which is true. These cases are, of course, by their very construction in many ways quite similar to unproblematic cases in which a person has good and true evidence for a true belief. As Norenzayan and Nisbett have shown, EAs are more inclined than Ws to make categorical judgments on the basis of similarity. Ws, on the other hand, are more disposed to focus on causation in describing the world and classifying things.[28] In a large class of Gettier cases, the evidence that *causes* the target to form a belief turns out to be false. This suggests that EAs might be much less inclined than Ws to withhold the attribution of knowledge in Gettier cases. And, indeed, they are.

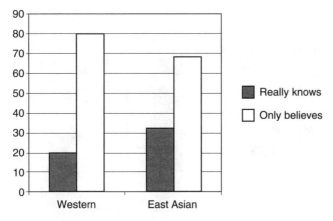

Figure 2.3. Community-Wide Truetemp Case ("Faluki").

The intuition probe we used to explore cultural differences on Gettier cases was the following:

Bob has a friend, Jill, who has driven a Buick for many years. Bob therefore thinks that Jill drives an American car. He is not aware, however, that her Buick has recently been stolen, and he is also not aware that Jill has replaced it with a Pontiac, which is a different kind of American car. Does Bob really know that Jill drives an American car, or does he only believe it?

REALLY KNOWS   ONLY BELIEVES

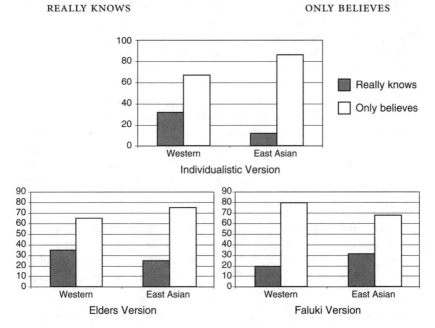

Figure 2.4. Comparison of Truetemp Cases.

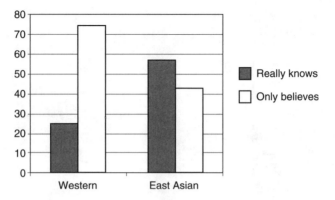

Figure 2.5. Gettier Case, Western and East Asian.

The striking finding in this case is that a large majority of Ws give the standard answer in the philosophical literature, viz., "Only Believes." But among EAs this pattern is actually *reversed*! A majority of EAs say that Bob really knows. The results are shown in figure 2.5.

Evidence from Another Ethnic Group

The experiments we have reported thus far were done in lower division classes and large lectures at Rutgers. Since Rutgers is the State University of New Jersey and New Jersey is home to many people of Indian, Pakistani, and Bangladeshi descent, in the course of the experiments we collected lots of data about these people's intuitions. Initially we simply set these data aside since we had no theoretical basis for expecting that the epistemic intuitions of people from the Indian subcontinent (hereafter SCs) would be systematically different from the epistemic intuitions of Westerners. But, after finding the extraordinary differences between Ws and EAs on the Gettier case, we thought it might be interesting to analyze the SC data as well. We were right. It turns out that the epistemic intuitions of SCs are even more different from the intuitions of Ws than the intuitions of EAs are. The SC results on the Gettier case are shown in figure 2.6. If these results are robust, then it seems that what counts as knowledge on the banks of the Ganges does not count as knowledge on the banks of the Mississippi!

There were two additional intuition probes that we used in our initial experiments which did not yield statistically significant differences between Ws and EAs. But when we analyzed the SC data, it turned out that there were significant differences between Ws and SCs. The text for one of these probes, the Cancer Conspiracy case, was as follows:

It's clear that smoking cigarettes increases the likelihood of getting cancer. However, there is now a great deal of evidence that just using nicotine

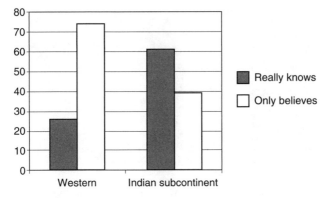

Figure 2.6. Gettier Case, Western and Indian.

by itself without smoking (for instance, by taking a nicotine pill) does not increase the likelihood of getting cancer. Jim knows about this evidence and as a result, he believes that using nicotine does not increase the likelihood of getting cancer. It is possible that the tobacco companies dishonestly made up and publicized this evidence that using nicotine does not increase the likelihood of cancer, and that the evidence is really false and misleading. Now, the tobacco companies did not actually make up this evidence, but Jim is not aware of this fact. Does Jim really know that using nicotine doesn't increase the likelihood of getting cancer, or does he only believe it?

REALLY KNOWS   **ONLY BELIEVES**

The results are shown in figure 2.7.

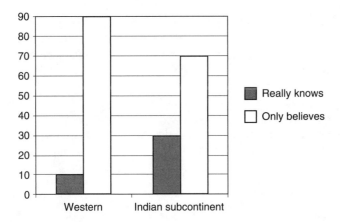

Figure 2.7. Conspiracy Case.

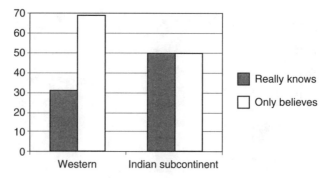

Figure 2.8. Zebra Case.

The other probe that produced significant differences is a version of Dretske's Zebra-in-Zoo case:[29]

> Mike is a young man visiting the zoo with his son, and when they come to the zebra cage, Mike points to the animal and says, "that's a zebra." Mike is right—it is a zebra. However, as the older people in his community know, there are lots of ways that people can be tricked into believing things that aren't true. Indeed, the older people in the community know that it's possible that zoo authorities could cleverly disguise mules to look just like zebras, and people viewing the animals would not be able to tell the difference. If the animal that Mike called a zebra had really been such a cleverly painted mule, Mike still would have thought that it was a zebra. Does Mike really know that the animal is a zebra, or does he only believe that it is?
>
> REALLY KNOWS   ONLY BELIEVES

The results are shown in figure 2.8.

What's going on in these last two cases? Why do SCs and Ws have different epistemic intuitions about them? The answer, to be quite frank, is that we are not sure how to explain these results. But, of course, for our polemical purposes, an explanatory hypothesis is not really essential. The mere fact that Ws, EAs, and SCs have different epistemic intuitions is enough to make it plausible that IDR strategies which take these intuitions as inputs would yield significantly different normative pronouncements as output. And this, we think, puts the ball squarely in the court of the defenders of IDR strategies. They must either argue that intuitive differences of the sort we've found would not lead to diverging normative claims, or they must argue that the outputs of an IDR strategy are genuinely normative despite the fact that they are different for different cultures. Nor is this the end of the bad news for those who advocate IDR strategies.

Epistemic Intuitions and Socioeconomic Status

Encouraged by our findings in these cross-cultural studies, we have begun to explore the possibility that epistemic intuitions might also be sensitive to the socioeconomic status of the people offering the intuitions. And while our findings here are also quite preliminary, the apparent answer is that SES does indeed have a major impact on subjects' epistemic intuitions.

Following Haidt (and much other research in social psychology) we used years of education to distinguish low and high SES groups. In the studies we will recount in this section, subjects were classified as low SES if they reported that they had never attended college. Subjects who reported that they had one or more years of college were coded as high SES. All the subjects were adults; they were approached near various commercial venues in downtown New Brunswick, New Jersey, and (since folks approached on the street tend to be rather less compliant than university undergraduates in classrooms) they were offered McDonald's gift certificates worth a few dollars if they agreed to participate in our study.

Interestingly, the two intuition probes for which we found significant SES differences both required the subjects to assess the importance of possible states of affairs that do not actually obtain. Here is the first probe, which is similar to the Dretske-type case discussed above:

> Pat is at the zoo with his son, and when they come to the zebra cage, Pat points to the animal and says, "That's a zebra." Pat is right—it is a zebra. However, given the distance the spectators are from the cage, Pat would not be able to tell the difference between a real zebra and a mule that is cleverly disguised to look like a zebra. And if the animal had really been a cleverly disguised mule, Pat still would have thought that it was a zebra. Does Pat really know that the animal is a zebra, or does he only believe that it is?
>
> REALLY KNOWS   ONLY BELIEVES

The results are shown in figure 2.9.

The second probe that produced significant (indeed enormous) differences between our two SES groups was the Cancer Conspiracy case that also generated

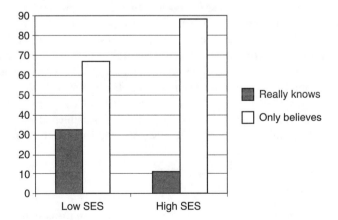

Figure 2.9. Zebra Case.

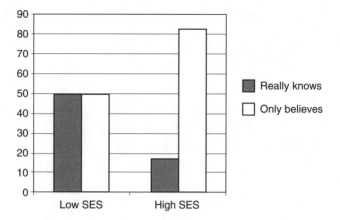

Figure 2.10. Cancer Conspiracy Case.

differences between Western subjects and subjects from the Indian subcontinent. The results are shown in figure 2.10.

Why are the intuitions in these two SES groups so different? Here again we do not have a well-worked-out theoretical framework of the sort that Nisbett and his colleagues have provided for the W vs. EA differences. So any answer we offer is only a speculation. One hypothesis is that one of the many factors that subjects are sensitive to in forming epistemic intuitions of this sort is the extent to which possible but nonactual states of affairs are relevant. Another possibility is that high SES subjects accept much weaker knowledge-defeaters than low SES subjects because low SES subjects have lower minimum standards for knowledge. More research is needed to determine whether either of these conjectures is correct. But whatever the explanation turns out to be, the data we've reported look to be yet another serious embarrassment for the advocates of IDR. As in the case of cultural difference, they must either argue that these intuitive differences, when plugged into an IDR black box, would not lead to different normative conclusions, or they must bite the bullet and argue that diverging normative claims are genuinely normative, and thus that the sorts of doxastic states that ought to be pursued by relatively rich and well-educated people are significantly different from the sorts of doxastic states that poor and less well-educated folks should seek. We don't pretend to have an argument showing that neither of these options is defensible. But we certainly don't envy the predicament of the IDR advocate who has to opt for one or the other.[30]

IV. OBJECTIONS AND REPLIES

In this section we propose to assemble some objections to the case against IDR that we've set out in the preceding sections along with our replies.

A. What's So Bad about Epistemic Relativism?

Objection

Suppose we're right. Suppose that epistemic intuitions *do* differ in different ethnic and SES groups, and that because of this IDR strategies will generate different normative conclusions depending on which group uses them. Why, the critic asks, should this be considered a problem for IDR advocates? At most it shows that different epistemic norms apply to different groups, and thus that epistemic relativism is true. But why, exactly, is that a problem? What's so bad about epistemic relativism? "Indeed," we imagine the critic ending with an *ad hominem* flourish, "one of the authors of this paper has published a book that *defends* epistemic relativism."[31]

Reply

We certainly have no argument that could show that *all* forms of epistemic relativism are unacceptable, and the one avowed relativist among us is still prepared to defend some forms of relativism. But if we are right about epistemic intuitions, then the version of relativism to which IDR strategies lead would entail that the epistemic norms appropriate for the rich are quite different from the epistemic norms appropriate for the poor, and that the epistemic norms appropriate for white people are different from the norms appropriate for people of color.[32] And that we take to be quite a preposterous result. The fact that IDR strategies lead to this result is, we think, a very strong reason to think that there is something very wrong with those strategies. Of course, a defender of an IDR strategy might simply bite the bullet and insist that the strategy he or she advocates is the right one for uncovering genuine epistemic norms, despite the fact that it leads to a relativistic consequence that many find implausible. But the IDR advocate who responds to our data in this way surely must offer some *argument* for the claim that the preferred IDR strategy produces genuine epistemic norms. And we know of no arguments along these lines that are even remotely plausible.

B. There Are Several Senses of "Knowledge"

Objection

The next objection begins with the observation that epistemologists have long been aware that the word "knows" has more than one meaning in ordinary discourse. Sometimes when people say that they "know" that something is the case, what they mean is that they have a strong sense of subjective certainty. So, for example, someone at a horse race might give voice to a strong hunch by saying: "I just know that Ivory Armchair is going to win." And even after Lab Bench comes in first, this colloquial sense of "know" still permits them to say, "Drat! I just knew that Ivory Armchair was going to win." At other times, though, when people use "know" and "knowledge," the sense they have in mind is the one that is of interest to epistemologists. The problem with our results, this objection maintains, is that we did nothing to ensure that when subjects answered "Really Knows" rather than "Only Believes" the sense of "know" that they had in mind was the one of philosophical interest rather than the subjective certainty sense. "So," the critic concludes, "for all you know, your subjects might have been offering you philosophically uninteresting judgments about people's sense of subjective certainty."

Reply

It is certainly possible that some of our subjects were interpreting the "Really Knows" option as a question about subjective certainty. But there is reason to think that this did not have a major impact on our findings. For all of our subject groups (W, EA, and SC in the ethnic studies and high and low SES in the SES study) we included a question designed to uncover any systematic differences in our subjects' inclination to treat mere subjective certainty as knowledge. The question we used was the following:

> Dave likes to play a game with flipping a coin. He sometimes gets a "special feeling" that the next flip will come out heads. When he gets this "special feeling," he is right about half the time, and wrong about half the time. Just before the next flip, Dave gets that "special feeling," and the feeling leads him to believe that the coin will land heads. He flips the coin, and it does land heads. Did Dave really know that the coin was going to land heads, or did he only believe it?
>
> REALLY KNOWS   ONLY BELIEVES

As shown in figure 2.11, there was no difference at all between the high and low SES groups on this question; in both groups almost none of our subjects judged that this was a case of knowledge. The results in the ethnic studies were basically the same.[33]

This might be a good place to elaborate a bit on what we are and are not claiming about epistemic intuitions and the psychological mechanisms or "knowledge structures" that may subserve them. For polemical purposes we have been emphasizing the diversity of epistemic intuitions in different ethnic and SES groups, since these quite different intuitions, when plugged into an IDR black box, will generate different normative claims. But we certainly do not mean to suggest that epistemic intuitions are completely malleable or that there are no constraints on the sorts of epistemic intuitions that might be found in different social groups. Indeed, the fact that subjects from all the groups we studied agreed in not classifying beliefs based on "special feelings" as knowledge suggests that there may well be a universal core to "folk epistemology." Whether or not this conjecture is true and, if it is, how this common core is best characterized are questions that will require a great deal more research. Obviously, these are not issues that can be settled from the philosopher's armchair.

C. The Effect Size We've Found Is Small and Philosophically Uninteresting

Objection

If it were the case that virtually all Ws judged various cases in one way and virtually all EAs or SCs judged the same cases in a different way, that might be genuine cause for concern among epistemologists. But that's not at all what you have found. Rather, what you've shown is merely that in various cases there is a 20 or 30 percent difference in the judgments offered by subjects in various groups. So, for example, a majority in all of your groups withhold knowledge attributions in all the Truetemp cases that were designed to test the degree to which subjects' intuitions reflected epistemic internalism. Since the majority in all groups agree, we can conclude that the correct account of epistemic norms is internalist. So it is far from clear why epistemologists should find the sort of cultural diversity you've found to be at all troubling, or even interesting.

Reply

Here we have two replies. First, the sizes of the statistically significant group differences that we've reported are quite comparable with the size of the differences that Nisbett, Haidt, and other social psychologists take to show important differences between groups. The second reply is more important. While in some cases what we've been reporting are just the brute facts that intuitions in different groups differ, in other cases what we've found is considerably more interesting. The differences between Ws and EAs look to be both systematic and explainable. EAs and Ws appear to be sensitive to different features of the situation, different *epistemic vectors*, as we will call them. EAs are much more sensitive to communitarian factors, while Ws respond to more individualistic ones. Moreover, Nisbett and his colleagues have given us good reason to think that these kinds of differences can be traced to deep and important differences in EA and W cognition. And we have no reason to think that equally important differences could not be found for SCs. Our data also suggests that both high and low SES Westerners stress the individualistic and noncommunitarian vector, since there was no difference between high and low SES groups on questions designed to emphasize this vector. What separates high and low SES subjects is some quite different vector—sensitivity to mere possibilities, perhaps. What our studies point to, then, is more than just divergent epistemic intuitions across groups; the studies point to divergent epistemic *concerns*—concerns which appear to differ along a variety of dimensions. It is plausible to suppose that these differences would significantly affect the output of just about any IDR process.

D. We Are Looking at the Wrong Sort of Intuitions; The Right Sort Are Accompanied by a Clear Sense of Necessity

Objection

The central idea of this objection is that our experiments are simply not designed to evoke the right sort of intuitions—the sort that the IDR process really requires. What we are collecting in our experiments are unfiltered spontaneous judgments about a variety of cases. But what is really needed, this objection maintains, are data about quite a different kind of intuitions. The right sort of intuitions are those that have modal import and are accompanied by a clear sense of necessity. They are the kind of intuitions that we have when confronted with principles like: If p, then not-not-p. Unless you show cultural or SES diversity in these sorts of intuitions, this objection continues, you have not shown anything that an IDR advocate needs to be concerned about, since you have not shown that the right sort of intuitions are not universal.[34]

Reply

It is true that the sorts of intuitions that our experiments collect are not the sorts that some IDR theorists would exploit. However, our findings do raise serious questions about the suggestion that intuitions which come with a clear sense of necessity and modal import—*strong intuitions,* as we propose to call them—are anything close to universal. Many epistemologists would no doubt insist that their own intuitions about many cases are strong intuitions. Simple Gettier case intuitions are a good example. Indeed, if these intuitions, which led a generation of epistemologists to seek something better than the traditional justified true belief analysis of knowledge, are not strong intuitions, then it is hard to believe that there are enough strong intuitions around to generate epistemic norms of any interest. But if philosophers' intuitions on simple Gettier cases *are* strong intuitions, then our data indicate that strong intuitions are far from universal. For, while our experiments cannot distinguish strong from weak intuitions, they do indicate that almost 30 percent of W subjects do not have either strong or weak intuitions that agree with those of most philosophers, since almost 30 percent of these subjects claim that, in our standard Gettier scenario, Bob really knows that Jill drives an American car. Among EA subjects, over 50 percent of subjects have the intuition (weak or strong) that Bob really knows, and among SC subjects the number is over 60! It may well be that upper-middle-class Westerners who have had a few years of graduate training in analytic philosophy do indeed all have strong, modality-linked intuitions about Gettier cases. But since most of the world's population apparently does not share these intuitions, it is hard to see why we should think that these intuitions tell us anything at all about the modal structure of reality or about epistemic norms or indeed about anything else of philosophical interest.

E. We Are Looking at the Wrong Sort of Intuitions; The Right Sort Require at Least a Modicum of Reflection

Objection

We have also heard a rather different objection about the type of intuitions examined in our study.[35] The proper input intuitions for the IDR strategy, the critics maintain, are not "first-off" intuitions—which may be really little better than mere guesses. Rather, IDR requires what might be called *minimally reflective intuitions*—intuitions resulting from some modicum of attention, consideration, and above all reflection on the particulars of the case at hand as well as one's other theoretical commitments. We have, this objection continues, done nothing to show that such minimally reflective intuitions would exhibit the sort of diversity we have been reporting, and until we show something along those lines, the IDR theorist need not worry.

Reply

This objection is right as far as it goes, since we have not (yet) examined intuitions produced under conditions of explicit reflection. But the objection really does not go very far, and certainly not far enough to allow IDR theorists to rest easy. First of all, many of our subjects clearly did reflect at least minimally before answering, as evidenced in the many survey forms on which the subjects wrote brief explanatory comments after their answers. Moreover, as we stressed in Reply 4.C, it is not just that we found group differences in epistemic intuition; much more interestingly, Western and East Asian subjects' intuitions seem to respond to quite different epistemic vectors. It is extremely likely that such differences in sensitivities would be recapitulated—or even strengthened—in any reflective process. If EA subjects have an inclination to take into account factors involving community beliefs, practices, and traditions, and W subjects do not have such an inclination, then we see no reason to expect that such vectors will not be differentially present under conditions of explicit reflection. IDR theorists who want to make use of any purported difference between first-off and minimally reflective intuitions had better go get some *data* showing that such differences would point in the direction they would want.

F. We Are Looking at the Wrong Sort of Intuitions; The Right Sort Are Those That Emerge after an Extended Period of Discussion and Reflection

Objection

The last objection we'll consider was proposed (though not, we suspect, endorsed) by Philip Kitcher. What IDR strategies need, this objection maintains, is neither first-off intuitions nor even minimally reflective intuitions, but rather the sorts of intuitions that people develop after a lengthy period of reflection and discussion—the sort of reflection and discussion that philosophy traditionally encourages. Kitcher suggested that they be called *Austinian intuitions.*

Your experiments, the objection insists, do nothing to show that Austinian intuitions would exhibit the sort of cultural diversity you've found in first-off intuitions or, indeed, that they would show any significant diversity at all. When sensible people reflect and reason together, there is every reason to suppose that they will ultimately reach a meeting of the minds.

Reply

We certainly concede that we have not shown that Austinian intuitions would not ultimately converge. However, to echo the theme of our previous reply, in the absence of any evidence we don't think there is any reason to suppose that the sorts of marked cultural differences in sensitivity to epistemic vectors that our experiments have demonstrated would simply disappear after reflection and discussion. Moreover, even if these cultural differences do dissipate after extended reflection, it might well be the case that they would be replaced by the sorts of order effects suggested in section 3.B by our Hypothesis 4. If that hypothesis is correct, then the Austinian intuitions on which a group of reflective people would converge would depend, in part, on the order in which examples and arguments happened to be introduced. And different groups might well converge on quite different sets of Austinian intuitions which then proved quite impervious to change. Experiments demonstrating the sort of path dependence that we suggest in Hypothesis 4 are much harder to design than experiments demonstrating cultural differences in initial intuitions. In the next stage of our ongoing empirical research on intuitions, we hope to run a series of experiments that will indicate the extent to which the evolution of people's intuitions is indeed a function of the order in which examples and counterexamples are encountered. Neither those experiments nor any of the evidence we've cited in this chapter will suffice to demonstrate that Austinian intuitions or IDR processes that propose to use them will fail to converge. But, to end with the theme with which we began, our goal has not been to establish that IDR strategies *will* lead to very different (putatively) normative conclusions, but simply to make it plausible that they *might*. The assumption that they won't is an empirical assumption; it is not an assumption that can be made without argument.

Our data indicate that when epistemologists advert to "our" intuitions when attempting to characterize epistemic concepts or draw normative conclusions, they are engaged in a culturally local endeavor—what we might think of as *ethnoepistemology*. Indeed, in our studies, some of the most influential thought experiments of twentieth-century epistemology elicited different intuitions in different cultures. In light of this, Intuition-Driven Romanticism seems a rather bizarre way to determine the correct epistemic norms. For it is difficult to see why a process that relies heavily on epistemic intuitions that are local to one's own cultural and socioeconomic group would lead to genuinely normative conclusions. Pending a detailed response to this problem, we think that the best reaction to the high-SES Western philosophy professor who tries to draw normative conclusions from the facts about "our" intuitions is to ask: What do you mean "we"?

APPENDIX

The Fisher Exact test was used to calculate statistical significance between groups.

Individualistic Truetemp Case (Figure 2.1)

	Really knows	Only believes
Western	61	128
East Asian	3	22

The p-exact = 0.020114

Elders Truetemp Case (Figure 2.2)

	Really knows	Only believes
Western	77	140
East Asian	5	15

The p-exact = 0.131784

Community-Wide Truetemp Case (Figure 2.3)

	Really knows	Only believes
Western	2	8
East Asian	10	21

The p-exact = 0.252681

Gettier Case: Western and East Asian (Figure 2.5)

	Really knows	Only believes
Western	17	49
East Asian	13	10

The p-exact = 0.006414

Gettier Case: Western and Indian (Figure 2.6)

	Really knows	Only believes
Western	17	49
Indian subcontinental	14	9

The p-exact = 0.002407

Cancer Conspiracy Case: Western and Indian (Figure 2.7)

	Really knows	Only believes
Western	7	59
Indian subcontinental	7	16

The p-exact = 0.025014

Zebra-in-Zoo Case: Western and Indian (Figure 2.8)

	Really knows	Only believes
Western	19	43
Indian subcontinental	12	12

The p-exact = 0.049898

Zebra-in-Zoo Case: Low and High SES (Figure 2.9)

	Really knows	Only believes
Low SES	8	16
High SES	4	30

The p-exact = 0.038246

Cancer Conspiracy Case: Low and High SES (Figure 2.10)

	Really knows	Only believes
Low SES	12	2
High SES	6	29

The p-exact = 0.006778

Special Feeling Case: Low and High SES (no figure)

	Really knows	Only believes
Low SES	3	32
High SES	3	21

The p-exact = 0.294004

Special Feeling Case: Western and East Asian (no figure)

	Really knows	Only believes
Western	2	59
East Asian	0	8

The p-exact = 0.780051

NOTES

We are grateful to Joe Cruz, Gilbert Harman, Philip Kitcher, and Joel Pust for helpful feedback on earlier versions of this essay. Our deepest debt is to Richard Nisbett, who provided us with invaluable advice and assistance in designing and interpreting the studies reported in section 3.

1. R. Samuels, "Naturalism and Normativity" (in preparation).

2. Alvin I. Goldman, "The Internalist Conception of Justification," in *Midwest Studies in Philosophy V: Epistemology,* ed. French, Uehling, and Wettstein (Minneapolis: University of Minnesota Press, 1980).

3. The literature on conceptual analysis in epistemology is vast. For an elite selection, see the essays assembled in E. Sosa, ed., *Knowledge and Justification* (Brookfield, Vt.: International Research Library of Philosophy, Dartmouth Publishing Company, 1994).

4. This is a view with a venerable history. In Plato's *Protagoras,* Socrates says that "knowledge is a noble and commanding thing," and Protagoras, not to be outdone,

replies that "wisdom and knowledge are the highest of human things." Plato, *The Dialogues of Plato*, trans. B. Jowett (New York: Random House, 1892/1937), 352.

5. Perhaps the most important advocate of extracting normative principles from analyses of our epistemic terms is Roderick Chisolm (*Theory of Knowledge* [Englewood Cliffs, N.J.: Prentice-Hall, 1977]). This approach is shared in projects as otherwise dissimilar as Bonjour and Pollock and Cruz. See, e.g., L. Bonjour, *The Structure of Empirical Knowledge* (Cambridge, Mass.: Harvard University Press, 1985); and J. Pollock and J. Cruz, *Contemporary Theories of Knowledge* (Lanham, Mass.: Rowman and Littlefield, 1999).

6. For further discussion of the Evaluative Project, see R. Samuels, S. Stich, and P. Tremoulet, "Rethinking Rationality: From Bleak Implications to Darwinian Modules," in *What Is Cognitive Science?* ed. E. LePore and Z. Pylyshyn (Oxford: Blackwell, 1999), 74–120; R. Samuels, S. Stich, and M. Bishop, "Ending the Rationality Wars: How to Make Disputes about Human Rationality Disappear," in *Common Sense, Reasoning and Rationality,* ed. Renee Elio, Vancouver Studies in Cognitive Science, vol. 11 (Oxford: Oxford University Press, in press); and R. Samuels, S. Stich, and L. Faucher, "Reasoning and Rationality," in *Handbook of Epistemology,* ed. I. Niiniluoto, M. Sintonen, and J. Wolenski (Dordrecht: Kluwer, in press). These papers are available on the Web site of the Rutgers University Research Group on Evolution and Higher Cognition: http://ruccs. rutgers.edu/ArchiveFolder/Research%20Group/research.html.

7. Note that as we've characterized them, epistemic intuitions are spontaneous judgments about *specific cases*. Some strategies for discovering or testing epistemic norms also take intuitions about general epistemic or inferential principles as input. These will count as Intuition-Driven Romantic strategies provided that the output is suitably sensitive to the intuitions about specific cases that are included in the input.

8. N. Goodman, *Fact, Fiction and Forecast* (Indianapolis, Ind.: Bobbs-Merrill, 1965), 66.

9. L. Cohen, "Can Human Irrationality Be Experimentally Demonstrated?" *Behavioral and Brain Sciences* 4 (1981): 317–70. For a useful discussion of the debate that Cohen's paper provoked, see E. Stein, *Without Good Reason: The Rationality Debate in Philosophy and Cognitive Science* (Oxford: Clarendon Press, 1996), ch. 5.

10. See, for example, C. Elgin, *Considered Judgment* (Princeton, N.J.: Princeton University Press, 1996), ch. 4; and Stein, *Without Good Reason*, chs. 5 and 7.

11. Alvin I. Goldman, *Epistemology and Cognition* (Cambridge, Mass.: Harvard University Press, 1986), 60.

12. Ibid., 64.

13. Ibid., 58.

14. Ibid., 66. In an insightful commentary on this paper, presented at the Conference in Honor of Alvin Goldman, Joel Pust notes that in his recent work Goldman (Alvin I. Goldman, "Epistemic Folkways and Scientific Epistemology," in *Liaisons* [Cambridge, Mass.: MIT Press, 1992]; Alvin I. Goldman, "A Priori Warrant and Naturalistic Epistemology," in *Philosophical Perspectives,* ed. James Tomberlin (a supplement to *Noûs*) 13 [1999]; and Alvin Goldman and J. Pust, "Philosophical Theory and Intuitional Evidence," in *Rethinking Intuition,* ed. M. DePaul and W. Ramsey (Lanham, Md.: Rowman and Littlefield, 1998]) has offered a rather different account of how epistemic intuitions are to be used:

> Very roughly, Goldman's more recent view treats the targets of philosophical analy-
> sis as concepts in the psychological sense of "concept," concrete mental represen-
> tations causally implicated in the production of philosophical intuitions. On this
> new view, intuitions serve primarily as reliable evidence concerning the intuitors
> internal psychological mechanisms.... Especially interesting in the context of [the

Weinberg, Nichols, and Stich paper] is the fact that Goldman *explicitly disavows* the common assumption of "great uniformity in epistemic subjects" judgments about cases, noting that this assumption may result from the fact that philosophers come from a "fairly homogeneous subculture" (Goldman, "Epistemic Folkways and Scientific Epistemology," 160).

This new psychologistic account makes it easier to explain why intuitions are reliable evidence of some sort. However, this reliability is gained by deflating the evidential pretensions of intuitions so that they are no longer treated as relevant to the *non-linguistic* or *non-psychological* question which is the central concern of the Normative Project: "What makes a belief epistemically justified?" While Goldman's approach solves *a* problem about the reliability of intuitions by telling us that *the fact that people have* certain intuitions is a reliable indicator of their psychological constitution, it does not resolve the problem which motivated Stich's argument since *that* problem was whether we are justified in treating *the content of* our epistemic intuitions as a reliable guide to the nature of justified belief. So, while Goldman's use of intuitions in his new project seems to me largely immune to [the criticisms in the paper by Weinberg, Nichols, and Stich], this is because that project has aspirations quite different from those of traditional analytic epistemology.

15. E. Gettier, "Is Justified True Belief Knowledge?" *Analysis* 23 (1963): 121–23. For a review of literature during the first two decades after Gettier's paper appeared, see R. Shope, *The Analysis of Knowing* (Princeton, N.J.: Princeton University Press, 1983). For more recent work in this tradition, see Plantinga, as well as the follow-up collection of papers in Kvanvig. A. Plantinga, *Warrant and Proper Function* (Oxford: Oxford University Press, 1993); A. Plantinga, *Warrant: The Current Debate* (Oxford: Oxford University Press, 1993); and J. Kvanvig, ed., *Warrant in Contemporary Epistemology: Essays in Honor of Plantinga's Theory of Knowledge* (Lanham, Md.: Rowman and Littlefield, 1996).

16. Stephen Stich, *The Fragmentation of Reason* (Cambridge, Mass.: MIT Press, 1990), sec. 4.6.

17. Cf. Pollock and Cruz, *Contemporary Theories of Knowledge,* 150.

18. The East Asian subjects were Chinese, Japanese, and Korean. Some of the experiments were conducted in Asia, others used East Asian students studying in the United States or first- and second-generation East Asian immigrants to the United States. The Western subjects were Americans of European ancestry.

19. R. Nisbett, K. Peng, I. Choi, and A. Norenzayan, "Culture and Systems of Thought: Holistic vs. Analytic Cognition," *Psychological Review* (2001): 293.

20. Nisbett (personal communication); M. Watanabe, *Styles of Reasoning in Japan and the United States: Logic of Education in Two Cultures* (Ph.D. thesis, Columbia University, 1999, Abstract). See also M. Watanabe, "Styles of Reasoning in Japan and the United States: Logic of Education in Two Cultures." Paper presented at the American Sociological Association Annual Meeting, San Francisco, August 1998.

21. Nisbett et al. (2001), 292–93.

22. J. Haidt, S. Koller, and M. Dias, "Affect, Culture and Morality," *Journal of Personality and Social Psychology* 65, 4 (1993): 613–28. We are grateful to Christopher Knapp for bringing Haidt's work to our attention.

23. See A. Clark, *Being There: Putting Brain, Body and World Together Again* (Cambridge, Mass.: MIT Press, 1997), 204–7.

24. Nisbett and Ross's work on "belief perseverance" shows that, sometimes at least, once a belief is formed, it can be surprisingly impervious to change. See, for example, R. Nisbett and L. Ross, *Human Inference: Strategies and Shortcomings of Social Judgment* (Englewood Cliffs, N.J.: Prentice-Hall, 1980), ch. 8.

25. K. Lehrer, *Theory of Knowledge* (Boulder, Colo.: Westview Press and Routledge, 1990).

26. In classifying subjects as East Asian or Western, we relied on the same ethnic identification questionnaire that Nisbett and his colleagues had used. We are grateful to Professor Nisbett for providing us with a copy of the questionnaire and for much helpful advice on its use.

27. The numerical data for all the experiments reported in this chapter are assembled in the appendix.

28. A. Norenzayan, R. E. Nisbett, E. E. Smith, and B. J. Kim, *Rules vs. Similarity as a Basis for Reasoning and Judgment in East and West* (Ann Arbor: University of Michigan, 1999).

29. F. Dretske, "Epistemic Operators," *Journal of Philosophy* 67, 24 (1970): 1007–23. Reprinted in F. Dretske, *Perception, Knowledge, and Belief* (Cambridge: Cambridge University Press, 2000).

30. We also checked for gender effects, and, while the data suggested some trends, we found significant differences on only one probe, the zebra case. On that probe, women were more likely to attribute knowledge than men ($p = .0487$). Without a larger set of data, we are not sure how to interpret this result, but we are confident that gender differences in philosophical intuitions will be an important area for further exploration.

31. Stich, *Fragmentation of Reason*, esp. ch. 6.

32. Though there is very little evidence on the point, we don't think the differences we've found are innate. Rather, we suspect, they are the product of deep differences in culture.

33. Another possible interpretation of "Really Knows" in our intuition probes would invoke what Ernest Sosa has termed merely "animal" or "servo-mechanical" knowledge. (E. Sosa, *Knowledge in Perspective* [Cambridge: Cambridge University Press, 1991], 953) We sometimes say that a dog knows that it's about to be fed, or that the thermostat knows the temperature in the room. But we philosophers are hunting different game—fully normative game which, the critic maintains, these surveys might not capture. However, if our subjects had this notion in mind, one would predict that they would overwhelmingly attribute such knowledge in the Truetemp cases, since the protagonists in each of the stories clearly has a reliable, thermostat-like information-registering capacity. Yet they did not do so—in none of the Truetemp cases did a majority of subjects opt for "Really Knows." So this rival gloss on "knows" will not help the IDR theorist to explain our data away.

34. See, for example, Bealer (G. Bealer, "A Theory of the *A Priori*," *Philosophical Perspectives, 13, Epistemology* [1999]: 29–55) who insists that "the work of cognitive psychologists such as Wason, Johnson-Laird, Nisbett, Kahneman, and Tversky tells us little about intuitions in our [philosophical] sense" (31).

35. This objection was offered by Henry Jackman, Ram Neta, and Jonathan Schaffer.

3

Semantics, Cross-Cultural Style

Edouard Machery, Ron Mallon, Shaun Nichols, & Stephen P. Stich

1. INTRODUCTION

Theories of meaning and reference have been at the heart of analytic philosophy since the beginning of the twentieth century. Two views, *the descriptivist view of reference* and *the causal-historical view of reference*, have dominated the field. The reference of names has been a key issue in this controversy. Despite numerous disagreements, philosophers agree that theories of reference for names have to be consistent with our *intuitions* regarding who or what the names refer to. Thus, the common wisdom in philosophy is that Kripke (1972/1980) has refuted the traditional descriptivist theories of reference by producing some famous stories which elicit intuitions that are inconsistent with these theories. In light of recent work in cultural psychology (Nisbett, Peng, Choi, & Norenzayan, 2001; Weinberg, Nichols, & Stich, 2001), we came to suspect that the intuitions that guide theorizing in this domain might well differ between members of East Asian and Western cultures. In this essay, we present evidence that probes closely modeled on Kripke's stories elicit significantly different responses from East Asians (EAs) (Hong Kong undergraduates) and Westerners (Ws) (American undergraduates), and we discuss the significance of this finding for the philosophical pursuit of a theory of reference.

1.1. Two Theories of Reference

Theories of reference purport to explain how terms pick out their referents. When we focus on proper names, two main positions have been developed, *the descriptivist view of reference* (e.g., Frege, 1892/1948; Searle, 1958) and *the causal-historical view* associated with Kripke (1972/1980).

Reprinted from *Cognition*, Vol. 92, "Semantics Cross-Cultural Style," B1–B12, 2004, with permission from Elsevier.

Two theses are common to all descriptivist accounts of the reference of proper names:[1]

D1. Competent speakers associate a *description* with every proper name. This description specifies a set of properties.

D2. An object is the referent of a proper name if and only if it *uniquely or best satisfies* the description associated with it. An object uniquely satisfies a description when the description is true of it and only it. If no object entirely satisfies the description, many philosophers claim that the proper name refers to the unique individual that satisfies most of the description (Lewis, 1970; Searle, 1958). If the description is not satisfied at all or if many individuals satisfy it, the name does not refer.

The causal-historical view offers a strikingly different picture (Kripke, 1972/1980):[2]

C1. A name is introduced into a linguistic community for the purpose of referring to an individual. It continues to refer to that individual as long as its uses are linked to the individual *via a causal chain* of successive users: every user of the name acquired it from another user, who acquired it in turn from someone else, and so on, up to the first user who introduced the name to refer to a specific individual.

C2. Speakers may associate descriptions with names. After a name is introduced, the associated description *does not play any role* in the fixation of the referent. The referent may *entirely* fail to satisfy the description.

1.2. The Gödel Case and the Jonah Case

There is widespread agreement among philosophers on the methodology for developing an adequate theory of reference. The project is to construct theories of reference that are consistent with our intuitions about the correct application of terms in fictional (and nonfictional) situations.[3] Indeed, Kripke's masterstroke was to propose some cases that elicited widely shared intuitions that were inconsistent with traditional descriptivist theories. Moreover, it has turned out that almost all philosophers share the intuitions elicited by Kripke's fictional cases, including most of his opponents. Even contemporary descriptivists allow that these intuitions have falsified traditional forms of descriptivism and try to accommodate them within their own sophisticated descriptivist frameworks (e.g., Evans, 1973, 1985; Jackson, 1998).

To make all of this a bit clearer we present two of Kripke's central cases in greater detail and describe the corresponding descriptivist[4] and causal-historical intuitions.

1.2.1. The Gödel Case (Kripke, 1972/1980, pp. 83–92)

Kripke imagines a case in which, because of some historical contingency, contemporary competent speakers associate with a proper name, "Gödel," a description that is entirely false of the original bearer of that name, person *a*.

Instead, it is true of a different individual, person b. Descriptivism implies that the proper name refers to b because b satisfies the description. The descriptivist intuition is that someone who uses "Gödel" under these circumstances is speaking about b. According to the causal-historical view, however, the name refers to its original bearer, since contemporary speakers are historically related to him. The Kripkean intuition is that someone who uses "Gödel" under these circumstances is speaking about a. According to Kripke (and many other philosophers), our semantic intuitions support the causal-historical view:

> Suppose that Gödel was not in fact the author of [Gödel's] theorem. A man called "Schmidt" ... actually did the work in question. His friend Gödel somehow got hold of the manuscript and it was thereafter attributed to Gödel. On the [descriptivist] view in question, then, when our ordinary man uses the name "Gödel," he really means to refer to Schmidt, because Schmidt is the unique person satisfying the description "the man who discovered the incompleteness of arithmetic." ... But it seems we are not. We simply are not. (Kripke, 1972/1980, pp. 83–84)

1.2.2. The Jonah Case (Kripke, 1972/1980, pp. 66–67)

Kripke imagines a case in which the description associated with a proper name, say "Jonah," is not satisfied at all. According to descriptivism, "Jonah" would then fail to have a referent. The descriptivist intuition is that someone who uses the name under these circumstances isn't speaking about any real individual.[5] On the contrary, on the causal-historical view, satisfying the description is not necessary for being the referent of a name. The Kripkean intuition is that someone can use the name to speak about the name's original bearer, whether or not the description is satisfied.[6] Again, our intuitions are supposed to support the causal-historical view:

> Suppose that someone says that no prophet ever was swallowed by a big fish or a whale. Does it follow, on that basis, that Jonah did not exist? There still seems to be the question whether the Biblical account is a legendary account of no person or a legendary account built on a real person. In the latter case, it's only natural to say that, though Jonah did exist, no one did the things commonly related to him. (Kripke, 1972/1980, p. 67)

1.3. Cultural Variation in Cognition and Intuitions

Philosophers typically share the Kripkean intuitions and expect theories of reference to accommodate them. As we discuss more fully in section 3, we suspect that most philosophers exploring the nature of reference assume that the Kripkean intuitions are universal. Suppose that semantic intuitions exhibit systematic differences between groups or individuals. This would raise questions about whose intuitions are going to count, putting in jeopardy philosophers' methodology.[7]

As researchers in history and anthropology have long maintained, one should be wary of simply assuming cultural universality without evidence. Recent work in cultural psychology has provided experimental results that underscore this cautionary note. In an important series of experiments, Richard Nisbett and his collaborators have found large and systematic differences between EAs and Ws on a number of basic cognitive processes, including perception, attention, and memory.[8] These groups also differ in the way they go about describing, predicting, and explaining events, in the way they categorize objects, and in the way they revise beliefs in the face of new arguments and evidence (for reviews, see Nisbett, 2003; Nisbett et al., 2001). This burgeoning literature in cultural psychology suggests that culture plays a dramatic role in shaping human cognition. Inspired by this research program, Weinberg et al. (2001) constructed a variety of probes modeled on thought experiments from the philosophical literature in epistemology. These thought experiments were designed to elicit intuitions about the appropriate application of epistemic concepts. Weinberg et al. found that there do indeed seem to be systematic cross-cultural differences in epistemic intuitions. In light of these findings on epistemic intuitions, we were curious to see whether there might also be cross-cultural differences in intuitions about reference.

We lack the space to offer a detailed account of the differences uncovered by Nisbett and his colleagues. But it is important to review briefly some of the findings that led to the studies we will report here. According to Nisbett and his colleagues, the differences between EAs and Ws "can be loosely grouped together under the heading of holistic vs. analytic thought." Holistic thought, which predominates among EAs, is characterized as "involving an orientation to the context or field as a whole, including attention to relationships between a focal object and the field, and a preference for explaining and predicting events on the basis of such relationships." Analytic thought, the prevailing pattern among Ws, is characterized as "involving detachment of the object from its context, a tendency to focus on attributes of the object in order to assign it to categories, and a preference for using rules about the categories to explain and predict the object's behavior" (Nisbett et al., 2001, p. 293).

One range of findings is particularly significant for our project. The cross-cultural work indicates that EAs are more inclined than Ws to make categorical judgments on the basis of similarity; Ws, on the other hand, are more disposed to focus on causation in describing the world and classifying things (Norenzayan, Smith, & Kim, 2002; Watanabe, 1998, 1999). This differential focus led us to hypothesize that there might be a related cross-cultural difference in semantic intuitions. On a description theory, the referent has to satisfy the description, but it need not be causally related to the use of the term. In contrast, on Kripke's causal-historical theory, the referent need not satisfy the associated description. Rather, it need only figure in the causal history (and in the causal explanation) of the speaker's current use of the word.

Given that Ws are more likely than EAs to make causation-based judgments, we predicted that when presented with Kripke-style thought experiments, *Ws would be more likely to respond in accordance with causal-historical accounts of reference, while EAs would be more likely to respond in accordance with descriptivist accounts of reference.*[9] To test this hypothesis, we assembled a range of intuition probes to explore whether such differences might be revealed. The probes were designed to parallel the Jonah case and the Gödel case.

2. EXPERIMENT

2.1. Method

2.1.1. Participants

Forty undergraduates at Rutgers University and 42 undergraduates from the University of Hong Kong participated. The University of Hong Kong is an English-speaking university in Hong Kong, and the participants were all fluent speakers of English. A standard demographics instrument was used to determine whether participants were Western or Chinese. Using this instrument, nine non-Western participants were excluded from the Rutgers sample, leaving a total of 31 Western participants from Rutgers (18 females, 13 males). One non-Chinese participant was excluded from the Hong Kong sample, leaving a total of 41 Chinese participants from Hong Kong (25 females, 16 males). One additional Hong Kong participant was excluded for failure to answer the demographic questions.

2.1.2. Materials and Procedure

In a classroom setting, participants were presented with four probes counterbalanced for order. The probes were presented in English both in the United States and in Hong Kong. Two were modeled on Kripke's Gödel case, and two were modeled on Kripke's Jonah case. One probe modeled on Kripke's Gödel case and one probe modeled on Kripke's Jonah case used names that were familiar to the Chinese participants. One of the Gödel probes was closely modeled on Kripke's own example (see appendix A for the other probes):

> Suppose that John has learned in college that Gödel is the man who proved an important mathematical theorem, called the incompleteness of arithmetic. John is quite good at mathematics and he can give an accurate statement of the incompleteness theorem, which he attributes to Gödel as the discoverer. But this is the only thing that he has heard about Gödel. Now suppose that Gödel was not the author of this theorem. A man called "Schmidt," whose body was found in Vienna under mysterious circumstances many years ago, actually did the work in questions. His friend Gödel somehow got hold of the manuscript and claimed credit for the work, which was thereafter attributed to Gödel. Thus, he has been known as the man who proved the incompleteness of arithmetic. Most people who have heard the name "Gödel" are like John; the claim that Gödel discovered the incompleteness theorem is the only thing they have ever heard about Gödel. When John uses the name "Gödel," is he talking about:
>
> (A) the person who really discovered the incompleteness of arithmetic? or
> (B) the person who got hold of the manuscript and claimed credit for the work?

2.2. Results and Discussion

2.2.1. Scoring

The scoring procedure was straightforward. Each question was scored binomially. An answer consonant with causal-historical accounts of reference (B) was given a score of 1; the other answer (A) was given a score of 0. The scores were then summed, so the cumulative score could range from 0 to 2. Means and standard deviation for summary scores are shown in table 3.1.

An independent samples t-test yielded a significant difference between Chinese and Western participants on the Gödel cases ($t(70) = -2.55$, $P < 0.05$) (all tests two-tailed). The Westerners were more likely than the Chinese to give causal-historical responses. However, in the Jonah cases, there was no significant difference between Chinese and Western participants ($t(69) = 0.486$, n.s.). In light of the dichotomous nature of the underlying distributions, we also analyzed each Gödel case nonparametrically, and the results were largely the same. Western participants were more likely than Chinese participants to give causal-historical responses on both the Tsu Ch'ung Chih probe ($\chi^2(1, N = 72)$ = 3.886, $P < 0.05$) and on the Gödel probe ($\chi^2(1, N = 72) = 6.023$, $P < 0.05$).[10]

Thus, we found that probes modeled on Kripke's Gödel case (including one that used Kripke's own words) elicit culturally variable intuitions. As we had predicted, Chinese participants tended to have descriptivist intuitions, while Westerners tended to have Kripkean ones. However, our prediction that the Westerners would be more likely than the Chinese to give causal-historical responses on the Jonah cases was not confirmed. There are a number of possible explanations for this. Setting out the Jonah cases precisely requires a lengthy presentation (see appendix A), so it is possible that our probes were simply too long and complex to generate interpretable data. Another, more interesting possibility hinges on the fact that in the Jonah cases, the descriptivist response is that the speaker's term fails to refer. It might be that for pragmatic reasons, both the Westerners and the Chinese reject the uncharitable interpretation that the speaker is not talking about anyone.

Table 3.1. Mean scores for experiment 1 (SD in parentheses)

	Score (SD)
Gödel cases	
Western participants	1.13 (0.88)
Chinese participants	0.63 (0.84)
Jonah cases	
Western participants	1.23 (0.96)
Chinese participants	1.32 (0.76)

3. THE END OF THE INNOCENCE

Our central prediction was that, given Westerners' greater tendency to make causation-based judgements, they would be more likely than the Chinese to have intuitions that fall in line with causal-historical accounts of reference. This prediction was borne out in our experiment. We found the predicted systematic cultural differences on one of the best known thought experiments in recent philosophy of language, Kripke's Gödel case. However, we have no illusions that our experiment is the final empirical word on the issue. Rather, our findings raise a number of salient questions for future research. For instance, we predicted that the Westerners would be more likely than the Chinese to have Kripkean intuitions *because they are more likely to make causation-based judgements*. Although our results are consistent with this hypothesis, they fail to support it directly. They do not establish unequivocally that the cultural difference results from a different emphasis on causation. In future work, it will be important to manipulate this variable more directly. Further, our experiment does not rule out various pragmatic explanations of the findings. Although we found the effect on multiple different versions of the Gödel case, the test question was very similar in all the cases. Perhaps the test question we used triggered different interpretations of the question in the two different groups. In addition, our focus in this essay has been on intuitions about proper names, since proper names have been at the center of debates about semantics. However, it will be important to examine whether intuitions about the reference of other sorts of terms, for example, natural kind terms (see, e.g., Putnam, 1975), also exhibit systematic cross-cultural differences. We hope that future work will begin to address these questions.

Although there are many empirical questions left open by the experiment reported here, we think that the experiment already points to significant philosophical conclusions. As we noted above, we suspect that philosophers employing these thought experiments take their own intuitions regarding the referents of terms, and those of their philosophical colleagues, to be universal. But our cases were modeled on some of the most influential thought experiments in the philosophy of reference, and we elicited culturally variable intuitions. Thus, the evidence suggests that it is wrong for philosophers to assume a priori the universality of their own semantic intuitions. Indeed, the variation might be even more dramatic than we have suggested. While our focus has been on cultural differences, the data also reveal considerable intracultural variation. The high standard deviations in our experiment indicate that there is a great deal of variation in the semantic intuitions within both the Chinese and Western groups. This might reflect smaller intracultural groups that differ in their semantic intuitions. A more extreme but very live possibility is that the variability exists even at the individual level, so that a given individual might have causal-historical intuitions on some occasions and descriptivist intuitions on other occasions. If so, then the assumption of universality is just spectacularly misguided.

Perhaps, however, philosophers do not assume the universality of semantic intuitions. In that case, philosophers of language need to clarify their project. One possibility is that philosophers of language would claim to have no interest in unschooled, folk semantic intuitions, including the differing intuitions of various cultural groups. These philosophers might maintain that, since they aim to find the *correct* theory of reference for proper names, only *reflective* intuitions, i.e., intuitions that are informed by a cautious examination of the philosophical significance of the probes, are to be taken into consideration.

We find it *wildly* implausible that the semantic intuitions of the narrow cross-section of humanity who are Western academic philosophers are a more reliable indicator of the correct theory of reference (if there is such a thing, see Stich, 1996, chap. 1) than the differing semantic intuitions of other cultural or linguistic groups. Indeed, given the intense training and selection that undergraduate and graduate students in philosophy have to go through, there is good reason to suspect that the alleged *reflective* intuitions may be *reinforced* intuitions. In the absence of a principled argument about why philosophers' intuitions are superior, this project smacks of narcissism in the extreme.

A more charitable interpretation of the work of philosophers of language is that it is a protoscientific project modeled on the Chomskyan tradition in linguistics. Such a project would employ intuitions about reference to develop an empirically adequate account of the implicit theory that underlies ordinary uses of names. If this is the correct interpretation of the philosophical interest in the theory of reference, then our data are especially surprising, for there is little hint in philosophical discussions that names might work in different ways in different dialects of the same language or in different cultural groups who speak the same language. So, on this interpretation, our data indicate that philosophers must radically revise their methodology. Since the intuitions philosophers pronounce from their armchairs are likely to be a product of their own culture and their academic training, in order to determine the implicit theories that underlie the use of names across cultures, philosophers need to get out of their armchairs. And this is far from what philosophers have been doing for the last several decades.

We are grateful to Vivian Chu, Max Deutsch, Tim German, Chad Hansen, Ping Lau, Philippe Schlenker, and an anonymous referee for advice, discussion, and helpful comments.

APPENDIX A

A.1. Gödel Case

Ivy is a high-school student in Hong Kong. In her astronomy class she was taught that Tsu Ch'ung Chih was the man who first determined the precise time of the summer and winter solstices. But, like all her classmates, this is the only thing she has heard about Tsu Ch'ung Chih. Now suppose that Tsu Ch'ung Chih did not really make this discovery. He stole it from an astronomer who died soon after making the discovery. But the theft remained entirely undetected and Tsu Ch'ung Chih became famous for the discovery of the precise times of the solstices. Many people are like Ivy; the claim that Tsu Ch'ung Chih determined the solstice times is the only thing they have heard about him. When Ivy uses the name "Tsu Ch'ung Chih," is she talking about:

(A) the person who really determined the solstice times? or
(B) the person who stole the discovery of the solstice times?

A.2. Jonah Cases

In high school, German students learn that Attila founded Germany in the second century A.D. They are taught that Attila was the king of a nomadic tribe that migrated from the east to settle in what would become Germany. Germans also believe that Attila was a merciless warrior and leader who expelled the Romans from Germany, and that after his victory against the Romans, Attila organized a large and prosperous kingdom.

Now suppose that none of this is true. No merciless warrior expelled the Romans from Germany, and Germany was not founded by a single individual. Actually, the facts are the following. In the fourth century A.D., a nobleman of low rank, called "Raditra," ruled a small and peaceful area in what today is Poland, several hundred miles from Germany. Raditra was a wise and gentle man who managed to preserve the peace in the small land he was ruling. For this reason, he quickly became the main character of many stories and legends. These stories were passed on from one generation of peasants to the next. But often when the story was passed on the peasants would embellish it, adding imaginary details and dropping some true facts to make the story more exciting. From a peaceful nobleman of low rank, Raditra was gradually transformed into a warrior fighting for his land. When the legend reached Germany, it told of a merciless warrior who was victorious against the Romans. By the eighth century A.D., the story told of an Eastern king who expelled the Romans and founded Germany. By that time, not a single true fact remained in the story.

Meanwhile, as the story was told and retold, the name "Raditra" was slowly altered: it was successively replaced by "Aditra," then by "Arritrak" in the sixth century, by "Arrita" and "Arrila" in the seventh, and finally by "Attila." The story about the glorious life of Attila was written down in the eighth century by a scrupulous Catholic monk, from whom all our beliefs are derived. Of course, Germans know nothing about these real events. They believe a story about a merciless Eastern king who expelled the Romans and founded Germany.

When a contemporary German high-school student says "Attila was the king who drove the Romans from Germany," is he actually talking about the wise and gentle nobleman, Raditra, who is the original source of the Attila legend, or is he talking about a fictional person, someone who does not really exist?

(A) He is talking about Raditra.
(B) He is talking about a fictional person who does not really exist.

Lau Mei Ling is a high-school student in the Chinese city of Guangzhou. Like everyone who goes to high school in Guangzhou, Mei Ling believes that Chan Wai Man was a Guangdong nobleman who had to take refuge in the wild mountains around Guangzhou in the eleventh century A.D., because Chan Wai Man was in love with the daughter of the ruthless Government Minister Lee, and the Minister did not approve. Everyone in Lau Mei Ling's high school believes that Chan Wai Man had to live as a thief in the mountains around Guangzhou, and that he would often steal from the rich allies of the Minister Lee and distribute their goods to the poor peasants.

Now suppose that none of this is true. No Guangdong nobleman ever lived in the mountains around Guangzhou, stealing from the wealthy people to help the peasants. The real facts are the following. In one of the monasteries around Guangzhou, there was a helpful monk called "Leung Yiu Pang." Leung Yiu Pang was always ready to help the peasants around his monastery, providing food in the winter, giving medicine to the sick, and helping the children. Because he was so kind, he quickly became the main character of many stories. These stories were passed on from one generation of peasants to the next. Over the years, the story changed slowly as the peasants would forget some elements of the story and add other elements. In one version, Leung Yiu Pang was described as a rebel fighting Minister Lee. Progressively the story came to describe the admirable deeds of a generous thief. By the late fourteenth century, the story was about a generous nobleman who was forced to live as a thief because of his love for the Minister's daughter. At length, not a single true fact remained in the story.

Meanwhile, the name "Leung Yiu Pang" was slowly altered: it was successively replaced by "Cheung Wai Pang" in the twelfth century, "Chung Wai Man" in the thirteenth, and finally by "Chan Wai Man." The story about the adventurous life of Chan Wai Man was written down in the fifteenth century by a scrupulous historian, from whom all our beliefs are derived. Of course, Mei Ling, her classmates, and her parents know nothing about these real events. Mei Ling believes a story about a generous thief who was fighting against a mean minister.

When Mei Ling says "Chan Wai Man stole from the rich and gave to the poor," is she actually talking about the generous monk, Leung Yiu Pang, who is the original source of the legend about Chan Wai Man, or is she talking about a fictional person, someone who does not really exist?

(A) She is talking about the generous monk, Leung Yiu Pang.
(B) She is talking about a fictional person who does not really exist.

NOTES

1. There are a variety of ways of developing description-theoretic accounts (e.g., Frege, 1892/1948; Garcia-Carpintero, 2000; Jackson, 1998; Lewis, 1970; Loar, 1976; Searle, 1958, 1983).

2. This picture has been refined in various ways (e.g., Devitt, 1981; Devitt & Sterelny, 1999; Salmon, 1986; Soames, 2001).

3. Philosophers typically assume that speakers know (perhaps implicitly) how the reference of proper names is picked out. The intuitive judgments of the speakers are supposed somehow to reflect that knowledge (Kripke, 1972/1980, pp. 42, 91; Segal, 2001).

4. We use "descriptivism" to refer to the simple, traditional versions of descriptivism and not to its recent, sophisticated elaborations. We call intuitions that are compatible with the causal-historical theory and incompatible with the traditional versions of descriptivism *Kripkean intuitions*. In contrast, we call those that are compatible with the traditional descriptivist theories and incompatible with the causal-historical theory *descriptivist intuitions*.

5. Or that the statement "Jonah exists" is false (given that the name has no referent).

6. Or that Jonah might have existed, whether or not the description is satisfied.

7. A few philosophers have acknowledged the possibility that there is variation in semantic intuitions (e.g., Dupré, 1993; Stich, 1990, 1996), but this possibility has not previously been investigated empirically.

8. The East Asian participants were Chinese, Japanese, and Korean.

9. There is a common concern that the labels "East Asian" and "Western" are too rough to do justice to the enormous diversity of cultural groups such labels encompass. We are sympathetic to this concern. However, the crudeness of these groupings does nothing to undermine the experiment we present. On the contrary, if we find significant results using crude cultural groupings, there is reason to believe more nuanced classifications should yield even stronger results.

10. It is worth noting that this result replicated an earlier pilot study in which we used two different cases modeled on Kripke's Gödel case. In the pilot study, we found that Western participants (at the College of Charleston, $N = 19$, $M = 1.42$, SD = 0.77) were more likely than Chinese participants (at Hong Kong University, $N = 32$, $M = 0.65$, SD = 0.75) to give causal-historical responses ($t(43) = -3.366$, $P < 0.01$, two-tailed). The results of the pilot study were also significant when analyzed nonparametrically.

REFERENCES

Devitt, M. (1981). *Designation*. New York: Columbia University Press.

Devitt, M., & Sterelny, K. (1999). *Language and reality: An introduction to the philosophy of language* (2nd ed.). Cambridge, MA: MIT Press.

Dupré, J. (1993). *The disorder of things: Metaphysical foundations of the disunity of science*. Cambridge, MA: Harvard University Press.

Evans, G. (1973). The causal theory of names. *Supplementary Proceedings of the Aristotelian Society, 47*, 187–208. Reprinted in Evans (1985) and Ludlow (1997).

Evans, G. (1985). *Collected papers*. Oxford: Oxford University Press.

Frege, G. (1892/1948). On sense and reference (M. Black, trans.). *Philosophical Review, 57*, 207–230. Reprinted in Ludlow (1997).

Garcia-Carpintero, M. (2000). A presuppositional account of reference fixing. *Journal of Philosophy, 97*(3), 109–147.

Jackson, F. (1998). Reference and description revisited. In J. Tomberlin (ed.), *Language, mind, and ontology* (12) (pp. 201–218). *Philosophical perspectives*. Oxford: Blackwell.

Kripke, S. (1972/1980). *Naming and necessity*. Cambridge, MA: Harvard University Press.

Lewis, D. (1970). How to define theoretical terms. *Journal of Philosophy, 67*, 427–446.

Loar, B. (1976). The semantics of singular terms. *Philosophical Studies, 30*, 353–377.

Nisbett, R. E. (2003). *The geography of thought: How Asians and Westerners think differently...and why*. New York: Free Press.

Nisbett, R. E., Peng, K., Choi, I., & Norenzayan, A. (2001). Culture and systems of thought: Holistic vs. analytic cognition. *Psychological Review, 108*, 291–310.

Norenzayan, A., Smith, E., & Kim, B. (2002). Cultural preferences for formal versus intuitive reasoning. *Cognitive Science, 26*, 653–684.

Putnam, H. (1975). The meaning of "meaning." In H. Putnam (ed.), *Mind, language, and reality* (2). *Philosophical papers*. New York: Cambridge University Press.

Salmon, N. (1986). *Frege's puzzle*. Cambridge, MA: MIT Press.

Searle, J. (1958). Proper names. *Mind, 67*, 166–173. Reprinted in Ludlow (1997).

Searle, J. (1983). *Intentionality: An essay in the philosophy of mind*. Cambridge: Cambridge University Press.

Segal, G. (2001). Two theories of names. *Mind and Language, 16*(5), 547–563.

Soames, S. (2001). *Beyond necessity: The unfinished semantic agenda of naming and necessity*. New York: Oxford University Press.

Stich, S. (1990). *The fragmentation of reason*. Cambridge, MA: MIT Press.

Stich, S. (1996). *Deconstructing the mind*. Oxford: Oxford University Press.

Watanabe, M. (1998). *Styles of reasoning in Japan and the United States: Logic of education in two cultures*. Paper presented at the American Sociological Association annual meeting, San Francisco, CA.

Watanabe, M. (1999). *Styles of reasoning in Japan and the United States: Logic of Education in two cultures*. Unpublished Ph.D. thesis, Columbia University, New York.

Weinberg, J., Nichols, S., & Stich, S. (2001). Normativity and epistemic intuitions. *Philosophical Topics, 29*(1&2), 429–459.

PART II

RESPONSIBILITY, DETERMINISM, AND LAY INTUITIONS

Philosophical discussions of free will and moral responsibility often involve explicit claims about people's ordinary intuitions. Experimental work in this area began as an attempt to explore such claims using empirical methods. Although different experimental philosophers have different views on many issues concerning free will and responsibility, they all share the goal of reaching a better understanding of the patterns of people's intuitions and the psychological processes that underlie them.

Woolfolk, Doris, and Darley look at cases in which an agent's behavior is governed by an absolute constraint. In some of the cases they examine, an external force completely controls the agent's behavior, so that the agent's own desires and values have no influence at all on the behaviors he or she ends up performing. To a first glance, it may appear that any normal person would say that the agents in such cases are in no way responsible for their behaviors and therefore not at all deserving of praise or blame. Yet the actual experimental findings reveal a far more complex and interesting pattern of intuitions. Even when an agent is under absolute constraint, participants find him more responsible, and hence more blameworthy, when he identifies with his actions than when he does not. The researchers suggest that this finding should lead to a substantial revision in our understanding of the way constraint and identification figure in ordinary attributions of moral responsibility.

Philosophers have often suggested that the intuitive view about the relationship between moral responsibility and determinism is *incompatibilism*. In essence, the claim here is that ordinary people believe that an agent can never be responsible for his or her behavior when that behavior is governed by deterministic laws. **Nahmias, Morris, Nadelhoffer, and Turner** put this claim to the test in a series of experimental studies. In each study, participants are given a story about an agent who performed a good or bad act in a deterministic universe. They are then asked to say whether or not this agent was morally responsible. Surprisingly, the results suggest that ordinary people are actually *compatibilists*. Across three different studies, using three different kinds of scenarios, the researchers consistently find that people regard the agent as morally responsible even though his or her actions are entirely determined.

Nichols and Knobe argue that people are pulled in different directions by different aspects of their psychology. Specifically, the suggestion is that people are pulled more toward incompatibilism by cool theoretical reasoning and more toward compatibilism by immediate affective reactions. Their studies are designed to manipulate the psychological factors underlying people's responses, with some conditions promoting abstract reasoning and others triggering emotional reactions. As predicted, people seem to give more incompatibilist responses when guided by abstract reasoning and more compatibilist responses when guided by emotional reactions.

SUGGESTED READINGS

Bloom, P. 2006. "My Brain Made Me Do It." *Journal of Cognition and Culture* 6: 209–214.
Knobe, J., and Doris, J. Forthcoming. "Strawsonian Variations: Folk Morality and the Search for a Unified Theory." In J. Doris et al. (eds.), *The Handbook of Moral Psychology*. Oxford: Oxford University Press.
Nahmias, E., Coates, J., and Kvaran, T. 2007. "Free Will, Moral Responsibility, and Mechanism: Experiments on Folk Intuitions." *Midwest Studies in Philosophy*.
Nichols, S. 2006. "Folk Intuitions about Free Will." *Journal of Cognition and Culture* 6.
Roskies, A. 2006. "Neuroscientific Challenges to Free Will." *Trends in Cognitive Sciences* 10: 419–423.
Sommers, T. Forthcoming. "Two Faces of Revenge." *Biology and Philosophy*.
Vargas, M. 2006. "Philosophy and the Folk: On Some Implications of Experimental Work for Philosophical Debates on Free Will." *Journal of Cognition and Culture* 6: 239–254.

4

Identification, Situational Constraint, and Social Cognition

Studies in the Attribution of Moral Responsibility

Robert L. Woolfolk, John M. Doris, & John M. Darley

1. INTRODUCTION

The ascription of moral responsibility is ubiquitous in both everyday social interaction and institutionalized social practices. The ways in which people understand and assign responsibility have been of great interest to psychologists and cognitive scientists studying social cognition and the attribution of responsibility, as well as to philosophers working in ethical theory. However, the folk theories that social perceivers employ in ascribing responsibility remain incompletely understood.

Empirical research on folk theories addressing the assignment of responsibility has its basis in attribution theory. Jones and Davis (1965) developed their theory of "correspondent inference" to articulate the conditions under which the observer of another person's actions would believe that those actions "corresponded" with or were indicative of the actor's underlying intentions, attitudes, or traits. They suggested that observers make correspondent inferences only after concluding that an actor is free to choose to perform the observed act, versus being constrained to do so by external factors. Kelley's (1972) "discounting principle" expresses the same conclusion. It maintains that attributions regarding characteristics of an actor, based on observations of that actor's behavior, are made only when the observed behavior is thought to be unconstrained. Conversely, in cases where an act is performed under extreme constraint, inferences about characteristics of the actor are expected to be "discounted."

The empirical research, however, has shown that observers sometimes fail to discount the informational value of behavior that is compelled or coerced.

Reprinted from *Cognition*, Vol. 100, 92, "Identification, situational constraint, and social cognition: Studies in the attribution of moral responsibility," 283–301, 2006, with permission from Elsevier.

In a long run of "no choice" experiments associated with Jones (1990), participants made correspondent inferences (attributed characteristics to the actor) even when it appeared to be obvious that the actions they observed were produced by strong and visible external constraints. In subsequent research, this tendency toward "overattribution" (Quattrone, 1982) has been demonstrated for a wide variety of attitudes and traits, leading Ross (1977) to coin the now famous "fundamental attribution error" term to describe this effect (cf. Darley & Cooper, 1998; Gilbert & Malone, 1995; Jones, 1990; Ross & Nisbett, 1991).

Recent work (e.g., Malle, 1999; McClure, 1998) has complicated the picture somewhat and has suggested that the person/situation dichotomy of causes, upon which much attribution research is predicated, is an overly simplistic framing of ordinary persons' thinking, and recent empirical studies indicate that overattribution may be less pervasive than suggested by early demonstrations of the "fundamental attribution error" (Fein, Hilton, & Miller, 1990; Hilton, Fein, & Miller, 1993; see Gilbert & Malone, 1995, for discussion). Although this recent research suggests important qualifications regarding the nature and extent of overattribution, the cumulative weight of evidence indicates that when behavior is constrained, perceivers regularly attribute more influence to characteristics of the person, as opposed to properties of the situation, than the discounting principle would predict.

According to various psychological theories (Darley & Shultz, 1990; Shaver, 1985; Shultz & Schleifer, 1983), the personal characteristic of actors that most influences observers' attributions is the actor's perceived *causal role* in an outcome. Some of the more recent psychological accounts of responsibility attribution emphasize the extent to which a given outcome is in the actor's "control" and is intentionally brought about (Alicke, 2000; Schlenker, Britt, Pennington, Murphy, & Doherty, 1994; Weiner, 1995). According to Schlenker et al.'s (1994) "triangle model" of responsibility, actors are likely to be held responsible when there is a perceived link between the event and the actor, such that the actor is viewed as having foreseen and "freely" brought about the event. Alicke's (2000) "culpable control" model of blame assignment posits various forms of personal control that are attended to by observers in attributing moral responsibility. One of these is "volitional outcome control," i.e., the extent to which the observer desired and foresaw the outcome of her action. Similarly, Reeder, Kumar, Hesson-McInnis, & Trafimow (2002) found that participants judging the morality of an actor paid more attention to the actors' motives, such as self-interest, than to "facilitating situational forces." Weiner's (1995) theory of responsibility also emphasizes the attribution of psychological states to the actor in the assessment of credit and blame; Weiner contends that in some circumstances observers may assign responsibility before evaluating mitigating contextual factors. While recent theories retain the familiar emphasis on the actor's causal role, especially causally efficacious psychological antecedents of behavior, these theories recognize that individuals can be connected to actions in highly complex ways that are not well summarized by relatively simplistic attributional principles, such as the discounting principle.

Philosophers often have maintained that individuals should not be held accountable for acting or failing to act when insufficient capacity for appropriate behavior is present, or when operating under constraints they could not be reasonably expected to resist (Smith, 1961; Wallace, 1994). These philosophical intuitions also are evident in legal practice (Robinson, 1996), in that we do not hold children accountable for acts that would constitute criminal conduct in an adult, nor do we court-martial military personnel who denounce their country while being tortured as prisoners of war. Indeed, many philosophers have endorsed a principle similar to the psychologist's causal discounting principle: if a behavior is determined by factors outside of the actor's control, the actor is not morally responsible for that behavior.

Here the philosophical discussion of "freedom and determinism" becomes relevant, and we will briefly review it. The problem is among the most controversial and recalcitrant in philosophy, and numerous commentators have observed that existing theoretical accounts of responsibility have difficulties, perhaps insoluble difficulties (e.g., Kane, 2002; Nagel, 1986). How can people act freely, it is asked, if, as the "scientific world view" holds, all behavior is causally determined by antecedent forces, forces beyond the actor's control?

There are three standard responses to this question. *Hard determinists* deny that people are ever responsible for their behavior, while *libertarians* insist that causal determinism is not always true in the case of human behavior, thereby allowing for the possibility of moral responsibility. These two groups are labeled *incompatibilist*, in that they both regard causal determination of behavior as incompatible with moral responsibility. Incompatibilists subscribe to the famous "principle of alternate possibilities," which states that one is morally responsible for what one has done only if one could have done otherwise. *Compatibilists*, on the other hand, assert that moral responsibility and causal determinism can be simultaneously maintained and that people may be legitimately held responsible in violation of this principle, even when they could *not* have done otherwise.

An influential compatibilist approach is associated with the philosopher Harry Frankfurt (1988; cf. Bratman, 1996; Velleman, 1992). Frankfurt contends that judgments of responsibility for behavior should be governed by the extent to which the actor "identifies" with the behavior and the motivations that produce the behavior (Doris, 2002; Frankfurt, 1988). An actor identifies with a behavior (or its motives) when she "embraces" that behavior (or its motives) or performs the behavior "wholeheartedly" (Bratman, 1996; Frankfurt, 1988); we might say that an actor identifies with a behavior to the extent that it expresses her "fundamental evaluative orientation" (Watson, 1996). When Dan happily donates some money to the office charity because he is deeply committed to giving, he identifies with his behavior and is, therefore, to be credited even if his boss has pressured him to donate. The converse of identification occurs when the actor is "alienated" from the desires or motives associated with the behavior, where the desires seem to result from factors external to the self. For example, when Julie grudgingly and unwillingly contributes to the office charity solely to appease her boss, she does not identify with the act of giving and therefore is not to be praised for the "charitable" deed.

While the kind of compatibilism described above has considerable intuitive appeal in these cases, it has implications that appear to be strikingly counter-intuitive when generalized: specifically, the theory appears to imply that persons may be held responsible even when they operated in the grip of forces compelling that action. In the studies we report in this article, we investigate whether participants attribute elevated responsibility to actors who are coerced to perform actions they also strongly desire to perform.

In the present study we examine empirically the following questions: (1) What is the effect of an actor's degree of identification with an act on observers' attributions of responsibility? (2) What is the effect of situational constraint on observers' attributions of responsibility? (3) To what degree do constraint and actor identification interact as influences on observers' attributions of responsibility? More specifically, does a high desire to commit the act increase attributions of responsibility even when the act seems compelled, or at least strongly coerced by external circumstances?

We use the term "identification" to denote the degree to which an actor wants or desires to perform behavior and maintains a positive "fundamental evaluative orientation" (Watson, 1996) toward that behavior. We investigate the variable of identification together with a more familiar causal factor, the degree to which the actor was coerced or compelled to perform the action. Our hypothesis is that an agent's identification with a behavior influences responsibility attributions to that actor, even when the actor is strongly constrained to do the action. The significance of this hypothesis, if supported, is twofold. First, it indicates that habits of responsibility attribution are influenced by factors other than the causal/explanatory factors implicated in the theories reviewed above. Second, it suggests that one philosophical account of responsibility, the "identificationist" account associated with Frankfurt, is reflected in the way ordinary people think.

Three experiments are described. In the first two experiments, we systematically varied identification, here operationalized as the extent to which an actor both endorses an action and desires to perform it. Identification was crossed with the level of constraint, or the degree to which the act was coerced. The third experiment includes a check on the independent variable manipulation of constraint employed in the first two experiments.

2. EXPERIMENT 1

In Experiment 1, we assessed the impact of varying levels of identification and situational constraint on the attribution of responsibility for a violent action, the killing of another person. We hypothesized that both external constraint and the actor's level of identification would affect judgments of responsibility for the action, even when the action was highly constrained.

2.1. Method

2.1.1. Participants and Procedure

Seventy-two (34 female and 38 male) University of California, Santa Cruz, under-graduates enrolled in philosophy classes participated in the experiment as volun-teers. Participants were randomly assigned to experimental conditions and were supervised as they completed the materials individually during class time.

2.1.2. Materials

Each participant read one of four different vignettes. The vignettes reflected a 2(Identification: low vs. high) × 2(Constraint: medium vs. high) between-participants design. The initial section of each vignette was common to all four conditions. In this section two married couples, Susan and Bill and Elaine and Frank, are depicted on a Caribbean vacation and subsequently on board an airliner returning home. It is revealed that Susan and Frank have been involved in a love affair and that Bill has discovered proof of the affair.

In the *High Identification* condition participants read:

> The humiliation and betrayal were almost more than he could bear. These were the two people he trusted most in the world. During the three days of the vacation that remained, he wrestled with the issue. He thought of many ways of retaliating. Finally, he decided that there was only one way he could deal with it. Bill decided that he would kill Frank.

In the *Low Identification* condition participants read:

> During the three days of the vacation that remained, he wrestled with the issue. Finally, he decided that if Susan and Frank wanted to be together, he would not stand in their way. He would confront them with the evi-dence and assume that whatever happened would be for the best. He really cared for both of them and wanted to be a forgiving person. He felt somewhat at peace with himself.

In the *High Constraint* condition, the next section of the narrative was the following:

> On the return trip home their plane was hijacked by a gang of eight kidnappers. The pilot was forced to land in Bermuda, where the hijack-ers demanded a ransom of $5 billion. To show the government their ruthlessness, the hijackers executed an elderly male passenger. They then seized two of the male passengers, Bill and Frank. The leader of the hijackers handed Bill a pistol with one bullet in it. With four machine guns pointed at him, Bill was ordered to shoot Frank in the head. He was told that if he did not obey, Frank, himself, and ten other passengers would be killed. Bill realized that there was no way to resist or overpower the hijackers, because he and the other passengers were no match for eight heavily armed men; any attempted heroics on his part would result in more loss of life than obeying the hijackers' orders.

In the *Moderate Constraint* condition, the same basic situation was depicted, but modified to lessen the degree to which Bill's shooting of Frank was compelled by the circumstances. The vignette in this condition altered the description to make resistance to and refusal of the hijackers' order appear a more viable behavioral option. It contained the following wording:

> On the return trip home their plane was hijacked by a gang of three kidnappers. The pilot was forced to land in Bermuda, where the hijackers demanded a ransom of $5 billion. To show the government their ruthlessness, the hijackers executed an elderly male passenger. They then seized two of the male passengers, Bill and Frank. The leader of the hijackers handed Bill a pistol with one bullet in it while another hijacker pointed a pistol at Bill. The third hijacker was in the pilot's cabin shouting angrily. At that moment, they were interrupted by an amplified voice ordering the hijackers to surrender immediately. Looking out the window, Bill saw that the plane was surrounded by heavily armed anti-terrorist forces. Bill quickly reviewed his options. He could try to persuade the hijackers that their situation was hopeless. He could stall until the anti-terrorist forces stormed the plane. The hijackers had been distracted by the arrival of the armed troops. Both the leader and the man holding a gun on Bill were nervous, frequently glancing out the windows of the plane. Perhaps, Bill thought, he could shoot the hijacker with the gun and the rest of the passengers could subdue the other two kidnappers. It was a risky move, but it could work. Bill thought he just might be able to pull it off, but the hijackers were angrily ordering him to "get on with it."

Next, in the *High Identification* condition, participants read:

> Despite the desperate circumstances, Bill understood the situation. He had been presented with the opportunity to kill his wife's lover and get away with it. And at that moment Bill was certain about his feelings. He wanted to kill Frank. Feeling no reluctance, he placed the pistol at Frank's temple and proceeded to blow his friend's brains out.

Alternatively, in the *Low Identification* condition, participants read:

> Bill was horrified. At that moment Bill was certain about his feelings. He did *not* want to kill Frank, even though Frank was his wife's lover. But although he was appalled by the situation and beside himself with distress, he reluctantly placed the pistol at Frank's temple and proceeded to blow his friend's brains out.

After reading the vignettes, participants completed an 8-item questionnaire (Likert-type, 7-point scale).

2.1.3. Dependent Variables

The study's principal dependent variable, the actor's degree of responsibility for his friend's death, was assessed by the first questionnaire item, "Bill is

Table 4.1. Factor loadings of dependent variables (Experiment 1)

Items	Factor 1	Factor 2
The hijackers are responsible for Frank's death.	−0.11	0.86
A person who does what Bill did should feel guilty.	0.87	0.05
Bill is a person of good character.	−0.39	0.26
The act Bill committed was wrong.	0.84	−0.08
Bill acted properly.	−0.64	0.13
Bill is to blame for Frank's death.	0.72	−0.17
The hijackers are to blame for Frank's death.	−0.05	0.89

responsible for Frank's death." Seven additional, supplementary items assessed the participants' attitudes regarding the propriety of the actor and the action. These items were included as vehicles for exploratory analyses intended to shed light on the social cognition that is correlated with the attribution of moral responsibility. We had asked various philosophers and psychologists to suggest, "What concepts are closely related to responsibility for an antisocial act?" These suggestions and our own intuitions were incorporated in the seven items, shown in table 4.1. Because these items were to be examined with multivariate statistics, we limited their number.

2.2. Results

To test the principal hypothesis of the study, an initial two-way (Identification × Constraint) univariate analysis of variance (ANOVA) was performed upon the item worded, "Bill is responsible for Frank's death." This variable will be referred to hereafter as Bill's Responsibility. As hypothesized, significant main effects were found for Identification, $F(1,68) = 6.83, P < 0.02$, and for Constraint, $F(1,68) = 5.02, P < 0.03$. As depicted in figure 4.1, when Bill was identified with the act, he was judged more responsible than when not identified. Also Bill was judged more responsible when he operated under less constraint.

An exploratory factor analysis was performed on the seven supplementary questionnaire items. A principal-components analysis with varimax rotation was employed. Two factors emerged with eigen values greater than 1.0, accounting for 63.6% of the variance. Factor loadings of the items are shown in table 4.1. An examination of the factor loadings for Factor 1 shows it to be constituted largely by items related to Bill's culpability and propriety. Factor 2 seems to be tapping the attribution of responsibility to sources other than Bill, namely, the hijackers.

A factor scale corresponding to each factor was constructed by an unweighted summation of the items that loaded higher than 0.50 on that factor. Four items were summed to produce the scale for Factor 1 and two items made up the scale for Factor 2 (values of items with negative loadings were reversed). The Factor 1 scale correlated highly with the study's primary dependent variable, Bill's Responsibility,

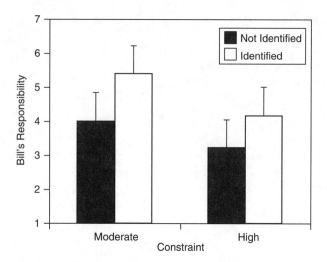

Figure 4.1. Mean levels of responsibility attributed to actor at different levels of identification and constraint.

$r(70) = 0.78$, $P < 0.001$. This scale was labeled Bill's Blameworthiness. The Factor 2 scale was labeled Hijacker Responsibility and was weakly correlated, negatively, with Bill's Responsibility, $r(70) = -0.11$, n.s. The scales for Factor 1 and Factor 2 were negatively correlated, $r(70) = -.24$, $P < 0.05$.

Each of the two scales corresponding to Bill's Blameworthiness and Hijacker Responsibility was subjected to the same analysis employed on Bill's Responsibility, a two-way univariate ANOVA (Identification × Constraint). Given that conducting these additional exploratory ANOVAs raises the probability of making a Type I error within the experiment, we made a BONFERRONI-like adjustment by setting the statistical significance levels for the exploratory analyses at 0.0166. A significant main effect for Identification, $F(1,68) = 11.74$, $P < 0.001$, emerged on Bill's Blameworthiness. Higher Identification was associated with the higher scores on Bill's Blameworthiness, indicating the assignment of greater culpability and impropriety. Higher scores on Bill's Blameworthiness also were assigned when Bill operated under less Constraint, $F(1,68) = 10.90$, $P < 0.002$. Means associated with these effects are depicted in figure 4.2.

Scores on Hijacker Responsibility were significantly higher when Identification was lower, $F(1,68) = 7.37$, $P < 0.009$, reflecting that more responsibility was attributed to the hijackers when Bill was not identified with the shooting. A significant Identification × Constraint interaction emerged, $F(1,68) = 13.78$, $P < 0.0004$, showing that responsibility assigned to the hijackers was diminished only when Bill was both identified and operated under less constraint. The main effect for Constraint on Factor 2 failed to achieve statistical significance ($P > 0.06$).

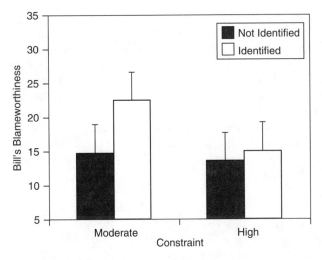

Figure 4.2. Mean Factor 1 scores (Bill's Blameworthiness) at different levels of identification and constraint.

2.3. Discussion

Despite the presence of coercive circumstances that involved strong constraint upon behavior, the level of the actor's identification appeared to influence variables measuring the assignment of responsibility for an action. These findings, coupled with the fact that varying the level of constraint also affected responsibility attribution, led us to conduct a second experiment to replicate the effects observed and to examine the influence of identification upon responsibility attribution when the degree of constraint was increased to levels in excess of those employed in Experiment 1.

3. EXPERIMENT 2

3.1. Method

In Experiment 2 we sought to extend the findings of Experiment 1 by further increasing the level of constraint under which the action was performed. The reader might be startled by the thought that multiple automatic weapons pointed at the actor would not constitute a maximally coercive situation. But some philosophers with whom we discussed our findings argued that, even in such circumstances, participants may have believed that it was possible for Bill to refrain from shooting Frank. These philosophers asserted that we had not produced a scenario in which the actor was *unable* to do otherwise, that we had not created a situation in which there was no alternate possibility.

To respond to this critique, we constructed a condition in which the actor operates under what we now term "absolute constraint," as contrasted with what we would now call the "practical constraint" operationalized in Experiment 1. In this Absolute Constraint condition Bill is administered a "compliance" drug that makes him unable to resist the demands of the hijackers. To ensure the validity of this condition we instructed participants to "suspend disbelief" as to the facts specified, especially in regard to the power of a drug to effect total compliance. This is a familiar technique in philosophical "thought experiments" (see Doris & Stich, 2004) designed to test intuitions that cannot be readily evaluated using responses to plausible naturalistic scenarios. It is difficult to create a scenario in which an intentional action occurs but is such that the actor indisputably could not have done otherwise, as indeed our philosophical interlocuters' comments on the previous experiment suggested. To this end, we asked participants to evaluate the behavior depicted in the vignette while assuming the absolute efficacy of the "compliance drug."

The design of the experiment was a 2 × 3 factorial. We examined the two levels of Identification: High and Low. The two Constraint conditions from Study 1 were replicated and a third condition, *Absolute Constraint*, was added.

3.1.1. Participants and Procedure

Forty-eight (27 female and 21 male) University of California, Santa Cruz, undergraduates enrolled in philosophy classes participated in the experiment as volunteers. Participants were randomly assigned to experimental conditions and were supervised as they completed the materials individually during class time.

3.1.2. Materials

Each participant read one of six different vignettes. The vignettes reflected a 2(Identification: low vs. high) × 3(Constraint: moderate vs. high vs. absolute) between-participants design.

The initial section of each vignette was common to all six conditions and was identical to that employed in Experiment 1, describing the relationships among the principals. High and Low Identification were depicted using the exact wording of Experiment 1. In the Moderate and High Constraint conditions the identical wording from Experiment 1 was employed. The *Absolute Constraint* condition was created by the following wording:

> On the return trip home their plane was hijacked by a gang of eight kidnappers....They then seized two of the male passengers, Bill and Frank. The leader of the kidnappers injected Bill's arm with a "compliance drug"—a designer drug similar to sodium pentathol, "truth serum." This drug makes individuals unable to resist the demands of powerful authorities. Its effects are similar to the impact of expertly administered hypnosis; it results in total compliance. To test the effects of the drug, the leader of the kidnappers shouted at Bill to slap himself. To his amazement, Bill observed his own right hand administering an open-handed blow to his own left cheek, although he had no sense of having willed his hand

to move. The leader then handed Bill a pistol with one bullet in it. Bill was ordered to shoot Frank in the head.... But when Bill's hand and arm moved again, placing the pistol at his friend's temple, Bill had no feeling that he had moved his arm to point the gun; it felt as though the gun had moved itself into position. Bill thought he noticed his finger moving on the trigger, but could not feel any sensations of movement. While he was observing these events, feeling like a puppet, passively observing his body moving in space, his hand closed on the pistol, discharging it and blowing Frank's brains out.

3.2. Results

The same dependent variables used in Experiment 1 were employed in this experiment. Because our primary experimental hypothesis involved the assignment of responsibility, as in Experiment 1, an initial two-way (Identification × Constraint) univariate analysis of variance was performed upon the item assessing Bill's Responsibility. Figure 4.3 depicts all the cell means of this analysis.[1] A significant main effect was found for Identification $F(1,42) = 9.89$, $P < 0.003$. When Bill was identified with the act, he was held more responsible than when not identified. A significant main effect for Constraint, $F(2,42) = 9.87$, $P < 0.0003$, indicated that when Constraint was higher, Bill was regarded as less responsible. A posteriori comparisons of the Constraint cell means, employing Tukey's HSD, determined all pairwise differences between cell means to be statistically significant, except that between Moderate Constraint and High Constraint, $Ps < 0.016$.

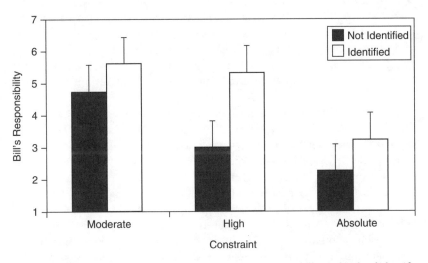

Figure 4.3. Mean levels of responsibility attributed to actor at different levels of identification and constraint.

Table 4.2. Factor loadings of dependent variables (Experiment 2)

Items	Factor 1	Factor 2
The hijackers are responsible for Frank's death.	−0.22	0.90
A person who does what Bill did should feel guilty.	0.71	−0.17
Bill is a person of good character.	−0.36	0.22
The act Bill committed was wrong.	0.74	−0.01
Bill acted properly.	−0.73	0.12
Bill is to blame for Frank's death.	0.84	−0.14
The hijackers are to blame for Frank's death.	−0.12	0.94

As in Experiment 1, a principal-components analysis with varimax rotation was performed on the questionnaire item scores. Two factors emerged with eigen values greater than 1.0, accounting for 67.1% of the variance. The factor structure derived in Experiment 1 was cross-validated, in that a very similar pattern of item loadings was observed (see table 4.2).

The factors again were named Bill's Blameworthiness and Hijacker Responsibility. Creating a factor scale for each factor by an unweighted summation of those items that loaded at 0.50 or higher produced two scales with identical item compositions to those of Experiment 1.

Each scale score for Bill's Blameworthiness and each for Hijacker Responsibility. Responsibility was subjected to the same univariate ANOVA described above. A main effect for Identification on Bill's Blameworthiness emerged, $F(1,42) = 7.95$, $P < 0.008$. Bill's Blameworthiness was higher when the actor was identified than when not identified. A main effect also was observed for Constraint on Bill's Blameworthiness, $F(2,42) = 4.79$, $P < 0.014$. As depicted in figure 4.4, means on this variable were inversely proportional to the level of Constraint. A posteriori pairwise comparisons (Tukey's HSD) among Constraint cell means determined the only significant difference ($P < 0.016$) to be that between the means of the Moderate Constraint and Absolute Constraint conditions.

Significant main effects on Hijacker Responsibility were observed for both Identification, $F(1,42) = 14.76$, $P < 0.0005$, and Constraint, $F(2,42) = 14.41$, $P < 0.0001$. Hijacker Responsibility was rated lower when Bill was identified with the act. Hijacker Responsibility scores were directly proportional to the level of Constraint. When Bill operated under Absolute Constraint, Hijacker Responsibility scores were highest ($M = 12.69$, SD = 1.92), under High Constraint ($M = 11.31$, SD = 2.09) scores were intermediate, and Moderate Constraint ($M = 8.69$, SD = 3.48) yielded the lowest scores on Hijacker Responsibility. A posteriori comparisons of every Constraint cell mean employing Tukey's HSD determined all pairwise differences between cell means to be statistically significant except that between Moderate Constraint and High Constraint, $Ps < 0.016$. As in Experiment 1, a significant Identification × Constraint inter-

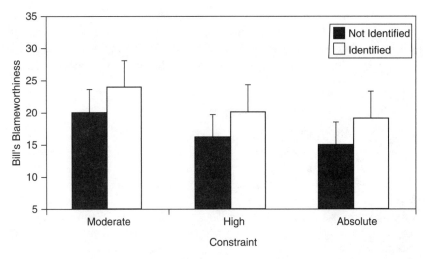

Figure 4.4. Mean factor 1 scores (Bill's Blameworthiness) at different levels of identification and constraint.

action occurred, $F(2,42) = 4.58$, $P < 0.016$, reflecting the disproportionately low assignment of responsibility to the hijackers when Bill was both identified and operating under the least constraint.

3.3. Discussion

The findings of Experiment 2 replicated and extended the principal findings of Experiment 1. Our data suggested that observers are inclined, under some circumstances, to hold actors who identify with an act more responsible than unidentified actors, even when it is highly plausible to suppose that the actor "could not have done otherwise." These findings are discussed at length in the General Discussion.

4. EXPERIMENT 3

In the previous two experiments, we created stories designed to cause experimental participants to perceive that the act of killing another person occurred under considerable constraint. We wrote different versions of the experimental scenarios designed to differ in the degree of constraint they depicted. Although many of our actor responsibility measures are indirect indications of the degree of constraint that the participants perceived, we did not directly ask participants in Experiments 1 and 2 to rate the degree to which the actor had been constrained, because we did not want to alert them to our interest in theoretical issues having to do with levels of constraint. So in the present study, we present data on the degree of constraint or coercion to which the actor was perceived to be subjected in the experimental vignettes.

We presented participants with three vignettes (with the identification manipulation removed), each containing one of the three levels of constraint used in the previous experiments. We also included a condition in which the actor shoots the victim under *no* ostensible constraint or coercion.

4.1. Method

4.1.1. Participants and Procedure

Forty-eight (28 female and 20 male) Princeton University students participated in the experiment in order to fulfill requirements for participation in Psychology Department research. Participants filled out various short "paper and pencil" research projects from various investigators. The projects were chosen for their theoretical and mundane dissimilarity and the order of the questionnaires randomized to minimize order effects. Participants reported to a specified room at set times and were given packets containing the various questionnaires by an experimenter.

4.1.2. Materials

Each participant read all four vignettes. The No Constraint vignette contained the material common to all vignettes and included the material below:

> Bill was shocked and upset. After wrestling with the issue, he purchased a black market handgun. On the last day of their vacation, Bill followed Frank as he walked through the back streets of the city they were visiting. When the opportunity presented itself, he placed the pistol at Frank's temple and proceeded to blow his friend's brains out.

The No Constraint vignette was presented first to all participants. The order of the remaining three vignettes was counterbalanced to yield six different orders of presentation.

Participants rated the conduct depicted in each vignette on a 6-item, manipulation-check questionnaire that assessed the degree to which Bill "was constrained," "was forced," "was free to do other than he did," "had a choice," "could have behaved differently," and whether it was "reasonable" to expect him to have behaved differently. Items were Likert-type, with 7-point scales.

4.2. Results

Because the six questionnaire items were highly correlated ($rs > \pm 0.28$), instead of univariate tests, a one-way repeated-measures multivariate analysis of variance was conducted. Constraint was the classification variable (four levels, within participants) and all six dependent variables were included. This analysis was significant, $F(3, 45) = 153.77$, $P < 0.001$. A posteriori Tukey's HSD tests indicated that each level of Constraint was significantly different from every other level, $Ps < 0.005$. No Constraint was associated with the greatest perceived freedom, Moderate Constraint linked with less freedom, High Constraint with still less freedom, and Absolute Constraint associated with the lowest ratings of

Table 4.3. Mean assignment of freedom to the actor (Bill) by level of situational constraint (7-point scale)

Item	No constraint	Moderate constraint	High constraint	Drug-induced, "absolute" constraint
Free "to do other than he did"	6.63	5.21	3.08	1.98

Table 4.4. Mean assignment of responsibility to the actor (Bill) by level of situational constraint and level of identification (7-point scale)

Actor's level of identification	Moderate constraint	High constraint	Drug-induced, "absolute" constraint	No constraint (identification not manipulated)
Identified	5.49	4.81	3.25	6.44
Not identified	4.38	3.11	2.25	

Means for moderate constraint and high constraint conditions are averaged across Experiments 1 and 2.

freedom. Table 4.3, which shows the means for Item 3 ("was free to do other than he did"), provides some sense of the relative degree of freedom that was attributed to Bill in the four conditions.

After reading the No Constraint vignette, participants also were asked to rate Bill's responsibility for Frank's death on the same item that was the principal dependent variable in Experiments 1 and 2. The mean rating of Bill's Responsibility ($M = 6.44$, SD = 1.38) in the No Constraint condition was higher than any cell mean rating on that item for any condition in Experiments 1 and 2. A somewhat more concrete understanding of the effect of the constraint manipulation in Experiments 1 and 2 upon responsibility ascriptions to the actor can be achieved by comparing the mean for Bill's Responsibility under No Constraint in Experiment 3 with the means associated with the different levels of Constraint in Experiments 1 and 2. This is done in table 4.4.

4.3. Discussion

The results of Experiment 3 provided support for the internal validities of Experiments 1 and 2. It would appear that our manipulation was successful, in that the degree of coercion in the circumstances we portrayed caused participants to adjust their ratings of the actor's freedom and responsibility accordingly.

5. GENERAL DISCUSSION

In the preceding experiments we attempted to elucidate some aspects of lay moral cognition. We found participants' attributions of responsibility for an action to be influenced by the actor's attitude toward that action, even when the action was causally constrained to such a degree that there were no other behavioral options. The degree to which actors "identified" with an action was strongly associated with responsibility for the action being assigned to them.

Our results have relevance to various discussions of responsibility attribution in the psychology literature. Attributional analyses employing a "discounting principle" would require assignments of moral responsibility to vary largely with the extent to which the actor exerts causal control on the outcome. But our data suggest that the attribution of moral responsibility takes into account noncausal elements, such as identification, in addition to causal factors. These data thus augment recent empirical work that emphasizes observers' perceptions of the desires and intended outcomes of the actor (Alicke, 2000; Schlenker et al. 1994; Weiner, 1995). Our data support the view that information about outcomes that an actor desires can moderate or override the attributional effects of the actor's perceived control over events.

Schlenker et al. (1994) describe a component of responsibility attribution they call the "identity-event linkage," which is the degree to which an actor is perceived as linked with an action, a link that has to do with intending to bring the action about or acting to bring it about, and doing so in the absence of excusing circumstances. Our findings are consistent with much of this formulation, but we would suggest a refinement of the authors' view that "personal control over the event" is required. In the present studies an actor who desired an outcome was judged to be to some extent responsible, even though there were extenuating circumstances of the most extreme sort. Here participants appear either to have perceived a link between the actor and the public event, based largely on the actor's attitudes, or to have assigned responsibility for the action based upon what participants construed to be an internal and private event over which the actor did have personal control: his internally desiring the outcome of an act that he was coerced to produce.

Alicke's (2000) theory of culpable control has deep roots in philosophy and therefore addresses issues relevant to our findings. Alicke treats intention as separate from causation in his analysis of his core construct of "personal control." His work suggests that the perceived linkages among a person's intentions, behavior, and the ultimate outcomes of that behavior are the key factors in judgments of culpability. Our work harmonizes with his approach, in that we can be viewed as exploring situations in which there is either consistency or inconsistency between an actor's desires and the actor's behavior, as well as circumstances in which there is either congruence or incongruence between desire and outcome. Alicke also stipulates that the same behavior can be judged as more or less culpable simply on the basis of the actor's relevant attitudes. Our case to be accounted for is the one in which some responsibility is attributed to an individual even when he was coerced to take an action, because the outcome of that action was one he desired. In Alicke's theory the machinery to account for this case is available in his constructs of "volitional behavior control" and "volitional outcome control." As do most models of responsibility attribution, his theory assigns an important role to the mitigating influence of external constraints in reducing the assignment of blame. This formulation is consistent with our general finding of reduced responsibility assigned for antisocial behavior as external coercion to commit that behavior increased. What is not clear is whether our finding of effects for identification in the presence of overwhelming constraint would be predicted by his theory. Some indication that the theory might allow for such phenomena is Alicke's assertion that observers tend to assume agency and assign blame as a default, subsequently adjusting attributions for mitigating factors. This then would be the classic anchor and adjustment process, in which it is known that the adjustment is generally insufficient to move the attributions appropriately far away from the initial anchor.

With respect to the philosophical literature, it appears that in at least some contexts the tacit theory of responsibility employed by social perceivers is not straightforwardly incompatibilist; in particular, actors may be held responsible even in circumstances where it is apparent they were coercively constrained to act as they did. For philosophers who believe theories of responsibility should be strongly informed by everyday social practice, as P. F. Strawson (1982) advocated, the data suggest that compatibilist theories may not be contrary to lay practices. Our data suggest that the assumption, made by many philosophers, that lay perceivers are "natural incompatibilists" (Kane, 2003, p. 300) is open to question.

This is not to argue that folk theories of responsibility are uniformly compatibilist. In fact, we would suggest that folk theories of responsibility are most likely *contextualist*, meaning that differing considerations are salient to moral responsibility attribution in different contexts, and that patterns of responsibility attribution may also vary culturally and developmentally. For example, recent empirical work by Nichols (2004) suggests that, at least in some situations, children (ages 3–6) treat the "could have done otherwise" condition of the principle of alternate possibilities as a precondition of human agency. The discourse of responsibility takes place in widely varying contexts and operates in connection with diverse human interests. We might suspect that along the broad spectrum of moral cognition related to responsibility ascription, which ranges from the determination of criminal liability, to the assignment of credit for scientific discovery, to deciding which sibling should have to clean up the spilled milk, complex considerations often come into play. How "responsibility" is assessed in varying contexts is a wonderful question for future research.

The present research supports some preliminary conclusions. We have provided evidence that lay attributions of responsibility may, in some circumstances, accord with philosophical views in which freedom and determinism are regarded to be compatible. We have shown also that the ascription of responsibility is an even more complex process than many theorists previously have contended. Adding the concept of identification to the other factors known to influence responsibility attribution may assist in understanding these complexities. Our findings indicate that further explorations of the construct of identification are warranted.

One question worthy of further exploration concerns what might be called the duration and depth of identification the actor has with the eventual outcome.

All of us can have fleeting desires to produce some morally negative outcome, such as seriously harming an individual who criticizes a manuscript of ours. If at that moment some external constraints cause us to injure the critic, do observers attribute the level of responsibility we have observed in the present data (where the intention to harm is more enduring) for this transitory intention to harm the other? Or do the observers treat the fleeting, emotion-produced intentions of the moment as not counting as "identifying" with coerced harms of the other? Questions such as these invite research attention.

The concept of identification, as we employ it, is somewhat broader than but seems to include elements of "intention" or "intentional behavior," as developed in the work of Malle, Knobe, & colleagues (e.g., Malle, 1999; Malle & Knobe, 1997a, b). The concept of identification also is related to that of "metadesire" or "second-order" desire, a desire to have certain desires, and to have those desires influence one's behavior. Recent research by Pizzaro, Uhlmann, and Salovey (2003) found that manipulating perceptions of actors' metadesires affected assignments of praise and blame for morally relevant conduct, a result consistent with our data. Future research should be directed toward exploring the connections between identification and such related concepts.

In summary, even in the case when an act was committed under conditions of absolute and overwhelming constraint, responsibility attributions were powerfully affected in the predicted direction by the identification manipulation. This finding is in violation of a venerable psychological principle of social cognition, the "discounting principle," and an equally venerable philosophical principle, the "principle of alternative possibilities." In our estimation the best explanation of this phenomenon is that the cognition involving moral attribution is strongly influenced by extra-causal factors, i.e., factors other than those that are likely to figure in the most careful and thoughtful *causal* explanation of the behavior in question. One such factor is the evaluative attitudes of the actor, what it is that the actor wants to come about or wants not to come about. As we remarked above, moral cognition involves evaluative as well as causal dimensions; it is an activity broader in scope than the activity ascribed to "the intuitive psychologist" familiar in the social cognition literature. What causes people to attribute responsibility, to praise or blame, is to some extent what is believed to be in the "heart" of the actor, and this is so even for actions committed under overwhelmingly coercive or constraining circumstances.

NOTES

The authors wish to express their gratitude to Lesley Allen, Joel Cooper, and Michael Gara for various forms of assistance in this research and to thank the editor and three anonymous reviewers for valuable comments on the manuscript.

1. The reader will note that even in the Absolute Constraint condition, when the actor also does not wish to commit the act, some responsibility is still attributed, suggesting something of a "floor effect" on the scale, i.e., that not all participants are willing to assign values at the extreme low end of the scale (see table 4.4). Although a similar, but smaller, "ceiling effect" will emerge in Experiment 3, at the high end of the responsi-

bility scale, we do not have data that tells us how much responsibility participants would assign to an actor who is both unconstrained in any apparent way and who also desires to commit the act.

REFERENCES

Alicke, M. D. (2000). Culpable control and the psychology of blame. *Psychological Bulletin, 126,* 556–574.

Bratman, M. E. (1996). Identification, decision, and treating as a reason. *Philosophical Topics, 24,* 1–18.

Darley, J. M., & Cooper, J. (eds.). (1998). *Attribution and social interaction: The legacy of Edward E. Jones.* Washington, DC: American Psychological Association.

Darley, J. M., & Shultz, T. R. (1990). Moral rules: Their content and acquisition. *Annual Review of Psychology, 41,* 525–556.

Doris, J. M. (2002). *Lack of character: Personality and moral behavior.* Cambridge: Cambridge University Press.

Doris, J. M., & Stich, S. P. (2004). As a matter of fact: Empirical perspectives on ethics. In F. Jackson & M. Smith (eds.), *The Oxford handbook of contemporary analytic philosophy.* Oxford: Oxford University Press.

Ekstrom, L. W. (2000). *Free will: A philosophical study.* Boulder: Westview Press.

Fein, S., Hilton, J. L., & Miller, D. T. (1990). Suspicion of ulterior motivation and the correspondence bias. *Journal of Personality and Social Psychology, 58,* 753–764.

Frankfurt, H. G. (1988). *The importance of what we care about: Philosophical essays.* Cambridge: Cambridge University Press.

Gilbert, D. T., & Malone, P. S. (1995). The correspondence bias. *Psychological Bulletin, 117,* 21–38.

Heider, F. (1958). *The psychology of interpersonal relations.* New York: Wiley.

Hilton, J. L., Fein, S., & Miller, D. T. (1993). Suspicion and dispositional inference. *Personality and Social Psychology Bulletin, 19,* 501–512.

Jones, E. E. (1990). *Interpersonal perception.* New York: W. H. Freeman and Company.

Jones, E. E., & Davis, K. E. (1965). From acts to dispositions: The attribution process in person perception. In L. Berkowitz (ed.), *Advances in experimental social psychology* (Vol. 2). New York: Academic Press, 219–266.

Kane, R. (2002). Introduction: The contours of contemporary free will debates. In R. Kane (ed.), *The Oxford handbook of free will.* New York: Oxford University Press, 3–41.

Kane, R. (2003). Responsibility, luck, and chance: Reflections on free will and determinism. In G. Watson (ed.), *Free will,* 2nd ed. New York: Oxford University Press, 299–321.

Kelley, H. H. (1972). Attribution in social interaction. In E. E. Jones, D. E. Kanouse, H. H. Kelley, R. Nisbett, S. Valins, & B. Weiner (eds.), *Attribution: Perceiving the causes of behavior.* Morristown, NJ: General Learning Press, 1–26.

Malle, B. F. (1999). How people explain behavior: A new theoretical framework. *Personality and Social Psychology Review, 3,* 23–48.

Malle, B. F., & Knobe, J. (1997a). The folk concept of intentionality. *Journal of Experimental Social Psychology, 33,* 101–121.

Malle, B. F., & Knobe, J. (1997b). Which behaviors do people explain? A basic actor-observer asymmetry. *Journal of Personality and Social Psychology, 72,* 288–304.

McClure, J. (1998). Discounting causes of behavior: Are two reasons better than one? *Journal of Personality and Social Psychology, 74,* 7–20.

McKenna, M. (2001). Source incompatibilism, ultimacy, and the transfer of non-responsibility. *American Philosophical Quarterly, 38*, 37–51.

Nagel, T. (1986). *The view from nowhere.* New York: Oxford University Press.

Nichols, S. (2004). The folk psychology of free will: Fits and starts. *Mind and Language, 19*, 473–502.

Pizzaro, D., Uhlmann, E., & Salovey, P. (2003). Asymmetry in judgments of moral praise and blame: The role of metadesires. *Psychological Science, 14*, 267–272.

Quattrone, G. A. (1982). Behavioral consequences of attributional bias. *Social Cognition, 1*, 358–378.

Reeder, G. D., Kumar, S., Hesson-McInnis, M. S., & Trafimow, D. (2002). Inferences about the morality of an aggressor: The role of perceived motive. *Journal of Personality and Social Psychology, 83*, 789–803.

Robinson, D. R. (1996). *Wild beasts and idle humours: The insanity defense from antiquity to the present.* Cambridge, MA: Harvard University Press.

Ross, L. (1977). The intuitive psychologist and his shortcomings: Distortions in the attribution process. In L. Berkowitz (ed.), *Advances in experimental social psychology* (Vol. 10). New York: Academic Press, 174–221.

Ross, L., & Nisbett, R. E. (1991). *The person and the situation: Perspectives of social psychology.* Philadelphia: Temple University Press.

Schlenker, B. R., Britt, T. W., Pennington, J., Murphy, R., & Doherty, K. (1994). The triangle model of responsibility. *Psychological Review, 101*, 632–652.

Shaver, K. G. (1985). *The attribution of blame: CAUSALITY, responsibility, and blameworthiness.* New York: Springer.

Shultz, T. R., & Schleifer, M. (1983). Towards a refinement of attribution concepts. In J. Jaspars, F. Fincham, & M. Hewstone (eds.), *Attribution theory and research: Conceptual, developmental, and social dimensions.* London: Academic Press, 37–62.

Smith, J. W. (1961). Impossibility and morals. *Mind, 70*, 362–375.

Strawson, P. F. (1982). Freedom and resentment. In G. Watson (ed.), *Free will.* New York: Oxford University Press, 59–80.

Velleman, J. D. (1992). What happens when someone acts? *Mind, 101*, 461–481.

Wallace, R. J. (1994). *Responsibility and the moral sentiments.* Cambridge, MA: Harvard University Press.

Watson, G. (1996). Two faces of responsibility. *Philosophical Topics, 24*, 227–248.

Weiner, B. (1995). *Judgments of responsibility: A foundation for a theory of social conduct.* New York: Guilford Press.

5

Is Incompatibilism Intuitive?

Eddy Nahmias, Stephen G. Morris, Thomas Nadelhoffer,
& Jason Turner

Incompatibilists believe that the freedom associated with moral responsibility is impossible if determinism is true, and they often claim that this is the natural view to take given that it is purportedly supported by ordinary intuitions. In this essay, we challenge the claim that incompatibilism is intuitive to most laypersons, and we discuss the significance of this challenge to the free will debate. In doing so, we first argue that it is particularly important for incompatibilists that their view of free will is intuitive given that it is more metaphysically demanding than compatibilist alternatives (§1). We then suggest that determining whether incompatibilism is *in fact* intuitive calls for empirical testing of pretheoretical judgments about relevant cases (§2). We therefore carried out some empirical studies of our own, and the results put significant pressure on the claim that incompatibilism is intuitive to the majority of laypersons (§3). Having examined the relevant data, we consider several potential objections to our approach and show why they fail to get incompatibilists off the hook (§4). We conclude that while our preliminary data suggest that incompatibilism is not as intuitive as incompatibilists have traditionally assumed, more work should be done both to determine what ordinary intuitions about free will and moral responsibility actually are and to understand what role these intuitions should play in the free will debate.

1. WHY IT MATTERS WHETHER INCOMPATIBILISM IS INTUITIVE

By calling the free will debate "the problem of free will and determinism," philosophers have traditionally assumed that there *is* a problem with the compatibility of free will and determinism unless and until proven otherwise. Accordingly, incompatibilists commonly lay claim to having the default position, with the two alternatives being either that we have free will—the libertarian view—or that we do not—the hard determinist (or skeptical) view. Carving out the philosophical territory in this way seems to place the burden of proof on compatibilists to provide an argument to show why what clearly seems to be a problem is not *really* a problem. Incompatibilists suggest that such attempts to analyze freedom along compatibilist lines betray common sense and fail to satisfy the intuitions of ordinary people. For instance, Robert Kane writes,

> In my experience, most ordinary persons start out as natural incompatibilists. They believe there is some kind of conflict between freedom and determinism; and the idea that freedom and responsibility might be compatible with determinism looks to them at first like a "quagmire of evasion" (William James) or "a wretched sub-terfuge" (Immanuel Kant). Ordinary persons have to be talked out of this natural incompatibilism by the clever arguments of philosophers. (1999: 217)

Similarly, Laura Ekstrom claims that "we come to the table, nearly all of us, as pretheoretic incompatibilists" (2002: 310). Galen Strawson contends that the incompatibilist conception of free will, though impossible to satisfy, is "just the kind of freedom that most people ordinarily and unreflectively suppose themselves to possess" (1986: 30), adding that it is "in our nature to take deter-minism to pose a serious problem for our notions of responsibility and free-dom" (89). And Thomas Pink tells us that "most of us start off by making an important assumption about freedom. Our freedom of action, we naturally tend to assume, must be incompatible with our actions being determined" (2004: 12).[1] On this view, because most people purportedly have the intuition that determinism conflicts with free will, any conception of freedom that does *not* require the falsity of determinism for agents to count as free and morally responsible is bound to be an evasion of—not a solution to—the problem. But are incompatibilists justified in assuming that the majority of laypersons share their own incompatibilist intuitions about free will?

Of course, if philosophers were concerned exclusively with a technical philo-sophical concept of free will, then appeals like those above to ordinary people's intuitions would be entirely irrelevant—just as they would be irrelevant for logi-cians debating the concept of validity or mathematicians analyzing the concept of infinity. But there is a reason why philosophers appeal to ordinary intuitions and common sense when they debate about free will: they are interested in devel-oping a theory of freedom that is relevant to our ordinary beliefs about moral responsibility. Given that most philosophers are concerned with the kinds of free will "worth wanting" (Dennett 1984), an acceptable theory of free will should elucidate the abilities presupposed by our practices of attributing praise and blame, our expressions of reactive attitudes such as indignation and gratitude, and our systems of punishment and reward. Often, such a conception of free-dom is also tied to our sense of dignity, individuality, creativity, hope, and love.[2] Because the free will debate is intimately connected to ordinary intuitions and beliefs via these values and practices, it is important that a philosophical theory of free will accounts for and accords with ordinary people's understanding of the concept and their judgments about relevant cases. Minimally, any theory of free-dom that conflicts with such intuitions should explain both why our intuitions are mistaken and why we have those misleading intuitions in the first place.[3]

It is especially important for incompatibilists that their view is supported by ordinary intuitions for the following three reasons. First, incompatibilism about any two concepts is *not* the default view. As William Lycan explains, "A theorist who maintains of something that is not obviously impossible that nonetheless that thing *is* impossible owes us an argument" (2003: 109). Either determinism obviously precludes free will or those who maintain that it does should offer an explanation as to why it does. The *philosophical* conception of determinism—i.e., that the laws of nature and state of the universe at one time entail the state of the universe at later times—has no obvious conceptual or logical bearing on human freedom and responsibility. So, by claiming that determinism *necessarily* precludes the existence of free will, incompatibilists thereby assume the argumentative burden.[4]

Second, the arguments that incompatibilists provide to explain why determinism necessarily precludes free will require conceptions of free will that are more metaphysically demanding than compatibilist alternatives. These libertarian conceptions demand more of the world in order for free will to exist: at a minimum, indeterministic event-causal processes at the right place in the human agent, and often, additionally, agent causation. To point out that incompatibilist theories are metaphysically demanding is not to suggest that they are thereby less likely to be true. Rather, it is simply to say that these theories require more motivation than less metaphysically demanding ones.

Consider an example. Suppose two philosophers—Hal and Dave—are debating what it takes for something to be an action. Hal claims that actions are events caused (in the right sort of way) by beliefs and desires. Dave agrees, but adds the further condition that the token beliefs and desires that cause an action cannot be identical to anything physical. Now Dave, by adding this condition, does not thereby commit himself to the claim that token beliefs and desires are *not* physical. But he *does* commit himself to the conditional claim that token beliefs and desires are not physical *if there are any actions.* On our view, if T_1 and T_2 are both theories of x, then to say that T_1 is more metaphysically demanding than T_2 is to say that T_1 requires more metaphysical theses to be true than T_2 does *in order for there to be any x's.* So, Dave's theory is more metaphysically demanding than Hal's because it requires more metaphysical theses to be true in order for there to be any actions. Likewise, incompatibilists—whether libertarians or skeptics—have more metaphysically demanding theories than compatibilists and other nonincompatibilists (e.g., Double 1991, 1996) since they say that special kinds of causation (indeterministic or agent-causation) must obtain *if there are any free actions.*[5]

Given that, on Dave's theory of action the existence of actions is incompatible with the token-identity of mental states, his theory will be harder to motivate than Hal's, which does not require extra metaphysical entities in order for actions to be possible.[6] Likewise, since incompatibilist theories of free will say the existence of free will is incompatible with determinism, these theories, other things being equal, will be harder to motivate than compatibilist theories, which do not require the existence of extra metaphysical processes, such as indeterminism or agent causation, in order for free actions to be possible. As we've seen, many incompatibilists have attempted to motivate their metaphysically demanding theories, at least in part, by suggesting that other things are *not* equal because our ordinary intuitions support incompatibilist views. This is not to say that incompatibilists *must* appeal to such intuitions in order to motivate their demanding theories (see §§4.2–4.3 below). Nonetheless, it is certainly unclear why, without wide-scale intuitive support for incompatibilism, the argumentative burden would be on *compatibilists*, as suggested by Kane above, and by Ekstrom when she claims that the compatibilist "needs a positive argument in favor of the compatibility thesis" (2000: 57).

Finally, *if* it were shown that people have intuitions that in fact support incompatibilism, it would still be open to foes of incompatibilism to argue that, relative to ordinary conceptions of freedom and responsibility, their view is a benign revision toward a more metaphysically tenable theory.[7] Incompatibilists, on the other hand, do not seem to have this move available to them in the event that their view is inconsistent with prephilosophical intuitions. After all, it is difficult to see why philosophers should revise the concept of free will to make it *more* metaphysically demanding than required by ordinary intuitions (see §4.3).[8] So, if incompatibilism is not the intuitive view, or if no premises that support incompatibilist conclusions are particularly intuitive, then there seems to be little motivation for advancing an incompatibilist theory of free will.

This is not to suggest that compatibilist, or other nonincompatibilist (see §4.2.3), theories are *correct*, nor is it to suggest that incompatibilist theories are *incorrect*—these claims go far beyond the scope of the present essay. We have simply set out to show why it makes sense for incompatibilists to claim that most people share their intuitions about free will and determinism. On the one hand, by aligning their view with commonsense, they thereby place the burden of proof on their opponents. On the other hand, by assuming that their theories are the most intuitive, they are able to motivate their metaphysically demanding conception of free will. This last point is particularly important, for if it turns out that incompatibilist theories are not nearly as intuitive as incompatibilists themselves commonly assume, then it becomes increasingly difficult to see why we should adopt these theories. However, so long as incompatibilists are allowed to *assume* that their theories best accord with and account for ordinary intuitions, they may also assume that they do not need to offer much by way of motivating their view.

But what evidence are incompatibilists relying on when they talk about the wide-scale intuitive plausibility of their theories? Usually, it is the same evidence philosophers typically give when they claim some idea is intuitive (or commonsensical or obvious)—namely, that it is intuitive *to them*. Unfortunately, because philosophers on differing sides of the debate disagree about the compatibility question and the proper analysis of 'free will,' they tend to disagree about the intuitive plausibility of many of the more basic premises or thought experiments that drive the debate as well—for instance, the effectiveness of Frankfurt cases, the analysis of 'could have done otherwise,' and the validity of inference rules employed in incompatibilist arguments, such as Peter van Inwagen's rule 'Beta' (1983). As a result, these philosophers find themselves at various argumentative impasses, often grounded in a conflict of intuitions.[9]

Given this stalemate of *philosophical* intuitions concerning free will and determinism, it is not surprising that philosophers often back up their position with appeals to *prephilosophical* intuitions. But since philosophers on both sides of the debate generally claim that their own intuitions are the natural, commonsensical ones, these opposing claims end in yet another stalemate. It would help, therefore, to know which position in fact accords best with the intuitions of philosophical laypersons who have not been significantly influenced by the relevant philosophical theories and arguments.

2. HOW TO DETERMINE WHETHER INCOMPATIBILISM IS INTUITIVE

Whether or not incompatibilism is intuitive to the majority of laypersons is a largely empirical question that we will examine accordingly. Here we depart from a standard philosophical methodology, whereby philosophers consult their *own* intuitions from the armchair and assume that they represent ordinary intuitions. While this practice may be appropriate when such an assumption is uncontroversial, it does not shed much light on the free will debate because, as we've suggested, philosophers have conflicting intuitions, intuitions that may well have been influenced by their own well-developed theories. So, we suggest that the free will debate calls for the kind of empirical research on 'folk intuitions' that has recently been carried out in other areas of philosophy—for instance, action theory (e.g., Nadelhoffer 2004, 2005; Knobe 2003, 2004), epistemology (e.g., Nichols, Weinberg, and Stich 2002), and ethics (e.g., Doris and Stich 2005). This type of research has produced some surprising and important results about what ordinary people's intuitions actually are. And given that such intuitions often play an important role in debates about freedom and responsibility, we believe that applying the same empirically informed methodology to these debates will be equally illuminating (see Nahmias, Morris, Nadelhoffer, and Turner 2004, 2005; Nichols 2004a).

It is important to keep in mind that we are not suggesting that any philosophical theory would be demonstrably confirmed (or disconfirmed) just because it aligns with (or conflicts with) folk intuitions and practices. After all, such intuitions and practices may be mistaken or contradictory and hence in need of elimination or revision. (Of course, to know the extent to which they need to be eliminated or revised, we must first know what these intuitions and practices actually are.) Nonetheless, on our view, a theory of free will that accords with those intuitions relevant to things we care about, such as ascriptions of moral responsibility, has, all else being equal, a theoretical advantage over a theory that demands revision or elimination of such intuitions. Though the nature of intuitions and their role in philosophical debates is controversial (see DePaul and Ramsey, 1998), many philosophers accept that, at a minimum, a theory that conflicts with widely shared intuitions takes on a cost that must be offset by other theoretical advantages, while a theory that accords with relevant intuitive judgments has "squatter's rights."[10]

Therefore, we believe that it is important to know what these intuitions actually are and that empirical research will sometimes be necessary to ascertain the answer. In this respect, we agree with Frank Jackson's claim that philosophers analyzing the concept of free will should "appeal to what seems most obvious and central about free action [and] determinism...as revealed by our intuitions about possible cases" (1998: 31), and we follow through on his suggestion that one should conduct "serious opinion polls on people's responses to various cases...when it is necessary" (36–37).[11] While such systematic studies may ultimately be work best left to psychologists and sociologists, philosophers are well situated to lay out the philosophical problems and to develop scenarios that probe the intuitions relevant to them. Moreover, in the event that psychologists and sociologists have not yet generated the data that philosophers need—as is the case with the free will debate—philosophers should not shy away from getting their hands dirty by trying to test folk intuitions themselves in a systematic way, even if their results will be merely preliminary. Having said this, we should now examine the results of our own attempts to probe laypersons' intuitions about free will and responsibility—with an eye toward ascertaining whether incompatibilism really is intuitive.

3. TESTING WHETHER INCOMPATIBILISM IS INTUITIVE

It is difficult to know what philosophers have in mind when they claim that ordinary people start out as 'natural incompatibilists.' For our purposes, we take intuitions to be propensities to make certain nondeductive, spontaneous judgments about, for instance, whether or not a particular concept applies in a particular situation.[12] So, one way to read the claim that incompatibilism is intuitive is as a *prediction* about the judgments laypersons would make in response to relevant thought experiments. Consider Kane's assertion that "ordinary persons...believe there is some kind of conflict between freedom and determinism" (Kane 1999: 217).[13] This suggests the following prediction:

> (P) When presented with a deterministic scenario, most people
>   will judge that agents in such a scenario do not act of their
>   own free will and are not morally responsible for their actions.

To see that (P) is a fair way of reading incompatibilist claims about people's intuitions, consider J. A. Cover and John O'Leary-Hawthorne's charge that any suggestion that "compatibilism does full justice to our ordinary conception of freedom...is at best poor anthropology" (1996: 50). Their supposed anthropological "evidence" to the contrary consists of the assertion that:

When ordinary people come to consciously recognize and understand that some action is contingent upon circumstances in an agent's past that are beyond that agent's control, they quickly lose a propensity to impute moral responsibility to the agent for that action. We can readily explain this fact by supposing that ordinary people have a conception of freedom, agency, and moral responsibility according to which an action is free and accountable only if that action is not fully determined by circumstances, past or present, that are beyond the agent's control. (50–51)[14]

We suggest that incompatibilists making these sorts of claims about the intuitions and beliefs of ordinary people are tacitly committed to something along the lines of (P). And since (P) is an empirically testable prediction, we tested it.

We surveyed people who had not studied the free will debate. In our first study, participants read the following scenario, drawn from a Laplacean conception of determinism:

> Imagine that in the next century we discover all the laws of nature, and we build a supercomputer which can deduce from these laws of nature and from the current state of everything in the world exactly what will be happening in the world at any future time. It can look at everything about the way the world is and predict everything about how it will be with 100% accuracy. Suppose that such a supercomputer existed, and it looks at the state of the universe at a certain time on March 25, 2150 A.D., twenty years before Jeremy Hall is born. The computer then deduces from this information and the laws of nature that Jeremy will definitely rob Fidelity Bank at 6:00 PM on January 26, 2195. As always, the supercomputer's prediction is correct; Jeremy robs Fidelity Bank at 6:00 PM on January 26, 2195.

Participants were asked to imagine that such a scenario were actual and then asked: "Do you think that, when Jeremy robs the bank, he acts of his own free will?" A significant majority (76%) of participants judged that Jeremy does act of his own free will.[15] One might worry that people are inclined to overlook mitigating factors when judging the freedom or responsibility of an agent who has performed an action they deem immoral. To test for the possibility that participants were influenced by the negative nature of the action, we replaced Jeremy's robbing the bank with a positive action (saving a child) for another set of participants and a neutral action (going jogging) for a third set. Changing the nature of the action had no significant effect on responses: 68% judged that Jeremy saves the child of his own free will, and 79% judged that he goes jogging of his own free will. We also asked additional sets of participants directly about moral responsibility: 83% responded that Jeremy is "morally blameworthy for robbing the bank," and 88% responded that "he is morally praiseworthy for saving the child."

Notice that we did not actually use the term 'determinism' in the scenario. This is in part because in prior surveys we found that most people either did not know what 'determinism' meant or they thought it meant, basically, the opposite of free will. If people have internalized the philosophical label "the problem of free will and determinism" and come to understand 'determinism' to *mean* the opposite of free will, that would count as support for the claim that incompatibilism is intuitive only at the cost of making incompatibilism an empty tautology. Rather, the claim that incompatibilism is intuitive should amount to the claim that ordinary intuitions about free will and moral responsibility indicate a conflict with the *philosophical* conception of 'determinism'—and it is irrelevant to *this* claim how laypersons happen to use the term 'determinism.' Hence, our goal was to describe determinism, roughly in the philosophical sense of the concept, without presenting determinism in a question-begging way as explicitly involving constraint, fatalism, reductionism, etc.[16] Of course, to test prediction (P), determinism should be as salient to participants as possible without being misleading. With this in mind, we developed a second scenario using a simpler, and perhaps more salient, presentation of determinism:

> Imagine there is a universe that is re-created over and over again, starting from the exact same initial conditions and with all the same laws of nature. In this universe the same conditions and the same laws of nature produce the exact same outcomes, so that every single time the universe is re-created, everything must happen the exact same way. For instance, in this universe a person named Jill decides to steal a necklace at a particular time, and every time the universe is re-created, Jill decides to steal the necklace at that time.[17]

The results were similar to those above. In this case the participants were asked both to judge whether Jill decided to steal the necklace of her own free will and whether "it would be fair to hold her morally responsible (that is, blame her) for her decision to steal the necklace."[18] Most participants offered consistent judgments; overall, 66% judged that Jill acted of her own free will, and 77% judged her to be morally responsible.

Finally, we developed a scenario meant to make salient the fact that the agents' actions were deterministically caused by factors outside their control (their genes and upbringing):

> Imagine there is a world where the beliefs and values of every person are caused completely by the combination of one's genes and one's environment. For instance, one day in this world, two identical twins, named Fred and Barney, are born to a mother who puts them up for adoption. Fred is adopted by the Jerksons and Barney is adopted by the Kindersons. In Fred's case, his genes and his upbringing by the selfish Jerkson family have caused him to value money above all else and to believe it is OK to acquire money however you can. In Barney's case, his (identical) genes and his upbringing by the kindly Kinderson family have caused him to value honesty above all else and to believe one should always respect others' property. Both Fred and Barney are intelligent individuals who are capable of deliberating about what they do.

One day Fred and Barney each happen to find a wallet containing $1,000 and the identification of the owner (neither man knows the owner). Each man is sure there is nobody else around. After deliberation, Fred Jerkson, because of his beliefs and values, keeps the money. After deliberation, Barney Kinderson, because of his beliefs and values, returns the wallet to its owner.

Given that, in this world, one's genes and environment completely cause one's beliefs and values, it is true that if Fred had been adopted by the Kindersons, he would have had the beliefs and values that would have caused him to return the wallet; and if Barney had been adopted by the Jerksons, he would have had the beliefs and values that would have caused him to keep the wallet.

Judgments about free will were consistent with the results in the other scenarios: 76% of the participants judged both that Fred kept the wallet of his own free will and that Barney returned it of his own free will. A different set of participants answered questions about moral responsibility, with 60% judging that Fred is morally blameworthy for keeping the wallet and 64% judging that Barney is morally praiseworthy for returning it.

The results from these three studies (table 5.1) offer considerable evidence for the falsity of the incompatibilist prediction (P)—i.e., the prediction that most ordinary people would judge that agents in a deterministic scenario do not act of their own free will and are not morally responsible. Instead, a significant majority of our participants judged that such agents *are* free and responsible for their actions.[19] If (P) represents the claim that incompatibilism is intuitive, then pending evidence to the contrary, incompatibilism is *not* intuitive. Obviously, these results do not thereby falsify incompatibilism. But they certainly raise a significant challenge for the common claim that ordinary people start out with incompatibilist intuitions and that, hence, the burden is on compatibilists to defend theories purported to be significant revisions of ordinary beliefs and practices. Rather, given this preliminary data, we suggest the burden is on incompatibilists to motivate a theory of free will that appears to be more metaphysically demanding than ordinary intuitions demand.

Table 5.1. Summary of Results

Subjects' judgments that the agents...	Scenario 1 (Jeremy)	Scenario 2 (Jill)	Scenario 3 (Fred & Barney)
...acted of their own **free will**	76% (robbing bank) 68% (saving child) 79% (going jogging)	66%	76% (stealing) 76% (returning)
...are **morally responsible** for their action	83% (robbing bank) 88% (saving child)	77%	60% (stealing) 64% (returning)

4. OBJECTIONS, REPLIES, AND IMPLICATIONS

We will now examine several moves incompatibilists might make in response to our approach: (1) garner empirical evidence in support of (P) that outweighs our evidence against it; (2) replace (P) with some other description of what it means to say that incompatibilism is intuitive and demonstrate that this alternative principle is supported by ordinary intuitions; or (3) give up the claim that incompatibilism is intuitive and argue that this does not affect the strength of the incompatibilist position.

4.1. Generate Empirical Evidence in Support of (P)

There are various methodological objections one might advance against our studies, and we address some of them elsewhere.[20] As mentioned above, one significant worry is that in order to test (P) the scenario must describe determinism in a way that is salient to the participants. Otherwise, many of them might fail to recognize the supposed threat to free will and responsibility.[21] We agree that the more salient determinism is in the scenarios, the more significant the results are. However, the descriptions of determinism cannot require untrained participants to understand the more technical aspects (e.g., modal operators) of the philosophical definitions of determinism. Nor can they describe determinism in ways that may mask any effects of determinism itself. For instance, suppose that a scenario illustrated determinism by involving a covert manipulator (e.g., a nefarious neurosurgeon) who ensures that an agent acts in a certain way, and suppose (as seems likely) that most people judge that the agent is not free or responsible. Would these judgments be issuing from an intuition that *determinism* undermines free will, or from an intuition that an agent's action is unfree if it is traceable to manipulation by another agent? Such judgments may be the result of freedom-defeating aspects of the case that are distinct from determinism.[22] Likewise, descriptions of determinism stating that the laws of nature constrain or compel us, that our actions are fated, or that our conscious deliberations are epiphenomenal are liable to generate negative judgments about freedom and responsibility, but such judgments would not help settle questions about the intuitiveness of incompatibilism—i.e., the view that the ordinary concepts of free will and moral responsibility are incompatible with the philosophical concept of determinism. Part of what we are trying to discover is whether unprimed subjects are prone to treat this concept of determinism as relevantly similar to constraint, compulsion, epiphenomenalism, or fate; to simply come out and *tell* them, in the scenarios, that such similarities hold is to undermine one of the goals of such studies.[23]

If one is able to find a way to increase the salience of determinism without inadvertently introducing a different threat to free will, we welcome the attempt. If turning up the volume on the 'determinism knob' *does* cause people to withdraw judgments of free will and moral responsibility (and if this is clearly not a result of factors extraneous to determinism), then we would withdraw our current interpretation of the data. If such cases do *not* result in most people judging the agents to be unfree and unresponsible, then our interpretation is strengthened.

As it stands, an incompatibilist who wants to show that our tests of prediction (P) are problematic (for this or other reasons) needs to offer alternative ways to test people's intuitions without presenting determinism in a questionable way.

4.2. (P) Does Not Capture the Content of the Claim That Incompatibilism Is Intuitive

A more promising response for the incompatibilist to make is that (P) does not accurately represent what it means to claim that incompatibilism is intuitive. One might argue that most people will *not* in fact recognize a conflict between determinism and freedom or responsibility, but will only come to see such a conflict once they understand the implications of determinism. Of course, "getting people to see these implications" is probably going to be a euphemism for "giving them a philosophical argument," and an incompatibilist one at that. These arguments will involve premises that are themselves controversial and also appeal to intuitions—for instance, about whether determinism conflicts with our ordinary conception of 'the ability to do otherwise.'[24] If it takes an argument to make incompatibilism the "intuitive view," then it seems Kane has it backward when he says, "ordinary persons have to be talked out of [their] natural incompatibilism by the clever arguments of philosophers" (1999: 218). Rather, it is the incompatibilist who is talking ordinary people *into* incompatibilism—or, at least, compatibilist philosophers are not talking them *out* of anything.[25] In any case, our primary target is represented by the incompatibilists who claim that ordinary people *begin* with the intuition that determinism precludes free will and moral responsibility. To the extent that our arguments and data force them to give up this claim and replace it with one of the alternatives we will outline below, we will have succeeded. To the extent that we also encourage philosophers on all sides of the free will debate to evaluate the role of intuitions in the debate and to consider the importance of gaining an empirical understanding of ordinary intuitions about free will and moral responsibility, we will also have achieved one of our aims.

4.2.1. Libertarian Intuitions Lead to Incompatibilism

Nonetheless, one route the incompatibilist might take is to argue that people have an intuitive conception of the sort of freedom necessary for moral responsibility that is in fact incompatible with determinism, but most people recognize this incompatibility only with some explanation. In other words, it is not that incompatibilism is intuitive and this suggests a libertarian conception of freedom; rather, the libertarian conception of freedom is intuitive, and the contours of this conception support premises in a philosophical argument for an incompatibilist conclusion. Instead of (P), such incompatibilists might advance:

> (L) Most people's intuitions about freedom and responsibility
> correspond to the libertarian conception—one that requires
> the ability to do otherwise in the exact same conditions and
> perhaps something like agent causal powers—and whether
> people realize it or not, such a conception is incompatible
> with determinism.

This claim marks a significant response to our tests of (P) in that it opens up the possibility that our participants were simply unable to recognize the conflict between their conception of free will and the deterministic scenarios.[26] However, establishing (L) requires evidence—e.g., against those compatibilists who claim the ordinary conception of free will is *not* the libertarian one (see note 3)—that laypersons in fact have a libertarian conception of free will, and one robust enough to require indeterminism (and perhaps agent causation). Such a claim will require empirical data sufficient to counter, for instance, our finding that most people consider an agent to be free and morally responsible in a deterministic setting.[27]

One way that incompatibilists have argued for the claim that people have a libertarian conception of freedom appeals to the phenomenology of decision making and action. They suggest that we experience the ability to choose otherwise associated with free will in an unconditional sense that commits us to a belief in indeterminism and perhaps also that we experience ourselves as agent causes of our actions.[28] No one suggests that this phenomenology establishes the *existence* of libertarian freedom, but they do suggest that it demonstrates a widespread belief in libertarian freedom such that, without it, free will would be an illusion.[29] However, we believe such appeals to phenomenology are controversial, supported only by philosophers' own theory-laden introspective reports but unsupported by any relevant research on the phenomenology of nonphilosophers.[30] It seems unlikely that our phenomenology of deliberation and action is rich or precise enough to entail a tacit commitment to the falsity of a theoretical view such as determinism.

4.2.2. More Basic Intuitions Lead to Incompatibilism

Another approach is for the incompatibilist to present an argument with premises that appeal to what might be considered more *basic* intuitions than those we have been discussing. Consider, for example, van Inwagen's famous Consequence argument (1983: ch. 3).[31] One version of the argument goes like this:

1. If determinism is true, then the past and the laws of nature strictly imply every truth about the future.
2. We have no choice about the past and we have no choice about the laws of nature.
3. If we have no choice about A and we have no choice about B, and A and B strictly imply C, then we have no choice about C.
4. Therefore, if determinism is true, we have no choice about any truth about the future (including any truth about what actions we take).

Given a few innocent assumptions about substituting in to premise (3), this argument is deductively valid. A proponent of it will be concerned to defend premise (2) and premise (3), the 'Transfer principle.' (The first premise is taken to be true by definition.)[32]

Suppose a philosopher—call her Liv—were to defend premises (2) and (3) by claiming that they are supported by pretheoretical intuitions. When faced with our results, Liv may respond as follows:

> Sure, you can get people to call deterministically caused actions free. But people have other intuitions too—intuitions that nobody has a choice about the past or the laws of nature, and intuitions that support the Transfer principle—and these intuitions entail incompatibilism. Your questions have a very broad scope—they were about free will and responsibility directly, and at the level of free will and responsibility. The intuitions supporting my premises are more basic—they are about the conceptual *components* of free will and responsibility, as it were—about *choice* or *control* and how they work. People may call Jeremy or Jill free and responsible, but they are mistaken, for they fail to take into account their *own* more basic intuitions about choice or control.

Liv, in essence, is arguing that the correct way to understand 'incompatibilism is intuitive' is as the claim:

(C) Most people have intuitions about a concept *C* (e.g., 'choice' or 'control'), which is distinct from the concept of free will but is an essential component of it, and these intuitions entail that free will is incompatible with determinism.

Since our studies do not directly investigate claims about *C*-intuitions—intuitions that are supposed to underwrite premises (2) and (3) of the Consequence argument—Liv can insist that our results are irrelevant to whether or not incompatibilism is intuitive in the *relevant* sense: the sense involved in (C).

It is true that our surveys do not directly consider *C*-intuitions. However, our results do offer some *indirect* evidence against the intuitive plausibility of the Consequence argument. Our scenarios present conditions in the past that, along with the laws of nature, are sufficient conditions for the agent's action. So, the fact that most participants judged that the agent in the scenarios *is* free and responsible seems to suggest either (a) that they have the intuition that the Transfer principle does *not* apply to free choices, or (b) that—regardless of the soundness of the Consequence argument—the concept of choice the argument invokes to reach the conclusion that "we have no choice about any truth about the future," does not accord with the concept ordinary people consider relevant to free will and moral responsibility.[33] In any case, if empirical data is relevant to the broad-scope claim that incompatibilism is the pretheoretically intuitive position, then similar data should be relevant to more narrow-scope claims about the intuitiveness of premises (2) and (3) of the Consequence argument. If an incompatibilist wants to support these premises by appealing to pretheoretical intuitions, then our methodology suggests that this move requires empirical investigation of the relevant intuitions no less than the questions we have set out to answer.

4.2.3. Conflicting Intuitions

There is another reason an incompatibilist like Liv should worry about our results. Even if it were shown to be true that people have the intuitions about, for instance, the concept of choice that would support premises (2) and (3) of the Consequence argument, it is not clear that this fact would secure the case for incompatibilism. Suppose that a majority of participants in our experiments are expressing intuitions to the effect that individuals may count as free and responsible even if determined. Furthermore, suppose for the sake of argument, that a large portion of these same people also have the intuitions needed to support premises (2) and (3). It then appears that these people have inconsistent intuitions—or, given the difficulty in individuating intuitions, perhaps they merely lack an intuition they ought to have. Either way, they are subject to a kind of intuitional inconsistency: their set of free-will-relevant intuitions fails to form a consistent whole. If so, their set of intuitions would fail to cohere in a way that we, as philosophers, could straight-forwardly use in constructing a philosophical theory of free will. Hence, in order to build a coherent, unified theory of free will, we would either need to accuse the folk of error in their judgments about our scenarios, to accuse them of error in the intuitive judgments meant to underwrite the Consequence argument, or, as above, to deny the link between the ordinary conception of free will and the concept of choice invoked in the Consequence argument.

Of course, if it turns out that there is no consistent set of pretheoretical intuitions relevant to free will, philosophers may decide not to provide a coherent, unified theory of free will after all. Richard Double, for instance, argues (1991, 1996) that, as a matter of empirical fact, our intuitions about free will are in serious conflict and that this conflict entails that there is no such thing as free will. More precisely, he holds that this "intuitional anarchy" (1991, ch. 5) about which choices count as free entails that the term 'free will' (and various cognates) lacks an extension and functions in much the same way that noncognitivists think ethical terms function. In his terminology, free will is "non-real" (1991), and "Our proclaiming choices to be free and persons to be morally responsible for their choices can be nothing more than our venting of non-truth-valued attitudes, none of which is 'more correct' or 'more rational' than competing attitudes" (1996: 3).[34]

Another route for denying that there is a unified account of free will—one which does not relegate our talk about 'free will' to the realm of non-truth-valued attitudes—draws on contextualist semantics and suggests that there are in fact a number of properties which, in different contexts, people mean when they use the concept of free will.[35] This is not just the mundane claim that 'free' is ambiguous between multiple meanings (e.g., political freedom, religious freedom, zero cost). Rather, it is the claim that when people use 'free will' in contexts and ways intimately tied up with practices of moral responsibility, sometimes it expresses one content, compatible with determinism, and other times—notably, in philosophical discussions when the criteria of applicability become more stringent—it expresses another content, incompatible with determinism.

However, it seems clear to us that neither the noncognitivist nor the contextualist approach to the kind of intuitional conflict discussed above will be satisfactory to incompatibilists. For we take it that incompatibilists, when stating their thesis, are making a claim about free will that has cognitive content and that is true in all contexts (or at least all contexts where interest in free will is tied to questions of moral responsibility). Thus, in the face of our data, and assuming empirical research showed people in fact have intuitions supporting (C), the incompatibilist will have to find a way of resolving this conflict of intuitions in a way that helps his or her case.[36]

As we have already seen, Liv's way of resolving this conflict is to suggest that our intuitions about choice are more 'basic' than the intuitions about free will evoked by our scenarios. However, it is not clear what 'basic' is supposed to mean in this context.[37] Liv may mean that they are more *explanatorily* basic, since (on her view) someone is morally responsible for x-ing only if he x-ed freely, and he x-ed freely only if he had a choice about whether or not he x-ed. This itself relies on further conceptual claims, though—claims which involve the relationship between free will and having a choice, and which are hotly contested.[38]

Furthermore, it is not clear that being more explanatorily basic is a sufficient reason for one intuition to trump another in the case of conflict. Judgments about cases *do* seem to override intuitions about the more explanatorily basic entities at least *some* of the time. Take, for instance, the example of intentional action. Intentional actions are explained, in part, by an agent's intentions; thus, intentions seem to be more explanatorily basic than intentional actions. Indeed, a popular theory of intentional action claims that one intentionally does x if and only if one has an intention to x and successfully executes that intention (see Adams and Steadman 2004). However, philosophers empirically testing folk intuitions have found that there are cases in which most laypersons will judge that an agent intentionally did x without having the intention to x. One interesting example involves a CEO who implements a program in order to increase profits, knowing that the program will harm the environment but not aiming to harm it. In experiments by Joshua Knobe (2003), 87% of respondents judged that the chairman intentionally harmed the environment, although only 29% said that he had the intention to harm the environment. In the action-theory literature, theories may aim to preserve people's intuitions about cases such as these and reject the intuition that intentionally doing x requires an intention to x (e.g., Bratman 1984). Yet the intuition about *intentions* would be the more explanatorily basic intuition, at least on the taxonomy of intuitions that Liv endorses.

The upshot is that, to the extent that a philosophical theory (e.g., of intentional action or free will) aims to account for and accord with ordinary intuitions, it is unclear what its proponents should do in the face of conflicting intuitions. One might try to explain the conflict with a contextualist approach, as we suggested above. One might also develop a theory that calls for the revision of some of our concepts and practices. Some theories of free will are revisionist in this way, suggesting that the more metaphysically demanding aspects of the ordinary conception of free will can be eliminated but that most of it can be preserved (see Vargas, 2005). But as we have already seen, it is unclear why a philosophical theory of free will should revise the ordinary conception to make it *more* metaphysically demanding.

In any case, if the claim that "incompatibilism is intuitive" is to be understood as (C), then the claim is no longer able to do the dialectical work it was supposed to do. We have argued that one dialectical role of incompatibilists' claims of intuitive support is to shift the burden of proof to the compatibilist. Roughly, incompatibilists cite the intuitiveness of their own view in an effort to show that compatibilism is counter-intuitive; compatibilists then have to explain why their own counter-intuitive claims are better warranted than the incompatibilist's intuitive claims. However, given our data, merely citing (C) does not show that incompatibilism is any more intuitive than its competitors. At best, it shows that people have conflicting intuitions about free will and that *neither* compatibilism nor incompatibilism is univocally intuitive; this hardly provides reason to favor one theory over another.

4.3. Give Up the Claim That Incompatibilism Is Intuitive

Once incompatibilists see their dialectical position, they may be inclined to give up on the claim that incompatibilism is supported by the intuitions of ordinary people and find some other way to defend incompatibilism that does not make use of this strategy. We have already suggested why this move puts the incompatibilist in the uncomfortable position of having to motivate a theory of free will that is both less intuitive and more metaphysically demanding than compatibilist alternatives. However, our main target in this essay is the claim that incompatibilism has wide-scale intuitive appeal. If incompatibilists back off of this claim, one of our goals has been accomplished. Consequently, we will not undertake a detailed discussion of the strengths and weaknesses of the strategy of entirely rejecting the role of intuitions in the free will debate.

That being said, we explained (in §1) why, given the connection between free will and things we care about, such as moral responsibility, ordinary intuitions and practices do matter to philosophical conceptions of free will. And we explained why we think incompatibilists cannot entirely eschew intuitions as support for their thesis. Incompatibilists have a metaphysically demanding theory of free will: in order to make ascriptions of free will and moral responsibility come out true, compatibilist theories set conditions that are consistent with the truth of determinism *or* indeterminism, whereas incompatibilist theories require the truth of indeterminism (occurring at just the right place in the agent), and perhaps also agent causation.[39] A conceptual corollary to Ockham's Razor suggests that when choosing among theories, all else being equal, we should choose the one that has less metaphysically demanding truth-conditions for its claims.[40] If this corollary is accepted, then incompatibilists will have to insist that all else is *not* equal. It is not clear how the incompatibilist can establish this other than by showing that incompatibilism simply does a better job of preserving intuitions—the *right* intuitions, whichever ones those may be—than compatibilism does.

This observation reinforces our general methodological point. In order to show that one theory preserves intuitions of a certain type better than another, we must be fairly certain exactly what the intuitions of those types actually *are*. We have argued that the best way to gain a handle on what those intuitions actually are will require empirical investigation, not solely a priori armchair speculation. After all, it appears that many incompatibilists, largely on the basis of such a priori reasoning, concluded that something like (P) was true—and yet, if our investigations are any indication, (P) is false. Likewise, incompatibilists who wish to defend some other claim, such as (L) or (C), would do well to look for empirical evidence in support of the claim that most people have the relevant intuitions. Without such support, incompatibilists run the risk of demanding more out of the universe than our ordinary intuitions about free will and moral responsibility require.

5. CONCLUSION

We have advanced several claims in this chapter. First, we demonstrated that incompatibilists often suggest that their conception of free will is intuitive to ordinary people and that the burden of proof is therefore on compatibilists to explain away incompatibilist intuitions or to offer deflationary accounts of these intuitions. We argued that, absent any appeal to intuitions, it is instead *incompatibilist* positions that must be motivated since (a) they are advancing a claim about conceptual necessity (i.e., that determinism necessarily entails the nonexistence of free will), and (b) they involve a conception of free will that is more metaphysically demanding than the alternatives. We suggested that incompatibilists' appeals to ordinary people's intuitions have served in part to motivate these demands and to situate the burden of proof on compatibilists. But, we argued, these claims about people's intuitions should be empirically tested rather than asserted based on philosophers' own post-theoretical intuitions or their informal polling of students. We offered our own experiments as an initial demonstration of this methodology and offered several responses to them. Our results suggest that most laypersons do *not* have incompatibilist intuitions, though this preliminary work should be supplemented in order to get a firmer grasp on the relevant intuitions. To the extent that our results have in fact uncovered what people's pretheoretical intuitions about free will are, we suggest that the incompatibilist carries the burden of explaining why these intuitions do *not* illuminate the proper conception of free will. We have not argued that "less intuitive" entails "incorrect"—which would admittedly be a bad argumentative strategy. Instead, we focused on the claim that, in the face of data suggesting incompatibilism is not the intuitive view, incompatibilist theories become increasingly difficult to motivate.

Minimally, we believe that empirical data about folk intuitions should (a) encourage philosophers to state more precisely whether or not they are interested in ordinary intuitions about free will and moral responsibility and why, (b) prevent philosophers from appealing to the wide-scale intuitive plausibility of their theories unless these claims can be empirically substantiated, and (c) encourage philosophers to reexamine some of their own assumptions concerning the role of intuitions in philosophy. And in the event that a particular theory fails to settle with ordinary intuitions, the onus will be on its proponents to explain why we should care about a technical notion rather than the ordinary one—especially when understanding the latter is an important philosophical goal in its own right.[41]

NOTES

1. See also Smilansky (2003: 259), Pereboom (2001: xvi), O'Connor (2000: 4), and Campbell (1951: 451).

2. See Kane (1996: ch. 6), as well as Clarke (2003: ch. 6) for helpful discussions of these issues.

3. Though some compatibilists present their view as an error theory of this sort or as a revision of ordinary conceptions of free will, most follow incompatibilists in claiming that their own theories of freedom and responsibility best accord with ordinary intuitions. For instance, Frankfurt cases (1969) are designed to pump the intuition that the freedom necessary for moral responsibility does not require the ability to do otherwise. See also Dennett (1984), Wolf (1990: 89), Lycan (2003), and Nowell-Smith (1949: 49).

4. See Warfield (2000) for an explanation of why the proper incompatibilist view is *not* the contingent claim, "If determinism is true then there is no freedom," but the stronger claim, "Necessarily, if determinism is true then there is no freedom" (169). Arguably, any claims about necessity (impossibility) are more contentious than claims about possibility. To illustrate, consider that quantifying over possible worlds, the claim "X is possible" is existential—there is at least one world where X obtains—whereas the claim "X is impossible" is universal—for *all* worlds, X fails to obtain (Lycan 2003). See also Chalmers (1996) who writes, "In general, a certain burden of proof lies on those who claim that a certain description is logically *impossible*.... If no reasonable analysis of the terms in question points towards a contradiction, or even makes the existence of a contradiction plausible, then there is a natural assumption in favor of logical possibility" (96).

5. Even though hard determinists or skeptics about free will are not committed to the *existence* of libertarian free will, they *are* committed to the libertarian *conception* of free will since their arguments require this conception to reach the conclusion that free will does not (or could not) exist. Hence, skeptics, like libertarians, require motivation for the accuracy of this conception, and they often do so by suggesting that incompatibilism is the commonsensical or intuitive view (see, for instance, Strawson 1986 and Smilansky 2003).

6. Of course, Dave may have an independent argument against the possibility of token-identity, in which case his further incompatibility claim becomes somewhat uninteresting. But this would be akin to a philosopher having an independent argument against the possibility of determinism and then concluding that, necessarily, if we have free will, determinism is false—this has, *prima facie*, nothing to do with the compatibility question and everything to do with the validity of the inference from "$\Box \sim p$" to

"□ $(q \supset \sim p)$." We take incompatibilism to be the statement of a thesis more substantial than this.

7. See Vargas (2005). Compatibilists may also be better situated to offer error theories to explain why people sometimes express incompatibilist intuitions even though this need not commit them to incompatibilist theories. See, for instance, Velleman (2000) and Graham and Horgan (1998).

8. There is a fourth reason that some incompatibilists should want their view to be intuitive to ordinary people. Peter Strawson (1962) offered a compatibilist argument to the effect that we cannot and should not attempt to provide metaphysical justifications for our practices of moral responsibility (e.g., praise and blame), which are grounded in reactive attitudes such as indignation and gratitude. He suggested such practices are subject to justifications and revisions based only on considerations *internal* to the relevant practices and attitudes, but not on considerations *external* to the practice, including, in his view, determinism. But incompatibilists, notably Galen Strawson, have responded to this argument by suggesting that the question of determinism is *not* external to our considerations of moral responsibility (see also Pereboom 2001). That is, they claim that our reactive attitudes themselves are sensitive to whether human actions are deterministically caused. As Galen Strawson puts it, the fact that "the basic incompatibilist intuition that determinism is incompatible with freedom...has such power for us is as much a natural fact about cogitative beings like ourselves as is the fact of our quite unreflective commitment to the reactive attitudes. What is more, the roots of the incompatibilist intuition lie deep in the very reactive attitudes that are invoked in order to undercut it. The reactive attitudes enshrine the incompatibilist intuition" (1986: 88). If it turned out that this claim is false—that most people's reactive attitudes are *not* in fact sensitive to considerations of determinism—then this particular incompatibilist response to the elder Strawson's argument would fail. While there are other responses to Peter Strawson's views, we interpret some of the claims that incompatibilism is intuitive as attempts to shore up this response that our ordinary reactive attitudes and attributions of moral responsibility are sensitive to determinism. And we accordingly view any evidence to the contrary as strengthening Peter Strawson's suggestion that determinism is irrelevant to debates about freedom and responsibility and, accordingly, as weakening incompatibilism.

9. See Fischer (1994) on what he calls "Dialectical Stalemates."

10. See Graham and Horgan (1998: 273). We will not be developing a defense of the role of intuitions in philosophical debates (though see §4.3), since our main target is incompatibilists who claim they have the support of ordinary intuitions and hence seem to accept that intuitions play some significant role in the debate.

11. See also Stich and Weinberg (2001), and Graham and Horgan (1998), who write, "philosophy should regard armchair-obtainable data about ideological [i.e., conceptual] questions as empirical, and hence defeasible" (277).

12. See Goldman and Pust (1998: 182) and Jackson (1998).

13. Or Pink's assertion that "the intuition that Incompatibilism is true...is very general. For most people who are new to philosophy, nothing else makes sense" (2004: 14).

14. Cover and Hawthorne draw this conclusion in part from discussions with their philosophy students (1996: 51). Similarly, Derk Pereboom writes, "Beginning students typically recoil at the compatibilist response to the problem of moral responsibility" (2001: xvi), and Timothy O'Connor writes, "Does freedom of choice have this implication [that causal determinism must be false]? It seems so to the typical undergraduate on first encountering the question" (2000: 4). We suspect that such responses from

students are influenced by the way the problem is presented to them, and we have our own unscientific "evidence" indicating that a compatibilist teacher can present the issue so that most students don't see a problem with determinism and raise their hands in support of a compatibilist conception of free will. Thus, we suggest surveying people who have not yet been exposed to the relevant philosophical arguments (and our own methodology follows this suggestion—see below).

15. For a complete description of this and other studies, including methodology, statistical significance, and various objections and replies, see Nahmias et al. (2005). For all of the studies, participants were students at Florida State University who had never taken a college philosophy course.

16. This is not to suggest that there is a univocal understanding of the philosophical conception of determinism (see, e.g., Earman 2004). However, incompatibilists tend to use the description of determinism offered by van Inwagen (1983: 65): a proposition expressing the state of the world at any instant conjoined with the laws of nature entails any proposition expressing the state of the universe at any other time. There are also debates about how to understand the laws of nature; see Beebee and Mele (2002) for an interesting discussion of the relationship between Humean conceptions of laws and the compatibility question.

17. We should point out that in this survey and all others, participants were instructed to reason conditionally from the assumption that the scenario is actual. For instance, in this one, we wrote: "In answering the following questions, assume that this scenario is an accurate description of the universe in which Jill steals the necklace (regardless of whether you think it might be an accurate description of the way *our* universe works)." We also used manipulation checks on the back of the surveys to ensure that participants understood the nature of the scenario and excluded those who missed the manipulation check. For instance, in this study participants were excluded if they responded "no" to the question: "According to the scenario, is it accurate to say that every time the universe is re-created, Jill makes the same decision?"

18. Questions were counterbalanced for order effects and none were found.

19. We recognize that participants may be employing various conceptions of moral responsibility in answering our questions. It would be helpful to run systematic tests on what conception people have in mind. On some pilot studies, we asked participants whether the agents in the scenarios *deserved* reward or punishment for their actions, and results were consistent with those reported above.

20. See Nahmias et al. (2005).

21. See Black and Tweedale (2002).

22. One could test which aspect of such cases drives negative judgments about freedom and responsibility by seeing if parallel manipulation scenarios that involve *indeterminism* garner similarly negative judgments. If so, it would suggest that it is *manipulation* rather than determinism that is causing the judgments that the agent is not free or responsible. See Mele's (2005) response to Pereboom's "generalization strategy" (2001: ch. 4).

23. Indeed, it seems that determinism has sometimes been conflated with other theses that *are* threatening to the ordinary conception of the sort of free will required for moral responsibility—theses that are neither entailed by, nor entail, determinism, such as predictability in practice (not just in theory), certain scientific accounts of human behavior, or any reductionist theories of mind that imply conscious deliberations are epiphenomenal. As with the example in the prior note, it would be useful to follow up our studies with ones that describe these theses in a way understandable to the folk. If

their responses suggest that they see these theses as threats to free will, then, given our results regarding folk judgments about determinism, we would have reason to believe that it is not the thesis of determinism per se that threatens people's ordinary notion of free will, but instead theses that are mistakenly conflated with determinism.

24. See Nahmias et al. (2005) for results regarding participants' judgments about the agents' ability to do otherwise in deterministic scenarios.

25. To test the influence of exposure to the philosophical arguments, we ran the Fred and Barney survey on a class of Intro students soon after a two-week section on the free will debate. The results, it turned out, were not significantly different from the results garnered from "untrained" participants: 83% of the "trained" participants judged that Fred and Barney acted of their own free will, where 76% of untrained participants had made such judgments.

26. One might point out that our studies consistently found a minority of participants (usually 20–30%) who offered incompatibilist responses and argue that these subjects "got it" while the majority were unable to recognize the connection between the determinism in the scenario and their own conception of freedom and responsibility. Perhaps some people were motivated not to recognize such a conflict because they are strongly attached to the idea that we are free and responsible and are thus inclined to avoid any cognitive dissonance involved in considering a possible threat to our own freedom. For instance, people's propensity to blame others for bad outcomes may skew some of their responses. We consider these issues more fully in Nahmias et al. (2005); see also Nichols and Knobe (2007).

27. See Nichols (2004b). He takes his results to suggest that both children and adults have a conception of agent causation. We appreciate Nichols empirical approach to these issues, but we do not think his results support the conclusion that people's intuitions suggest agent causation (see Turner and Nahmias, 2006).

28. Note, however, that a phenomenological commitment to agent causation alone would not be enough to support (L): one can believe in agent causation and still be a compatibilist (see Markosian 1999). On the phenomenology of choice and action, see also Horgan, Tienson, and Graham (2003).

29. See, e.g., Clarke (2003: ch. 6) and van Inwagen (1983: ch. V).

30. See Nahmias et al. (2004).

31. The version below is drawn from Warfield (2000: 168). In van Inwagen's argument, the Transfer principle that corresponds to premise (3) is treated as an inference rule called 'Beta.'

32. The incompatibilist will also have to establish that the concept of choice involved in the conclusion is in fact the one relevant to our interest in freedom and responsibility. Some have challenged this claim, suggesting that we can be morally responsible even if we cannot choose otherwise in the sense entailed by the Consequence argument (see, for instance, Fischer 1994). See discussion in text below.

33. Thanks to Al Mele for help with this point. See Lycan (2003) for a Moorean argument to the effect that we should reject controversial philosophical premises (e.g., the Transfer principle) when they commit us to a highly counterintuitive conclusion (e.g., that we would lack—and would have always lacked—free will and moral responsibility if physicists discover determinism to be true).

34. We think this conclusion is too hasty for several reasons. For instance, even if ordinary intuitions suggest conflicting concepts of free will, that would not entail that there are no free choices. It might just mean that the concept is indeterminate in meaning (compare Sider 2001, on the concept of personal identity).

35. See, e.g., Graham and Horgan (1998) and Hawthorne (2001).

36. Admittedly, it is not immediately obvious that conflicting intuitions provide any succor to compatibilists, either, especially if compatibilism is committed to the existence of a univocal meaning for 'free' on which claims like "Joe was determined and acted freely" can come out true. However, the thesis we are defending is not that ordinary intuitions support compatibilism, but merely that they do not support incompatibilism. (Thanks to an anonymous referee for pressing us on this point.)

37. Perhaps it means that the intuitions about choice are stronger than the intuitions we elicited to the extent that people would be less likely to give up the former rather than the latter. (We owe this point to Tom Crisp.) If so, this claim would require empirical support that will certainly be difficult to garner.

38. If 'having a choice' is equated with having alternative possibilities, this claim will be undermined if Frankfurt-style counterexamples are possible (that is, if it is possible for someone to freely A without being able to avoid A-ing.) The success or failure of these counterexamples seems itself a matter deeply tied up with intuition; see Doris and Stich (2005) and Woolfolk, Doris, and Darley (2006) for empirical examinations of such examples.

39. Recent compatibilists generally reject the claim made by earlier compatibilists that free will *requires* determinism. For an event-causal libertarian view that requires quantum indeterminism in the agent's brain at precisely the moment of choice, see Kane (1996). See O'Connor (2000) and Clarke (2003) for discussions of agent causation.

40. More precisely: if, for every sentence S_1 in theory T_1 and its counterpart S_2 in T_2, if S_1's truth-conditions are no more metaphysically demanding than S_2's, and if some sentence S_2 in T_2 has more demanding truth-conditions than its counterpart S_1 in T_1, then, *all else being equal*, T_1 ought to be accepted.

41. For their helpful suggestions as we developed this project, we would like to thank John Doris, Joshua Knobe, Tamler Sommers, Bill Lycan, and George Graham. In addition, we are especially grateful for beneficial advice on earlier drafts of this chapter from two anonymous referees, and Shaun Nichols, Manuel Vargas, Tom Crisp, and Al Mele.

REFERENCES

Adams, F., and Steadman, A. 2004. "Intentional Action in Ordinary Language: Core Concept or Pragmatic Understanding?" *Analysis* 64: 173–181.

Beebee, H., and Mele, A. 2002. "Humean Compatibilism." *Mind* 111: 201–223.

Black, S., and Tweedale, J. 2003. "Responsibility and Alternative Possibilities: The Use and Abuse of Examples." *Journal of Ethics* 6: 281–303.

Campbell, C. A. 1951. "Is 'Freewill' a Pseudo-Problem?" *Mind* 60 (240): 441–465.

Chalmers, D. 1996. *The Conscious Mind: In Search of a Fundamental Theory*. New York: Oxford University Press.

Clarke, R. 2003. *Libertarian Accounts of Free Will*. New York: Oxford University Press.

Cover, J. A., and O'Leary-Hawthorne, J. 1996. "Free Agency and Materialism." In *Faith, Freedom and Rationality*, J. Jordan and D. Howard-Snyder (eds.), 47–71. Lanham, MD: Roman and Littlefield.

DePaul, M. R., and Ramsey, W. (eds.). 1998. *Rethinking Intuition: The Psychology of Intuition and Its Role in Philosophical Inquiry*. Lanham, MD: Rowman & Littlefield.

Dennett, D. 1984. *Elbow Room: The Varieties of Free Will Worth Wanting*. Cambridge, MA: MIT Press.

Doris, J., and Stich, S. 2005. "As a Matter of Fact: Empirical Perspectives on Ethics." In *The Oxford Handbook of Contemporary Philosophy*, F. Jackson & M. Smith (eds.).

Double, R. 1991. *The Non-Reality of Free Will*. New York: Oxford University Press.

Double, R. 1996. *Metaphilosophy and Free Will*. New York: Oxford University Press.

Earman, J. 2004. "Determinism: What We Have Learned and What We Still Don't Know." In *Freedom and Determinism*, J. K. Campbell, M. O'Rourke, and D. Shier (eds.). Cambridge, MA: MIT Press.

Ekstrom, L. 2002. "Libertarianism and Frankfurt-Style Cases." In *The Oxford Handbook of Free Will*, R. Kane (ed.). New York: Oxford University Press.

Ekstrom, L. 2000. *Free Will*. Boulder, CO: Westview Press.

Fischer, J. 1994. *The Metaphysics of Free Will*. Cambridge: Blackwell.

Frankfurt, H. 1969. "Alternate Possibilities and Moral Responsibility." In *The Importance of What We Care About*. Cambridge: Cambridge University Press, 1988.

Goldman, A., and Pust, J. 1998. "Philosophical Theory and Intuitional Evidence." In DePaul and Ramsey (eds.).

Graham, G., and Horgan, T. 1998. "Southern Fundamentalism and the End of Philosophy." In Depaul and Ramsey (eds.).

Hawthorne, J. 2001. "Freedom in Context." *Philosophical Studies* 104: 63–79.

Horgan, T., Tienson, J., and Graham, G. 2003. "The Phenomenology of First-Person Agency." In *Physicalism and Mental Causation*, S. Walter and H. Heckman (eds.). Charlottesville, VA: Imprint Academic.

Jackson, F. 1998. *From Metaphysics to Ethics: A Defense of Conceptual Analysis*. New York: Oxford University Press.

Kane, R. 1999. "Responsibility, Luck, and Chance: Reflections on Free Will and Indeterminism." *Journal of Philosophy* 96: 217–240.

Kane, R. 1996. *The Significance of Free Will*. New York: Oxford University Press.

Knobe, J. 2003. "Intentional Action and Side-effects in Ordinary Language." *Analysis* 63: 190–193.

Knobe, J. 2004. "Intention, Intentional Action and Moral Considerations." *Analysis* 64: 181–187.

Lycan, W. 2003. "Free Will and the Burden of Proof." In *Proceedings of the Royal Institute of Philosophy for 2001–02*, Anthony O'Hear (ed.), 107–122. Cambridge: Cambridge University Press.

Markosian, N. 1999. "A Compatibilist Version of the Theory of Agent Causation." *Pacific Philosophical Quarterly* 80: 257–277.

Mele, A. 2005. "A Critique of Pereboom's 'Four Case Argument' for Incompatibilism." *Analysis* 65.

Nadelhoffer, T. 2004. "The Butler Problem Revisited." *Analysis* 64(3): 277–284.

Nadelhoffer, T. 2005. "Skill, Luck, and Folk Ascriptions of Intentional Action." *Philosophical Psychology* 24: 196–213.

Nahmias, E., Morris, S., Nadelhoffer, T., and Turner, J. 2004. "The Phenomenology of Free Will." *Journal of Consciousness Studies* 11(7–8): 162–179.

Nahmias, E., Morris, S., Nadelhoffer, T., and Turner, J. 2005. "Surveying Freedom: Folk Intuitions about Free Will and Moral Responsibility." *Philosophical Psychology* 18(5): 561–584.

Nichols, S. 2004a. "After Objectivity." *Philosophical Psychology* 17: 5–28.

Nichols, S. 2004b. "The Folk Psychology of Free Will: Fits and Starts." *Mind and Language* 19: 473–502.

Nichols, S., and Knobe, J. 2007. "Moral Responsibility and Determinism: The Cognitive Science of Folk Intuitions." *Noûs*.

Nichols, S., Weinberg, J., and Stich, S. 2002. "Metaskepticism: Meditations in Ethno-Epistemology." In *The Skeptics*, S. Luper (ed.). Burlington, VT: Ashgate.

Nowell-Smith, P. H. 1949. "Free Will and Moral Responsibility." *Mind* 57: 45–65.

O'Connor, T. 2000. *Persons and Causes: The Metaphysics of Free Will*. New York: Oxford University Press.

Pereboom, D. 2001. *Living without Free Will*. Cambridge: Cambridge University Press.

Pink, T. 2004. *Free Will: A Very Short Introduction*. New York: Oxford University Press.

Sider, T. 2001. "Criteria of Personal Identity and the Limits of Conceptual Analysis." *Philosophical Perspectives 15, Metaphysics*. James E. Livberlin, ed., 189–209.

Smilansky, S. 2003. "Compatibilism: The Argument from Shallowness." *Philosophical Studies* 115(3): 257–282.

Stich, S., and Weinberg, J. M. 2001. "Jackson's Empirical Assumptions." *Philosophy and Phenomenological Research* 62: 637–643.

Strawson, G. 1986. *Freedom and Belief*. Oxford: Oxford University Press.

Strawson, P. 1962. "Freedom and Resentment." *Proceedings of the British Academy* 48.

Turner, J., and Nahmias, E. 2006. "Are the Folk Agent-Causationists?" *Mind and Language* 21(5): 597–609.

Vargas, M. 2005. "The Revisionist's Guide to Moral Responsibility." *Philosophical Studies* 125(3): 399–429.

van Inwagen, P. 1983. *An Essay on Free Will*. Oxford: Clarendon Press.

Velleman, D. 2000. "Epistemic Freedom." In *The Possibility of Practical Reason*. New York: Oxford University Press.

Warfield, T. 2000. "A New Argument for Incompatibilism." *Philosophical Perspectives* 14: 167–180.

Wolf, S. 1990. *Freedom within Reason*. New York: Oxford University Press.

Woolfolk, R., Doris, J., and Darley, J. 2006. "Identification, Situational Constraint, and Social Cognition: Studies in the Attribution of Moral Responsibility." *Cognition* 100(2): 283–306.

6

Moral Responsibility and Determinism

The Cognitive Science of Folk Intuitions

Shaun Nichols & Joshua Knobe

1. INTRODUCTION

The dispute between compatibilists and incompatibilists must be one of the most persistent and heated deadlocks in Western philosophy. Incompatibilists maintain that people are not fully morally responsible if determinism is true, that is, if every event is an inevitable consequence of the prior conditions and the natural laws. By contrast, compatibilists maintain that even if determinism is true, our moral responsibility is not undermined in the slightest, for determinism and moral responsibility are perfectly consistent.[1]

The debate between these two positions has invoked many different resources, including quantum mechanics, social psychology, and basic metaphysics. But recent discussions have relied heavily on arguments that draw on people's intuitions about particular cases. Some philosophers have claimed that people have incompatibilist intuitions (e.g., Kane 1999, 218; Strawson 1986, 30; Vargas 2006); others have challenged this claim and suggested that people's intuitions actually fit with compatibilism (Nahmias et al. 2005). But although philosophers have constructed increasingly sophisticated arguments about the implications of people's intuitions, there has been remarkably little discussion about *why* people have the intuitions they do. That is to say, relatively little has been said about the specific psychological processes that generate or sustain people's intuitions. And yet, it seems clear that questions about the sources of people's intuitions could have a major impact on debates about the compatibility of responsibility and determinism. There is an obvious sense in which it is important to figure out whether people's intuitions are being produced by a process that is generally reliable or whether they are being distorted by a process that generally leads people astray.

Our aim here is to present and defend a hypothesis about the processes that generate people's intuitions concerning moral responsibility. Our hypothesis is that people have an incompatibilist theory of moral responsibility that is elicited in some contexts but that they also have psychological mechanisms that can lead them to arrive at compatibilist judgments in other contexts.[2] To support this hypothesis, we report new experimental data. These data show that people's responses to questions about moral responsibility can vary dramatically depending on the way in which the question is formulated. When asked questions that call for a more abstract, theoretical sort of cognition, people give overwhelmingly incompatibilist answers. But when asked questions that trigger emotions, their answers become far more compatibilist.

2. AFFECT, BLAME, AND THE ATTRIBUTION OF RESPONSIBILITY

In their attempts to get a handle on folk concepts and folk theories, naturalistic philosophers have proceeded by looking at people's intuitions about particular cases (e.g., Knobe 2003a, 2003b; Nahmias et al 2005; Nichols 2004a; Weinberg et al. 2001; Woolfolk et al. 2006). The basic technique is simple. The philosopher constructs a hypothetical scenario and then asks people whether, for instance, the agent in the scenario is morally responsible. By varying the details of the case and checking to see how people's intuitions are affected, one can gradually get a sense for the contours of the folk theory. This method is a good one, but it must be practiced with care. One cannot simply assume that all of the relevant intuitions are generated by the same underlying folk theory. It is always possible that different intuitions will turn out to have been generated by different psychological processes.

Here we will focus especially on the role of *affect* in generating intuitions about moral responsibility. Our hypothesis is that when people are confronted with a story about an agent who performs a morally bad behavior, this can trigger an immediate emotional response, and this emotional response can play a crucial role in their intuitions about whether the agent was morally responsible. In fact, people may sometimes declare such an agent to be morally responsible despite the fact that they embrace a theory of responsibility on which the agent is not responsible.

Consider, for example, Watson's (1987) interesting discussion of the crimes of Robert Harris. Watson provides long quotations from a newspaper article about how Harris savagely murdered innocent people, showing no remorse for what he had done. Then he describes, in equally chilling detail, the horrible abuse Harris had to endure as he was growing up. After reading all of these vivid details, it would be almost impossible for a reader to respond by calmly working out the implications of his or her theory of moral responsibility. Any normal reader will have a rich array of reactions, including not only abstract theorizing but also feelings of horror and disgust. A reader's intuitions about such a case might be swayed by her emotions, leaving her with a conclusion that contravened her more abstract, theoretical beliefs about the nature of moral responsibility.

Still, it might be thought that this sort of effect would be unlikely to influence people's reactions to ordinary philosophical examples. Most philosophical examples are purely hypothetical and thinly described (often only a few sentences in length). To a first glance at least, it might seem that emotional reactions are unlikely to have any impact on people's intuitions about examples like these. But a growing body of experimental evidence indicates that this commonsense view is mistaken. This evidence suggests that affect plays an important role even in people's intuitions about thinly described, purely hypothetical cases (Blair 1995; Greene et al. 2001; Nichols 2002; Haidt et al. 1993).

It may seem puzzling that affect should play such a powerful role, and a number of different models of the role of emotion in evaluative thought have been proposed. We will discuss some of these models in further detail in sections 5, 6, and 7. In the meantime, we want to point to one factor that appears to influence people's affective reactions. A recent study by Smart and Loewenstein (2005) shows that when a transgressor is made more 'determinate' for subjects, subjects experience greater negative affect and are more punitive toward that agent as a result. In the study, subjects play a game in which they can privately cooperate or defect. Each subject is assigned an identifying number, but none of the subjects knows anyone else's number. The experimenter puts the numbers of the defectors into an envelope. The cooperators are subsequently allowed to decide whether to penalize a defector. The cooperator is informed that he will pick a number out of the envelope to determine which defector will be penalized (or not). The manipulation was unbelievably subtle. In the *indeterminate* condition, subjects decide how much to penalize *before* they draw the number; in the *determinate* condition, subjects decide how much to penalize *after* they draw the number. Despite this tiny difference, Smart and Loewenstein found a significant effect—subjects in the determinate condition gave worse penalties than subjects in the indeterminate condition. Furthermore, subjects filled out a self-report questionnaire on how much anger, blame, and sympathy they felt, and subjects in the determinate condition felt more anger and blame than subjects in the indeterminate condition. Finally, using mediational statistical analysis, Smart and Loewenstein found that determinateness impacts punitiveness by virtue of provoking stronger emotions.

As we shall see, previous studies of people's moral responsibility intuitions all featured determinate agents and therefore were designed in a way that would tend to trigger affective reactions. Our own study provides an opportunity to see how people's intuitions are altered when the stimuli are designed in a way that keeps affective reactions to a minimum.

3. INTUITIONS ABOUT FREE WILL AND RESPONSIBILITY

Incompatibilist philosophers have traditionally claimed both that ordinary people believe that human decisions are not governed by deterministic laws and that ordinary people believe that determinism is incompatible with moral responsibility (e.g., Kane 1999; Strawson 1986). These claims have been based, not on systematic empirical research, but rather on anecdote and informal observation. For example, Kane writes, "In my experience, most ordinary persons start out as natural incompatibilists" (1999, 217). (As will be clear below, we think Kane is actually getting at something deep about our intuitions here.) In recent years, philosophers have sought to put claims like this one to the test using experimental methods. The results have sometimes been surprising.

First, consider the claim that ordinary people believe that human decisions are not governed by deterministic laws. In a set of experiments exploring the lay understanding of choice, both children and adults tended to treat moral choices as indeterminist (Nichols 2004a). Participants were presented with cases of moral choice events (e.g., a girl steals a candy bar) and physical events (e.g., a pot of water comes to a boil), and they were asked whether, if everything in the world was the same right up until the event occurred, the event *had to* occur. Both children and adults were more likely to say that the physical event had to occur than that the moral choice event had to occur. This result seems to vindicate the traditional claim that ordinary people in our culture believe that at least some human decisions are not determined.

Experimental study has not been so kind to the traditional claim that ordinary people are incompatibilists about responsibility. Woolfolk, Doris, and Darley (2006) gave participants a story about an agent who is captured by kidnappers and given a powerful 'compliance drug.' The drug makes it impossible for him to disobey orders. The kidnappers order him to perform an immoral action, and he cannot help but obey. Subjects in the 'low identification condition' were told that the agent did not want to perform the immoral action and was only performing it because he had been given the compliance drug. Subjects in the 'high identification condition' were told that the agent wanted to perform the immoral action all along and felt no reluctance about performing it. The results showed a clear effect of identification: subjects in the high identification condition gave higher ratings of responsibility for the agent than subjects in the low identification condition. This result fits beautifully with the compatibilist view that responsibility depends on identification (e.g., Frankfurt 1988). However, subjects in both conditions showed an overall tendency to give low ratings of responsibility for the agent. So these results don't pose a direct threat to the view that people are incompatibilists about responsibility.

The final set of studies we'll review poses a greater problem for the view that people are intuitive incompatibilists. Nahmias, Morris, Nadelhoffer, and Turner (2005) find that participants will hold an agent morally responsible even when they are told to assume that the agent is in a deterministic universe. For instance, they presented participants with the following scenario:

> Imagine that in the next century we discover all the laws of nature, and we build a supercomputer which can deduce from these laws of nature and from the current state of everything in the world exactly what will be happening in the world at any future time. It can look at everything about the way the world is and predict everything about how it will be with 100% accuracy. Suppose that such a supercomputer existed, and it looks at the state of the universe at a certain time on March 25th, 2150 A.D., twenty years before Jeremy Hall is born. The com-

puter then deduces from this information and the laws of nature that Jeremy will definitely rob Fidelity Bank at 6:00 PM on January 26th, 2195. As always, the supercomputer's prediction is correct; Jeremy robs Fidelity Bank at 6:00 PM on January 26th, 2195.

Participants were subsequently asked whether Jeremy is morally blameworthy for robbing the bank. The results were striking: 83% of subjects said that Jeremy was morally blameworthy for robbing the bank. In two additional experiments with different scenarios, similar effects emerged, suggesting that lay people regard moral responsibility as compatible with determinism. These findings are fascinating, and we will try to build on them in our own experiments.

Of course, it is possible to challenge the experiments on methodological grounds. For instance, the scenarios use technical vocabulary (e.g., "laws of nature," "current state"), and one might wonder whether the subjects really understood the scenarios. Further, one might complain that determinism is not made sufficiently salient in the scenarios. The story of the supercomputer focuses on the predictability of events in the universe, and many philosophers have taken the predictability of the universe to be less threatening to free will than causal inevitability. Although one might use these methodological worries to dismiss the results, we are not inclined to do so. For we think that Nahmias and colleagues have tapped into something of genuine interest.[3] They report three quite different scenarios that produce much the same effect. In each of their experiments, most people (60–85%) say that the agent is morally responsible even under the assumption that determinism is true. Moreover, the results coincide with independent psychological work on the assignment of punishment. Viney and colleagues found that college students who were identified as determinists were no less punitive than indeterminists (Viney et al. 1982) and no less likely to offer retributivist justifications for punishments (Viney et al. 1988).[4] So, we will assume that Nahmias et al. are right that when faced with an agent intentionally doing a bad action in a deterministic setting, people tend to hold the agent morally responsible.

But if people so consistently give compatibilist responses on experimental questionnaires, why have some philosophers concluded that ordinary people are incompatibilists?[5] Have these philosophers simply been failing to listen to their own undergraduate students? We suspect that something more complex is going on. On our view, most people (at least in our culture) really do hold incompatibilist theories of moral responsibility, and these theories can easily be brought out in the kinds of philosophical discussions that arise, for example, in university seminars. It's just that, in addition to these theories of moral responsibility, people also have immediate affective reactions to stories about immoral behaviors. What we see in the results of the experiments by Nahmias and colleagues is, in part, the effect of these affective reactions. To uncover people's underlying theories, we need to offer them questions that call for more abstract, theoretical cognition.

4. EXPERIMENTAL EVIDENCE: FIRST PHASE

We conducted a series of experiments to explore whether participants will be more likely to report incompatibilist intuitions if the emotional and motivational factors are minimized. In each experiment, one condition, the *concrete* condition, was designed to elicit greater affective response; the other condition, the *abstract* condition, was designed to trigger abstract, theoretical cognition. We predicted that people would be more likely to respond as compatibilists in the concrete condition.

Before we present the details of the experiments, we should note that there are many ways to characterize determinism. The most precise characterizations involve technical language about, for example, the laws of nature. However, we think it's a mistake to use technical terminology for these sorts of experiments, and we therefore tried to present the issue in more accessible language.[6] Of course, any attempt to translate complex philosophical issues into simpler terms will raise difficult questions. It is certainly possible that the specific description of determinism used in our study biased people's intuitions in one direction or another. Perhaps the overall rate of incompatibilist responses would have been somewhat higher or lower if we had used a subtly different formulation.

One should keep in mind, however, that our main focus here is on the *difference* between people's responses in the concrete condition and their responses in the abstract condition. Even though we use exactly the same description of determinism in these two conditions, we predict that people will give compatibilist responses in the concrete condition and incompatibilist responses in the abstract condition. Such an effect could not be dismissed as an artifact of our description of determinism. If a difference actually does emerge, we will therefore have good evidence for the view that affect is playing some role in people's compatibilist intuitions.

All of our studies were conducted on undergraduates at the University of Utah,[7] and all of the studies began with the same setup. Participants were given the following description of a determinist universe and an indeterminist universe:

> Imagine a universe (Universe A) in which everything that happens is completely caused by whatever happened before it. This is true from the very beginning of the universe, so what happened in the beginning of the universe caused what happened next, and so on right up until the present. For example one day John decided to have French fries at lunch. Like everything else, this decision was completely caused by what happened before it. So, if everything in this universe was exactly the same up until John made his decision, then it *had to happen* that John would decide to have French fries.
>
> Now imagine a universe (Universe B) in which *almost* everything that happens is completely caused by whatever happened before it. The one exception is human decision making. For example, one day Mary decided to have French fries at lunch. Since a person's decision in this universe is

not completely caused by what happened before it, even if everything in the universe was exactly the same up until Mary made her decision, it *did not have to happen* that Mary would decide to have French fries. She could have decided to have something different.

The key difference, then, is that in Universe A every decision is completely caused by what happened before the decision—given the past, each decision *has to happen* the way that it does. By contrast, in Universe B, decisions are not completely caused by the past, and each human decision *does not have to happen* the way that it does.

1. Which of these universes do you think is most like ours? (circle one)

UNIVERSE A   UNIVERSE B

Please briefly explain your answer.

The purpose of this initial question was simply to see whether subjects believe that our own universe is deterministic or indeterministic. Across conditions, nearly all participants (over 90%) judged that the indeterministic universe is more similar to our own.

After answering the initial question, subjects received a question designed to test intuitions about compatibilism and incompatibilism. Subjects were randomly assigned either to the *concrete* condition or to the *abstract* condition. We ran several different versions, but we will focus on the most important ones. In one of our concrete conditions, subjects were given the following question:

In Universe A, a man named Bill has become attracted to his secretary, and he decides that the only way to be with her is to kill his wife and three children. He knows that it is impossible to escape from his house in the event of a fire. Before he leaves on a business trip, he sets up a device in his basement that burns down the house and kills his family.

Is Bill fully morally responsible for killing his wife and children?

YES   NO

In this condition, most subjects (72%) gave the compatibilist response that the agent was fully morally responsible. This is comparable to results obtained in experiments by Nahmias and colleagues. But now consider one of our abstract conditions:

In Universe A, is it possible for a person to be fully morally responsible for their actions?

YES   NO

In this condition, most subjects (86%) gave the *incompatibilist* response!

In short, most people give the compatibilist response to the concrete case, but the vast majority give the *incompatibilist* response to the abstract case. What on earth could explain this dramatic difference? Let's first consider a deflationary possibility. Perhaps the concrete condition is so long and complex that subjects lose track of the fact that the agent is in a determinist universe. This is a perfectly sensible explanation. To see whether this accounts for the difference, we ran another concrete condition in which the scenario was short and simple. Subjects were given all the same initial descriptions and then given the following question:

> In Universe A, Bill stabs his wife and children to death so that he can be with his secretary. Is it possible that Bill is fully morally responsible for killing his family?
>
> YES   NO

Even in this simple scenario, 50% of subjects gave the compatibilist response, which is still significantly different from the very low number of compatibilist responses in the abstract condition.[8]

As we noted above, there are many ways of describing determinism, and the overall rate of incompatibilist responses might have been higher or lower if we had used a somewhat different description. Still, one cannot plausibly dismiss the high rate of incompatibilist responses in the abstract condition as a product of some subtle bias in our description of determinism. After all, the concrete condition used precisely the same description, and yet subjects in that condition were significantly more likely to give compatibilist responses.[9]

These initial experiments replicated the finding (originally due to Nahmias et al.) that people have compatibilist intuitions when presented with vignettes that trigger affective responses. But they also yielded a new and surprising result. When subjects were presented with an abstract vignette, they had predominantly *incompatibilist* intuitions. This pattern of results suggests that affect is playing a key role in generating people's compatibilist intuitions.

5. PSYCHOLOGICAL MODELS

Thus far, we have been providing evidence for the claim that different folk intuitions about responsibility are produced by different kinds of psychological processes. But if it is indeed the case that one sort of process leads to compatibilist intuitions and another leads to incompatibilist intuitions, which sort of process should we regard as the best guide to the true relationship between moral responsibility and determinism?

Before we can address this question, we need to know a little bit more about the specific psychological processes that might underlie different types of folk intuitions. We therefore consider a series of possible models. We begin by looking at three extremely simple models and then go on to consider ways that elements of these simple models might be joined together to form more complex models.

The Performance Error Model

Perhaps the most obvious way of explaining the data reported here would be to suggest that strong affective reactions can bias and distort people's judgments. On this view, people ordinarily make responsibility judgments by relying on a tacit theory, but when they are faced with a truly egregious violation of moral norms (as in our concrete cases), they experience a strong affective reaction that makes them unable to apply the theory correctly. In short, this hypothesis posits an *affective performance error*. That is, it draws a distinction between people's underlying representations of the criteria for moral responsibility and the performance systems that enable them to apply those criteria to particular cases. It then suggests that people's affective reactions are interfering with the normal operation of the performance systems.

The performance error model draws support from the vast literature in social psychology on the interaction between affect and theoretical cognition. This literature has unearthed numerous ways in which people's affective reactions can interfere with their ability to reason correctly. Under the influence of affective or motivational biases, people are less likely to recall certain kinds of relevant information, less likely to believe unwanted evidence, and less likely to use critical resources to attack conclusions that are motivationally neutral (see Kunda 1990 for a review). Given that we find these biases in so many other aspects of cognition, it is only natural to conclude that they can be found in moral responsibility judgments as well.

More pointedly, there is evidence that affect sometimes biases attributions of responsibility. Lerner and colleagues found that when subjects' negative emotions are aroused, they hold agents more responsible and more deserving of punishment, *even when the negative emotions are aroused by an unrelated event* (Lerner et al. 1998). In their study, subjects in the *anger* condition watched a video clip of a bully beating up a teenager, while subjects in the *emotion-neutral* condition watched a video clip of abstract figures (Lerner et al. 1998, 566). All subjects were then presented with what they were told was a different experiment designed to examine how people assess responsibility for negligent behaviors. Subjects in the anger condition (i.e., those who had seen the bully video) gave higher responsibility ratings than subjects in the emotion-neutral condition. So, although the subjects' emotions were induced by the film, these emotions impacted their responsibility judgments in unrelated scenarios. The most natural way to interpret this result is that the emotion served to bias the reasoning people used in making their assessments of responsibility.

Proponents of the performance error model might suggest that a similar phenomenon is at work in the experiments we have reported here. They would concede that people give compatibilist responses under certain circumstances, but they would deny that there is any real sense in which people can be said to hold a compatibilist view of moral responsibility. Instead, they would claim that the compatibilist responses we find in our concrete conditions are to be understood in terms of performance errors brought about by affective reactions. In the abstract condition, people's underlying theory is revealed for what it is—incompatibilist.

The Affective Competence Model

There is, however, another possible way of understanding the role of affect in the assessment of moral responsibility. Instead of supposing that affect serves only to bias or distort our theoretical judgments, one might suggest that people's affective reactions actually lie at the core of the process by which they ordinarily assign responsibility. Perhaps people normally make responsibility judgments by experiencing an affective reaction that, in combination with certain other processes, enables an assessment of moral responsibility. Of course, it can hardly be denied that some people also have elaborate theories of moral responsibility and that they use these theories in certain activities (e.g., in writing philosophy papers), but the proponents of this second view would deny that people's cold cognitive theories of responsibility play any real role in the process by means of which they normally make responsibility judgments. This process, they would claim, is governed primarily by affect.

This 'affective competence' view gains some support from recent studies of people with deficits in emotional processing due to psychological illnesses. When these people are given questions that require moral judgments, they sometimes offer bizarre patterns of responses (Blair 1995; Blair et al. 1997; Hauser et al. 2006). In other words, when we strip away the capacity for affective reactions, it seems that we are not left with a person who can apply the fundamental criteria of morality in an especially impartial or unbiased fashion. Instead, we seem to be left with someone who has trouble understanding what morality is all about. Results from studies like these have led some researchers to conclude that affect must be playing an important role in the fundamental competence underlying people's moral judgments (Blair 1995; Haidt 2001; Nichols 2004b; Prinz 2007).

Proponents of this view might suggest that the only way to really get a handle on people's capacity for moral judgment is to look at their responses in cases that provoke affective reactions. When we examine these cases, people seem to show a marked tendency to offer compatibilist responses, and it might therefore be suggested that the subjects in our studies should be regarded as compatibilists. Of course, we have also provided data indicating that these subjects provide incompatibilist answers when given theoretical questions, but it might be felt that studying people's theoretical beliefs tells us little or nothing about how they really go about making moral judgments. (Think of what would happen if we tried to study the human capacity for language by asking people theoretical questions about the principles of syntax!) Thus, affective competency theorists might maintain that the best way to describe our findings would be to say that people's fundamental moral competence is a compatibilist one but that some people happen to subscribe to a theory that contradicts this fundamental competence.

The Concrete Competence Model

Finally, we need to consider the possibility that people's responses are not being influenced by affect in any way. Perhaps people's responses in the concrete conditions are actually generated by a purely cognitive process. Even if we assume that the process at work here can only be applied to concrete cases, we should not necessarily conclude that it makes essential use of affect. It might turn out that we have an entirely cognitive, affect-free process that, for whatever reason, can be applied to concrete questions but not to abstract ones.

One particularly appealing version of this hypothesis would be that people's intuitions in the concrete conditions are generated by an innate 'moral responsibility module.'[10] This module could take as input information about an agent and his or her behavior and then produce as output an intuition as to whether or not that agent is morally responsible. Presumably, the module would not use the same kinds of processes that are used in conscious reasoning. Instead, it would use a process that is swift, automatic, and entirely unconscious.

Here, the key idea is that only limited communication is possible between the module and the rest of the mind. The module takes as input certain very specific kinds of information about the agent (the fact that the agent is a human being, the fact that he knows what he is doing, etc.), but the vast majority of the person's beliefs would be entirely inaccessible to processes taking place inside of the module. Thus, the module would not be able to make use of the person's theory about the relationship between determinism and moral responsibility. It might not even be able to make use of the person's belief that the agent is in a deterministic universe. Because these beliefs would be inaccessible inside of the module, the conclusions of the module could differ dramatically from the conclusions that the person would reach after a process of conscious consideration.

Hybrid Models

Thus far, we have been considering three simple models of responsibility attribution. It would be possible, however, to construct more complex models by joining together elements of the three simple ones we have already presented. So, for example, it might turn out that moral responsibility judgments are subserved by a module but that the workings of this module are sometimes plagued with affective performance errors, or that the fundamental competence underlying responsibility judgments makes essential use of affect but that this affect somehow serves as input to a module, and many other possible hybrids might be suggested here.

Since we are unable to consider all of the possible hybrid models, we will focus on one that we find especially plausible. On the hybrid model we will be discussing, affect plays two distinct roles in the assignment of moral responsibility. Specifically, affect serves *both* as part of the fundamental competence underlying responsibility judgments *and* as a factor that can sometimes lead to performance errors. To get a sense for what we mean here, imagine that you are trying to determine whether certain poems should be regarded as 'moving,' and now suppose you discover that one of the poems was actually written by your best friend. Here, it seems that the basic competence underlying your judgment would involve one sort of affect (your feelings about the poems) but the performance systems enabling your judgment could be derailed by another sort of affect (your feelings about the friend). The hybrid model in question would suggest that a similar sort of process takes place in judgments of moral responsibility. The competence underlying these judgments does make use of affect, but affect can also be implicated in processes that ultimately lead to performance errors.

Proponents of this model might suggest that affect does play an important role in the competence underlying moral responsibility judgments but that the effect obtained in the experiments reported here should still be treated as a performance error.[11] In other words, even if we suppose that affect has an important role to play in moral responsibility judgments, we can still conclude that the basic competence underlying these judgments is an incompatibilist one and that the responses we find in our concrete conditions are the result of a failure to apply that competence correctly.

6. EXPERIMENTAL EVIDENCE: SECOND PHASE

Now that we have described some of the psychological models that might explain our results, we can explore a bit more deeply whether experimental evidence counts against any of the models. One key question is whether or not the compatibilist responses in our experiments are really the product of affect. We compared concrete conditions with abstract conditions, and we suggested that the concrete descriptions triggered greater affective response, which in turn pushed subjects toward compatibilist responses. However, it's possible that what really mattered was concreteness itself, not any affect associated with concreteness. That is, it's possible that the compatibilist responses were not influenced by affect but were elicited simply because the scenario involved a particular act by a particular individual. Indeed, this is exactly the sort of explanation one would expect from the responsibility module account. Fortunately, there is a direct way to test this proposal.

To explore whether concreteness alone can explain the compatibilist responses, we ran another experiment in which the affective salience varied across the two questions, but concreteness was held constant. Again, all subjects were given the initial descriptions of the two universes, A and B, and all subjects were asked which universe they thought was most similar to ours. Subjects were randomly assigned either to the *high affect* or *low affect* condition. In the *high affect* condition, subjects were asked the following:

> As he has done many times in the past, Bill stalks and rapes a stranger. Is it possible that Bill is fully morally responsible for raping the stranger?

In the *low affect* condition, subjects were asked:

> As he has done many times in the past, Mark arranges to cheat on his taxes. Is it possible that Mark is fully morally responsible for cheating on his taxes?

In addition, in each condition, for half of the subjects, the question stipulated that the agent was in Universe A; for the other half, the agent was in Universe B. Thus, each subject was randomly assigned to one of the cells in table 6.1.

Table 6.1

	Agent in indeterminist universe	Agent in determinist universe
High affect case		
Low affect case		

What did we find? Even when we used these exclusively concrete scenarios, there was a clear difference between the high affect and low affect cases. Among subjects who were asked about agents in a *determinist* universe, people were much more likely to give the incompatibilist answer in the low affect case than in the high affect case. Indeed, most people said that it is *not* possible that the tax cheat is fully morally responsible, and a clear majority said that it *is* possible that the rapist is fully morally responsible. By contrast, for subjects who were asked about an agent in an indeterminist universe, most people said that it is possible for the agent to be fully morally responsible, regardless of whether he was a tax cheat or a rapist.[12] See table 6.2.

Table 6.2

	Agent in indeterminist universe	Agent in determinist universe
High affect case	95%	64%
Low affect case	89%	23%

These results help to clarify the role that affect plays in people's responsibility attributions. Even when we control for concreteness, we still find that affect impacts people's intuitions about responsibility under determinism. The overall pattern of results therefore suggests that affect is playing an important role in the process that generates people's compatibilist intuitions.

We now have good evidence that affect plays a role in compatibilist judgments. But there remains the difficult question of whether what we see in these responses is the result of an affective competence or an affective performance error. Let's consider whether one of these models provides a better explanation of the experiment we just reported.

We think that the affective performance error model provides quite a plausible explanation of our results. What we see in the tax cheat case is that, when affect is minimized, people give dramatically different answers depending on whether the agent is in a determinist or indeterminist universe. On the performance error hypothesis, these responses reveal the genuine competence with responsibility attribution, for in the low affect cases, the affective bias is minimized. When high affect is introduced, as in the serial rapist case, the normal competence with responsibility attribution is skewed by the emotions; that explains why there is such a large difference between the high and low affect cases in the determinist conditions.

Now let's turn to the affective competence account. It's much less clear that the affective competence theorist has a good explanation of the results. In particular, it seems difficult to see how the affective competence account can explain why responses to the low affect case drop precipitously in the determinist condition, since this doesn't hold for the high affect case. Perhaps the affective competence theorist could say that low affect cases like the tax cheat case fail to trigger our competence with responsibility attribution, and so we should not treat those responses as reflecting our normal competence. But obviously it would take significant work to show that such everyday cases of apparent responsibility attribution don't really count as cases in which we exercise our competence at responsibility attribution. Thus, at first glance, the performance error account provides a better explanation of these results than the affective competence account.

Of course, even if it is true that our results are best explained by the performance error account, this doesn't mean that affect is irrelevant to the normal competence. As noted in the previous section, one option that strikes us as quite plausible is a hybrid account on which (i) our normal competence with responsibility attribution does depend on affective systems, but (ii) affect also generates a bias leading to compatibilist responses in our experiments.

Although our experiment provides some reason to favor the performance error account of the compatibilist responses we found, it seems clear that deciding between the affective performance error and the affective competence models of compatibilist responses is not the sort of issue that will be resolved by a single crucial experiment. What we really need here is a deeper understanding of the role that affect plays in moral cognition more generally. (Presumably, if we had a deeper understanding of this more general issue, we would be able to do a better job of figuring out how empirical studies could address the specific question about the role of affect in judgments of moral responsibility.) But our inability to resolve all of the relevant questions immediately is no cause for pessimism. On the contrary, we see every reason to be optimistic about the prospects for research in this area. Recent years have seen a surge of interest in the ways in which affect can influence moral cognition—with new empirical studies and theoretical developments coming in all the time—and it seems likely that the next few years will yield important new insights into the question at hand.

7. PHILOSOPHICAL IMPLICATIONS

Our findings help to explain why the debate between compatibilists and incompatibilists is so stubbornly persistent. It seems that certain psychological processes tend to generate compatibilist intuitions, while others tend to generate incompatibilist intuitions. Thus, each of the two major views appeals to an element of our psychological makeup.

But the experimental results do not serve merely to give us insight into the causal origins of certain philosophical positions; they also help us to evaluate some of the arguments that have been put forward in support of those positions. After all, many of these arguments rely on explicit appeals to intuition. If we find that different intuitions are produced by different psychological mechanisms, we might conclude that some of these intuitions should be given more weight than others. What we need to know now is which intuitions to take seriously and which to dismiss as products of mechanisms that are only leading us astray.

Clearly, the answer will depend partly on which, if any, of the three models described above turns out to be the right one, and since we don't yet have the data we need to decide between these competing models, we will not be able to offer a definite conclusion here. Our approach will therefore be to consider each of the models in turn and ask what implications it would have (if it turned out to be correct) for broader philosophical questions about the role of intuitions in the debate over moral responsibility.

The Performance Error Model

If compatibilist intuitions are explained by the performance error model, then we shouldn't assign much weight to these intuitions. For on that model, as we have described it, compatibilist intuitions are a product of the distorting effects of emotion and motivation. If we could eliminate the performance errors, the compatibilist intuitions should disappear.

Note that the performance error model does not claim that people's compatibilist intuitions are actually *incorrect*. What it says is simply that the process that generates these intuitions involves a certain kind of error. It is certainly possible that, even though the process involves this error, it ends up yielding a correct conclusion. Still, we feel that the performance error model has important philosophical implications. At the very least, it suggests that the fact that people sometimes have compatibilist intuitions does not itself give us reason to suppose that compatibilism is correct.

The philosophical implications of the performance error model have a special significance because the experimental evidence gathered thus far seems to suggest that the basic idea behind this model is actually true. But the jury is still out. Further research might show that one of the other models is in fact more accurate, and we therefore consider their philosophical implications as well.

The Affective Competence Model

On the affective competence model, people's responses in the concrete conditions of our original experiment are genuine expressions of their underlying competence. The suggestion is that the compatibilist responses people give in these conditions are not clouded by any kind of performance error. Rather, these responses reflect a successful implementation of the system we normally use for making responsibility judgments, and that system should therefore be regarded as a compatibilist one.

In many ways, this affective competence model is reminiscent of the view that P. F. Strawson (1962) puts forward in his classic paper "Freedom and Resentment." On that view, it would be a mistake to go about trying to understand the concept of moral responsibility by seeking to associate it with some sort of metaphysical theory. Rather, the best place to start is with an examination of the 'reactive attitudes' (blame, remorse, gratitude, etc.) and the role they play in our ordinary practice of responsibility attribution.

Yet, despite the obvious affinities between the affective competence model and Strawson's theory, it is important to keep in mind certain respects in which the affective competence model is making substantially weaker claims. Most importantly, the model isn't specifically claiming that people proceed *correctly* in the concrete conditions. All it says is that people's responses in these conditions reflect a successful implementation of their own underlying system for making responsibility judgments. This claim then leaves it entirely open whether the criteria used in that underlying system are themselves correct or incorrect.

For an analogous case, consider the ways in which people ordinarily make probability judgments. It can be shown that people's probability judgments often involve incorrect inferences, and one might therefore be tempted to assume that people are not correctly applying their own underlying criteria for probabilistic inference. But many psychologists reject this view. They suggest that people actually are correctly applying their underlying criteria and that the mistaken probabilistic inferences only arise because people's underlying criteria are themselves faulty (see, e.g., Tversky and Kahneman 1981; 1983).

Clearly, a similar approach could be applied in the case of responsibility judgments. Even if people's compatibilist intuitions reflect a successful implementation of their underlying system for making responsibility judgments, one could still argue that this underlying system is itself flawed. Hence, the affective competence model would vindicate the idea that people's core views about responsibility are compatibilist, but it would be a mistake to regard the model as an outright vindication of those intuitions.

The Concrete Competence Model

The implications of the concrete competence model depend in a crucial way on the precise details of the competence involved. Since it is not possible to say anything very general about all of the models in this basic category, we will focus specifically on the implications of the claim that people's responsibility attributions are subserved by an encapsulated module.

As a number of authors have noted, modularity involves a kind of trade-off. The key advantages of modules are that they usually operate automatically, unconsciously, and extremely quickly. But these advantages come at a price. The reason why modules are able to operate so quickly is that they simply ignore certain sources of potentially relevant information. Even when we know that the lines in the Müller-Lyer illusion are the same length, we still have the visual illusion. Perhaps in the assignment of moral responsibility, we are dealing with a similar sort of phenomenon—a 'moral illusion.' It might be that people have a complex and sophisticated theory about the relationship between determinism and moral responsibility but that the relevant module just isn't able to access this theory. It continues to spit out judgments that the agent is blameworthy even when these judgments go against a consciously held theory elsewhere in the mind.

Of course, defenders of compatibilism might point out that this argument can also be applied in the opposite direction. They might suggest that the module itself contains a complex and sophisticated theory to which the rest of the mind has no access. The conclusion would be that, unless we use the module to assess the relationship between determinism and moral responsibility, we will arrive at an impoverished and inadequate understanding. This type of argument definitely seems plausible in certain domains (e.g., in the domain of grammatical theory). It is unclear at this point whether something analogous holds true for the domain of responsibility attribution.[13]

Reflective Equilibrium

Our concern in this section has been with philosophical questions about whether knowledge of particular mental processes is likely to give us valuable insight into complex moral issues. Clearly, these philosophical questions should be carefully distinguished from the purely psychological question as to whether people *think* that particular mental processes give them insight into these issues. Even if people think that a given process is affording them valuable moral insight, it might turn out that this process is actually entirely unreliable and they would be better off approaching these issues in a radically different way.

Still, we thought it would be interesting to know how people themselves resolve the tension between their rival intuitions, and we therefore ran one final experiment. All subjects were given a brief description of the results from our earlier studies and then asked to adjudicate the conflict between the compatibilist and incompatibilist intuitions. Given that people's intuitions in the concrete conditions contradict their intuitions in the abstract conditions, would they choose to hold on to the concrete judgment that Bill is morally responsible or the abstract judgment that no one can be responsible in a deterministic universe?[14] The results showed no clear majority on either side. Approximately half of the subjects chose to hold onto the judgment that the particular agent was morally responsible, while the other half chose to hold onto the judgment that no one can be responsible in a deterministic universe.[15] Apparently, there is no more consensus about these issues among the folk than there is among philosophers.

8. CONCLUSION

As we noted at the outset, participants in the debate over moral responsibility have appealed to an enormous variety of arguments. Theories from metaphysics, moral philosophy, philosophy of mind, and even quantum mechanics have all been shown to be relevant in one way or another, and researchers are continually finding new ways in which seemingly unrelated considerations can be brought to bear on the issue. The present essay has not been concerned with the full scope of this debate. Instead, we have confined ourselves to just one type of evidence—evidence derived from people's intuitions.

Philosophers who have discussed lay intuitions in this area tend to say either that folk intuitions conform to compatibilism or that they conform to incompatibilism. Our actual findings were considerably more complex and perhaps more interesting. It appears that people have *both* compatibilist *and* incompatibilist intuitions. Moreover, it appears that these different kinds of intuitions are generated by different kinds of psychological processes. To assess the importance of this finding for the debate over moral responsibility, one would have to know precisely what sort of psychological process produced each type of intuition and how much weight to accord to the output of each sort of process. We have begun the task of addressing these issues here, but clearly far more remains to be done.

NOTES

Several people gave us great feedback on an early draft of this essay. We'd like to thank John Doris, Chris Hitchcock, Bob Kane, Neil Levy, Al Mele, Stephen Morris, Thomas Nadelhoffer, Eddy Nahmias, Derk Pereboom, Lynne Rudder-Baker, Tamler Sommers, Jason Turner, and Manuel Vargas. Thanks also to John Fischer for posting a draft of this essay on the Garden of Forking Paths Weblog (http://gfp.typepad.com/). Versions of this essay were delivered at the UNC/Duke workshop on Naturalized Ethics, the Society for Empirical Ethics, the Society for Philosophy and Psychology, Yale University, the University of Arizona, and the Inland Northwest Philosophy Conference. We thank the participants for their helpful comments.

1. Actually, compatibilists and incompatibilists argue both (1) about whether determinism is compatible with moral responsibility and (2) about whether determinism is compatible with *free will*. As Fischer (1999) has emphasized, these two questions are logically independent. One might maintain that determinism is compatible with moral responsibility but not with free will. Here, however, our concern lies entirely with the first of the two questions—whether determinism is compatible with moral responsibility.

2. We use the term 'theory' here loosely to refer to an internally represented body of information. Also, when we claim that the folk have an incompatibilist theory, we are not suggesting that this theory has a privileged status over the psychological systems that generate compatibilist intuitions. As will be apparent, we think that it remains an open question whether the system that generates incompatibilist intuitions has a privileged status.

3. One virtue of Nahmias and colleagues' question about moral responsibility is that the notion of 'moral responsibility' is supposed to be common between philosophers and the folk. That is, philosophers tend to assume that the notion of moral responsibility deployed in philosophy closely tracks the notion that people express when they attri-

bute moral responsibility. Furthermore, incompatibilists often specify that the relevant incompatibilist notion of free will is precisely the notion of free will that is required for moral responsibility (e.g., Campbell 1951). Nahmias and colleagues also ask questions about whether the agent in the deterministic scenario "acts of his own free will," and they find that people give answers consonant with compatibilism. We find these results less compelling. For the expression 'free will' has become a term of philosophical art, and it's unclear how to interpret lay responses concerning such technical terms. Moreover, incompatibilists typically grant that there are compatibilist notions of freedom that get exploited by the folk. Incompatibilists just maintain that there is also a commonsense notion of freedom that is not compatibilist.

4. Although these results from Viney and colleagues are suggestive, the measure used for identifying determinists is too liberal, and as a result, the group of subjects coded as 'determinists' might well include indeterminists. (See McIntyre et al. 1984 for a detailed description of the measure.) It remains to be seen whether this result will hold up using better measures for identifying determinists.

5. A related problem for the incompatibilist concerns the history of philosophy—if incompatibilism is intuitive, why has compatibilism been so popular among the great philosophers in history? An incompatibilist-friendly explanation is given in Nichols (2007).

6. In our deterministic scenario, we say that given the past, each decision *has to happen* the way that it does. This scenario allows us to test folk intuitions about the type of compatibilism most popular in contemporary philosophy. Most contemporary compatibilists argue, following Frankfurt (1969), that an agent can be morally responsible for her behavior even if she *had to* act the way she did. (As we shall see, most subjects in our concrete condition give responses that conform to this view.) However, it would also be possible for a compatibilist to maintain that (1) we can never be responsible for an event that had to occur the way it did but also that (2) even if a particular behavior is determined to occur by the laws of nature, the agent does not necessarily *have to* perform that behavior. Our experiment does not address the possibility that the folk subscribe to this type of compatibilism. With any luck, that possibility will be investigated in future research.

7. It will, of course, be important to investigate whether our results extend to other populations. However, as we will stress throughout, we are primarily looking at how subjects from the same population give different answers in the different conditions.

8. $\chi^2 (1, N = 41) = 6.034, p < .05$, two-tailed.

9. We also ran an experiment that used a more real-world kind of case than the deterministic set up described in our main experiments. This was sparked by some perceptive comments from Daniel Batson, who also gave us extremely helpful suggestions in designing the study. Again, the idea was to test whether abstract conditions were more likely to generate incompatibilist responses than affect-laden concrete conditions. All subjects were told about a genetic condition that leads a person to perform horrible actions, but they were also told that there is now an inexpensive pill that counteracts the condition and that now everyone with the condition gets this pill. In the abstract condition, subjects were then asked to indicate whether the people who had this condition before the pill was created could be held morally responsible for their actions. In the concrete condition, subjects were told that Bill had this condition before the pill was invented, and Bill killed his wife and children to be with his secretary. Subjects were then asked to indicate whether Bill was morally responsible for his action. The results were quite clear, and they were in concert with all of our earlier findings. Subjects given the abstract question gave

significantly lower ratings of responsibility than subjects given the concrete question. Thus, the basic effect can be obtained using quite different materials.

10. As far as we know, no prior research has posited a moral responsibility module, but there has been considerable enthusiasm for the more general idea that many basic cognitive capacities are driven by modules (Fodor 1983; Leslie 1994), and a number of authors have suggested that certain aspects of moral judgment might be subserved by module-like mechanisms (Dwyer 1999; Harman 1999; Hauser 2006).

11. We are grateful to Jesse Prinz for suggesting this possibility.

12. As in our previous experiments, the vast majority of subjects said that our universe was most similar to the indeterminist universe. We suspect that being a determinist might actually lead people to have more compatibilist views (see Nichols 2006), and as a result, we antecedently decided to exclude the minority who gave the determinist response from our statistical analyses. The statistical details are as follows. The contrast between high and low affect for the determinist condition was significant (χ^2 (1, $N = 44$) = 8.066, $p < .01$). That is, people were more likely to say that it's possible for the rapist to be fully morally responsible. The contrast between the two high affect conditions was also significant (χ^2 (1, $N = 45$) = 7.204, $p < .01$); that is, people were more likely to say that it's possible that the rapist is fully morally responsible in the indeterminist universe. The contrast between the two low affect conditions was very highly significant (χ^2 (1, $N = 45$) = 26.492, $p < 0.0001$). Subjects were dramatically more likely to say that it's possible for the tax cheat to be fully morally responsible in the indeterminist universe.

13. The distinction between modularity hypotheses and affective hypotheses first entered the philosophical literature in the context of the debate about the role of moral considerations in intentional action (Knobe 2006; Malle and Nelson 2003; Nadelhoffer 2004; Young et al. 2006). In that context, modularity hypotheses are usually regarded as vindicating folk intuitions. However, there is a key difference between that context and the present one. The difference is that information about the moral status of the action might be accessible in an intentional action module, but information about determinism is unlikely to be accessible in a moral responsibility module.

14. The design of the pilot study was modeled on the initial experiments described in section 3. Participants were asked both the high affect (Bill stabbing his wife) and the abstract questions (counterbalanced for order). They then answered the reflective equilibrium question:

> Previous research indicates that when people are given question 3 above, they often say that Bill is fully morally responsible for killing his family. But when people are given question 2 above, most people say that it is not possible that people in Universe A are fully morally responsible for their actions. Clearly these claims are not consistent. Because if it is not possible to be fully morally responsible in Universe A, then Bill can't be fully morally responsible.
>
> We are interested in how people will resolve this inconsistency. So, regardless of how you answered questions 2 and 3, please indicate which of the following you agree with most:
> i. In Universe A, it is *not* possible for people to be morally responsible for their actions.
> ii. Bill, who is in Universe A, *is* fully morally responsible for killing his family.

15. There were 19 subjects. Of these, 10 gave incompatibilist responses to the reflective equilibrium question; 9 gave compatibilist responses.

REFERENCES

Blair, R. 1995. "A Cognitive Developmental Approach to Morality: Investigating the Psychopath." *Cognition* 57.

Blair, R., Jones, L., Clark, F., Smith, M., and Jones, L. 1997. "The Psychopathic Individual: A Lack of Responsiveness to Distress Cues." *Psychophysiology* 34.

Campbell, C. A. 1951. "Is 'Free Will' a Pseudo-problem?" *Journal of Philosophy* 60.

Dwyer, S. 1999. "Moral Competence." In K. Murasugi and R. Stainton (eds.), *Philosophy and Linguistics*. Westview Press.

Fischer, J. 1999. "Recent Work on Moral Responsibility." *Ethics* 110.

Fodor, J. 1983. *Modularity of Mind*. MIT Press.

Frankfurt, H. 1969. "Alternate Possibilities and Moral Responsibility." *Journal of Philosophy* 66.

Frankfurt, H. 1988. *The Importance of What We Care About: Philosophical Essays*. Cambridge University Press.

Greene, J., Sommerville, R., Nystrom, L., Darley, J., and Cohen, J. 2001. "An fMRI Investigation of Emotional Engagement in Moral Judgment." *Science* 293.

Haidt, J. 2001. "The Emotional Dog and Its Rational Tail: A Social Intuitionist Approach to Moral Judgment." *Psychological Review* 108.

Haidt, J., Koller, S. H., and Dias, M. G. 1993. "Affect, Culture, and Morality, or Is It Wrong to Eat Your Dog?" *Journal of Personality and Social Psychology* 65.

Harman, G. 1999. "Moral Philosophy and Linguistics." In K. Brinkmann (ed.), *Proceedings of the 20th World Congress of Philosophy: Volume 1: Ethics*. Philosophy Documentation Center.

Hauser, M. 2006. *Moral Minds: The Unconscious Voice of Right and Wrong*. HarperCollins.

Hauser, M., Young, L., and Cushman, F. 2008. "Reviving Rawls' Linguistic Analogy: Operative Principles and the Causal Structure of Moral Actions." In W. Sinnott-Armstrong (ed.), *Moral Psychology*. MIT Press.

Hume, D. 1740/1978. *A Treatise of Human Nature*. Oxford University Press.

Kane, R. 1999. "Responsibility, Luck, and Chance: Reflections on Free Will and Indeterminism." *Journal of Philosophy* 96.

Knobe, J. 2003a. "Intentional Action and Side-Effects in Ordinary Language." *Analysis* 63.

Knobe, J. 2003b. "Intentional Action in Folk Psychology: An Experimental Investigation." *Philosophical Psychology* 16.

Knobe, J. 2006. "The Concept of Intentional Action: A Case Study in the Uses of Folk Psychology." *Philosophical Studies* 130.

Kunda, Z. 1990. "The Case for Motivated Reasoning." *Psychological Bulletin* 108.

Lerner, J., Goldberg, J., and Tetlock, P. 1998. "Sober Second Thought: The Effects of Accountability, Anger, and Authoritarianism on Attributions of Responsibility." *Personality and Social Psychology Bulletin* 24.

Leslie, A. 1994. "ToMM, ToBY and Agency: Core Architecture and Domain Specificity." In L. Hirschfeld and S. Gelman (eds.), *Mapping the Mind*. Cambridge University Press.

Malle, B., and Nelson, S. 2003. "Judging Mens Rea: The Tension between Folk Concepts and Legal Concepts of Intentionality." *Behavioral Sciences and the Law* 21.

McIntyre, R., Viney, D., and Viney, W. 1984. "Validity of a Scale Designed to Measure Beliefs in Free Will and Determinism." *Psychological Reports* 54.

Nadelhoffer, T. 2004. "Praise, Side Effects, and Folk Ascriptions of Intentional Action." *Journal of Theoretical and Philosophical Psychology* 24.

Nahmias, E., Morris, S., Nadelhoffer, T., and Turner, J. 2005. "Surveying Freedom: Folk Intuitions about Free Will and Moral Responsibility." *Philosophical Psychology* 18.

Nichols, S. 2002. "Norms with Feeling," *Cognition* 84.

Nichols, S. 2004a. "The Folk Psychology of Free Will: Fits and Starts." *Mind and Language* 19.

Nichols, S. 2004b. *Sentimental Rules: On the Natural Foundations of Moral Judgment.* Oxford University Press.

Nichols, S. 2006. "Folk Intuitions about Free Will." *Journal of Cognition and Culture* 6.

Nichols, S. 2007. "The Rise of Compatibilism: A Case Study in the Quantitative History of Philosophy." *Midwest Studies in Philosophy* 31.

Prinz, J. 2007. *The Emotional Construction of Morals.* Oxford University Press.

Pylyshyn, Z. 1999. "Is Vision Continuous with Cognition? The Case for Cognitive Impenetrability of Visual Perception." *Behavioral and Brain Sciences 22.*

Smart, D., and Loewenstein, G. 2005. "The Devil You Know: The Effect of Identifiability on Punitiveness." *Journal of Behavioral Decision Making* 18.

Strawson, G. 1986. *Freedom and Belief.* Oxford University Press.

Strawson, P. 1962. "Freedom and Resentment." *Proceedings of the British Academy* 48. Reprinted in G. Watson (ed.), *Free Will.* Oxford University Press, 1980. Page references are to the reprinted version.

Tversky, A., and Kahneman, D. 1981. "The Framing of Decisions and the Psychology of Choice." *Science* 211.

Tversky, A., and Kahneman, D. 1983. "Extensional versus Intuitive Reasoning: The Conjunction Fallacy in Probabilistic Reasoning." *Psychological Review* 90.

Van Inwagen, P. 1983. *An Essay on Free Will.* Oxford University Press.

Vargas, M. 2006. "On the Importance of History for Responsible Agency." *Philosophical Studies* 127.

Viney, W., Waldman, D., and Barchilon, J. 1982. "Attitudes toward Punishment in Relation to Beliefs in Free Will and Determinism." *Human Relations* 35.

Viney, W., Parker-Martin, P., and Dotten, S. D. H. 1988. "Beliefs in Free Will and Determinism and Lack of Relation to Punishment Rationale and Magnitude." *Journal of General Psychology* 115.

Watson, G. 1987. "Responsibility and the Limits of Evil: Variations on a Strawsonian Theme." In F. Schoeman (ed.), *Responsibility, Character, and the Emotions: New Essays in Moral Psychology.* Cambridge University Press.

Weinberg, J., Nichols, S., and Stich, S. 2001. "Normativity and Epistemic Intuitions." *Philosophical Topics* 29.

Woolfolk, R., Doris, J., and Darley, J. 2006. "Identification, Situational Constraint, and Social Cognition." *Cognition* 100.

Young, L., Cushman, F., Adolphs, R., Tranel, D., and Hauser, M. 2006. "Does Emotion Mediate the Effect of an Action's Moral Status on Its Intentional Status? Neuropsychological Evidence." *Journal of Cognition and Culture* 6.

PART III

FOLK PSYCHOLOGY AND MORAL COGNITION

People ordinarily come to understand each other by ascribing beliefs, desires, intentions, emotions, and so forth. The conceptual framework used to ascribe these states is known as 'folk psychology.' One surprising finding to come out of recent work in experimental philosophy is the discovery that moral judgments can sometimes influence folk psychology. In other words, people's judgments as to whether certain actions are morally right or morally wrong can impact the way they apply certain folk-psychological concepts. This is a puzzling effect, and experimental philosophers have offered a broad array of different hypotheses to explain it.

Knobe suggests that this effect should lead us to revise our understanding of the function of folk psychology itself. Instead of regarding folk psychology as a device for predicting and explaining behavior, we should regard it as a multipurpose tool—suited to the task of prediction and explanation, but also to the task of facilitating moral judgment.

By contrast, **Nadelhoffer** argues that the effect should be understood as a bias, that is, as a kind of mistake. On this view, folk psychology itself might be a purely descriptive conceptual framework in which moral judgment plays no role, but people sometimes end up applying this framework incorrectly, thereby allowing moral judgments to influence folk-psychological ascriptions.

These two essays both focus specifically on the concept of *intentional action*. Subsequent research has shown that similar effects arrive for other folk-psychological concepts, including the concept of reason explanation, the concept of valuing, and the concept of happiness. The phenomenon appears to be quite broad in scope.

SUGGESTED READINGS

Adams, F., and Steadman, A. 2004. "Intentional Action in Ordinary Language: Core Concept or Pragmatic Understanding?" *Analysis* 64: 173–181.

Harman, G. 2006. "Intending, Intention, Intent, Intentional Action, and Acting Intentionally: Comments on Knobe and Burra." *Journal of Cognition and Culture* 6: 269–276.

Knobe, J. 2007. "Reason Explanation in Folk Psychology." *Midwest Studies in Philosophy*.

Leslie, A., Knobe, J., and Cohen, A. 2006. "Acting Intentionally and the Side-Effect Effect: 'Theory of Mind' and Moral Judgment." *Psychological Science* 17: 421–427.

Machery, E. 2008. "The Folk Concept of Intentional Action: Philosophical and Experimental Issues." *Mind and Language* 23: 165–189.

Malle, B. 2006. "Intentionality, Morality, and Their Relationship in Human Judgment." *Journal of Cognition and Culture* 6: 87–113.

Nichols, S., and Ulatowski, J. 2007. "Intuitions and Individual Differences: The Knobe Effect Revisited." *Mind and Language*.

Phelan, M., and Sarkissian, H. 2008. "The Folk Strike Back; Or, Why You Didn't Do It Intentionally, Though It Was Bad and You Knew It." *Philosophical Studies*.

Young, L., Cushman, F., Adolphs, R., Tranel, D., and Hauser, M. 2006. "Does Emotion Mediate the Effect of an Action's Moral Status on Its Intentional Status? Neuropsychological Evidence." *Journal of Cognition and Culture* 6: 291–304.

7

The Concept of Intentional Action

A Case Study in the Uses of Folk Psychology

Joshua Knobe

The twentieth century saw the rise of a new discipline that we might call *scientific psychology*. Practitioners of this new discipline develop detailed theories, conduct systematic experiments, and publish their results in academic journals.

But long before the rise of scientific psychology, people had ways of making sense of the goings-on in each other's minds. These ordinary ways of understanding the mind did not involve any detailed theories or systematic experiments, but they constituted a kind of psychology all the same. This ordinary, everyday psychology was expressed in sentences like: 'She is feeling angry.' 'He wishes he could go.' 'They think that it is going to rain.' The basic conceptual framework underlying these sorts of everyday psychological ascriptions is usually known as *folk psychology*.

A question now arises about the relationship between folk psychology and scientific psychology. To what extent are they similar, and to what extent different? Over time, researchers working on this question have arrived at a sort of limited consensus. Although considerable disagreement remains about whether or not folk-psychological reasoning actually proceeds using the same kinds of methods one finds in scientific psychology, almost all researchers now agree that the two kinds of psychology serve more or less the same basic function. Specifically, it is now widely agreed that both kinds of psychology serve primarily to help us predict and explain behavior.

There is something extremely plausible and convincing about the claim that folk psychology plays much the same role in our lives that scientific psychology does. Nonetheless, I think we now have good reason to believe that this claim is not quite right. As I try to show here, certain aspects of folk psychology do not appear to be best understood as tools for predicting and explaining behavior. Instead, these aspects of folk psychology appear to be serving a function that we would never expect to find in a systematic science.

In arguing for this conclusion, I will focus on just one aspect of folk psychology—our folk-psychological concept of *intentional action*. People normally distinguish between behaviors that are performed intentionally (e.g., raising a glass of wine to one's lips) and those that are performed unintentionally (e.g., spilling the wine all over one's shirt). The key question to be addressed here is whether the competencies underlying people's use of this distinction are to be understood primarily in terms of the kinds of aims we normally associate with scientific concepts. I review evidence that indicates that the answer is *no*—in other words, that these competencies have been shaped in a very fundamental way by a quite different sort of function.

By focusing in this way on just one concept, one gains the opportunity for greater depth. That is, one gains the opportunity to examine this one concept in detail and gain real insight into questions about the role it plays in folk psychology. But, of course, to gain this kind of depth, one must sacrifice a certain amount of breadth. It is conceivable (at least in principle) that the concept of intentional action is completely different from every other aspect of folk psychology. Hence, it is conceivable that every other aspect of folk psychology really was shaped almost entirely by its role in 'scientific' tasks (like prediction and explanation) and that the concept of intentional action is the sole exception to this general rule. Although this seems to me to be a somewhat implausible conclusion, I will not be arguing against it explicitly here. The claim is simply that the competencies underlying our folk-psychological concept of intentional action constitute a counterexample to the view that all of folk psychology should be understood as a device for prediction and explanation.

I

I begin with some straightforward data about people's intuitions concerning specific cases. The key claim here will be that—strange as it may seem—people's intuitions as to whether or not a behavior was performed intentionally can sometimes be influenced by *moral* considerations. That is to say, when people are wondering whether or not a given behavior was performed intentionally, they are sometimes influenced by their beliefs about whether the behavior itself was good or bad. To find evidence for this claim, we can construct pairs of cases that are almost exactly alike except that one involves a harmful behavior and the other a helpful behavior. It can then be shown that these different behaviors elicit different intuitions.

For a simple example, consider the following story:

> The vice-president of a company went to the chairman of the board and said, "We are thinking of starting a new program. It will help us increase profits, but it will also harm the environment."
>
> The chairman of the board answered, "I don't care at all about harming the environment. I just want to make as much profit as I can. Let's start the new program."
>
> They started the new program. Sure enough, the environment was harmed.
>
> Now ask yourself: Did the chairman of the board *intentionally* harm the environment?

Faced with this question, most people (though certainly not all) say that the answer is yes. And when asked why they think that the chairman intentionally harmed the environment, they tend to mention something about the chairman's psychological state—for example, that he decided to implement the program even though he specifically knew that he would thereby be harming the environment.

But it seems clear that these facts about the agent's psychological state cannot be all there is to the story. For suppose that we replace the word 'harm' with 'help,' so that the vignette becomes:

> The vice-president of a company went to the chairman of the board and said, "We are thinking of starting a new program. It will help us increase profits, and it will also help the environment."
>
> The chairman of the board answered, "I don't care at all about helping the environment. I just want to make as much profit as I can. Let's start the new program."
>
> They started the new program. Sure enough, the environment was helped.

This one change in the vignette leads to a quite radical change in people's intuitions. Faced with this second version, most people say that the chairman did *not* intentionally help the environment.

To confirm these claims about people's intuitions, I presented the two vignettes to subjects in a controlled experiment (Knobe 2003a). The results were clear and compelling: 82 percent of subjects who received the story about environmental harm said that the chairman harmed the environment intentionally, whereas only 23 percent of subjects who received the story about environmental help said that the chairman helped the environment intentionally. This result provides preliminary evidence for the view that people's beliefs about the moral status of a behavior have some influence on their intuitions about whether or not the behavior was performed intentionally.

Of course, it would be a mistake to base such a broad claim on evidence from just one vignette. But the claim becomes plausible when one sees how robust the effect is. The effect continues to emerge when the whole experiment is translated into Hindi and run with Indian subjects (Knobe and Burra 2006); it emerges when subjects are only four years old (Leslie et al. 2006); it emerges even when the experiment is run on subjects who suffer deficits in emotional processing due to lesions in the ventromedial prefrontal cortex (Young et al. 2006). Moreover, philosophers have constructed other, very different cases in which moral considerations appear to influence people's intuitions about whether or not a given behavior is intentional (Harman 1976; Lowe 1978), and when these other kinds of cases have been put to an experimental test, the effect emerges on them as well (Knobe 2003b).

To some degree at least, it seems that these results should come as a surprise to those who think of people's concept of intentional action as a tool for predicting and explaining behavior. After all, it seems that the best way to accomplish these "scientific" goals would be to ignore all the moral issues and focus entirely on a different sort of question (e.g., on questions about the agent's mental states). How then are we to make sense of the fact that moral considerations sometimes influence people's application of the concept of intentional action?

By now, it should be clear where I am heading. What I want to suggest is that there is another use of the concept of intentional action in light of which the influence of moral considerations really does make sense. The claim is that people's concept of intentional action should not be understood simply as a tool for predicting and explaining behavior. The concept has also been shaped in a very fundamental way by a different kind of use, and it is only by considering this second use that we will be able to reach an adequate understanding of the surprising results we have just described.

II

Before taking up this issue in more detail, let us pause to consider the structure of the cases in which people's intuitions appear to be influenced by moral considerations. Here our aim is simply to amass some useful data about people's intentional action intuitions. We will defer to a later section all questions about *why* people have these intuitions and what these intuitions indicate about the role of intentional action in folk psychology.

In describing the factors that influence people's intuitions, it will often prove helpful to make reference to the various features that philosophers have discussed in their analyses of the concept of intentional action. Here we shall be principally concerned with the features *trying*, *foresight*, and *skill*. There has been a great deal of controversy in the philosophical literature about the role that each of these features plays in the concept of intentional action (for an excellent review, see Mele 1992). In the present context, however, it will not be necessary to discuss these controversies in any real detail. Instead, what we want to show is that, in the cases under dispute, people's intuitions are influenced by the moral status of the behavior.

First, let us consider the debate surrounding the role of *trying* and *foresight*. Some philosophers think that trying is a necessary condition for intentional action (Adams 1986; McCann 1986); others argue that a certain kind of foresight can actually be sufficient even in the absence of trying (Ginet 1990).

The distinction between these two views comes out most clearly in cases of what might be called *side effects*. An outcome can be considered a 'side effect' when (1) the agent was not specifically trying to bring it about but (2) the agent chose to do something that she foresaw would involve bringing it about. The question is: Will people think that the agent brought about such an outcome *intentionally?*

An examination of such cases can help us understand the roles played by judgments of trying and foresight in generating people's intentional action intuitions. If people take trying to be a necessary condition, they should think that the agent did not bring about the side effect intentionally. By contrast, if they take foresight to be sufficient, they should think that the agent did bring about the effect intentionally. But when we study these cases systematically, we end up with a surprising result: people's intuitions appear to be influenced by the *moral* qualities of the side effect itself. Specifically, people seem to be considerably more willing to say that the agent brought about the side effect intentionally when they regard that side effect as bad than when they regard the side effect as good.

This is the key result of the experiment described above—where a vignette about environmental harm elicited very different intuitions from a quite similar vignette about environmental help. And the same effect arises for other cases that have the same basic structure. So, for example, when we transpose the story from a corporate boardroom to a battlefield—with a lieutenant helping or harming his troops in place of a chairman helping or harming the environment—we still get the same basic effect. People say that the lieutenant acted intentionally if he harmed the troops as a side effect but that he did not act intentionally if he helped the troops as a side effect (Knobe 2003a).

Cases of side effects are not the only ones in which moral considerations play a role. Similar issues arise in cases where the agent lacks *skill*. Consider a case in which an agent is trying to perform a behavior and actually does succeed in performing that behavior. And now suppose that the agent didn't really have the skill to perform that behavior in any reliable fashion, so that ultimately the agent only manages to succeed through sheer luck. Has the agent performed the behavior intentionally? According to some philosophical analyses, the answer is yes (e.g., Brand 1984); according to others, the answer is no (e.g., Mele and Moser 1994). But once again, it appears that neither view correctly predicts people's intuitions in all cases. People's intuitions about these cases seem to depend in part on the moral status of the behavior itself.

Here it may be helpful to consider another series of cases. First, take a case in which the agent's behavior might be regarded as an *achievement*:

> Jake desperately wants to win the rifle contest. He knows that he will only win the contest if he hits the bulls-eye. He raises the rifle, gets the bull's-eye in the sights, and presses the trigger.
>
> But Jake isn't very good at using his rifle. His hand slips on the barrel of the gun, and the shot goes wild...
>
> Nonetheless, the bullet lands directly on the bull's-eye. Jake wins the contest.

Faced with this case, most people think that it would be wrong to say that Jake hit the bull's-eye intentionally.

But now suppose that we consider a case that is quite similar in certain respects but in which the behavior would normally be regarded as *immoral*:

> Jake desperately wants to have more money. He knows that he will inherit a lot of money when his aunt dies. One day, he sees his aunt walking by the window. He raises his rifle, gets her in the sights, and presses the trigger.
>
> But Jake isn't very good at using his rifle. His hand slips on the barrel of the gun, and the shot goes wild...
>
> Nonetheless, the bullet hits her directly in the heart. She dies instantly.

Changing the moral significance of the behavior in this way leads to a quite substantial change in the pattern of people's intuitions. Faced with this second vignette, people overwhelmingly say that Jake hit his aunt intentionally.

Finally, let us consider a case in which the agent's behavior would normally be seen as *morally good:*

> Klaus is a soldier in the German army during World War II. His regiment has been sent on a mission that he believes to be deeply immoral. He knows that many innocent people will die unless he can somehow stop the mission before it is completed. One day, it occurs to him that the best way to sabotage the mission would be to shoot a bullet into his own regiment's communication device.
>
> He knows that if he gets caught shooting the device, he may be imprisoned, tortured, or even killed. He could try to pretend that he was simply making a mistake—that he just got confused and thought the device belonged to the enemy—but he is almost certain that no one will believe him.
>
> With that thought in mind, he raises his rifle, gets the device in his sights, and presses the trigger. But Klaus isn't very good at using his rifle. His hand slips on the barrel of the gun, and the shot goes wild...
>
> Nonetheless, the bullet lands directly in the communications device. The mission is foiled, and many innocent lives are saved.

Here most people feel that Klaus did hit the communications device intentionally.

In fact, the differences among these vignettes have been demonstrated experimentally—with 23 percent of subjects saying that Jake intentionally hit the target in the achievement vignette, 91 percent in the immoral vignette, and 92 percent in the morally good vignette (Knobe 2003b). Once again, it appears that people's intentional action intuitions are in some way influenced by their beliefs about the moral status of the behavior itself.

Thus far, we have reported results from only two experiments. But these results have been replicated and extended in a considerable body of work by both philosophers and psychologists (Feltz and Cokely 2007; Leslie et al. 2006; Malle 2006; McCann 2005; Nadelhoffer 2004a, 2005; Nichols and Ulatowski 2007; Pizarro et al. 2007; Sverdlik 2004; Young et al. 2006). At this point, there can be little doubt that moral considerations have an impact on people's use of the word 'intentionally.' The key remaining questions are about how this effect is to be understood.

III

In particular, a question arises as to whether moral considerations are actually playing a role in the fundamental competencies underlying our use of the concept of intentional action. After all, it is possible that moral considerations could have a decisive impact on our use of words like 'intentionally' even if they have no impact at all in these underlying competencies. Some additional process could be intervening between the underlying competencies and our use of words, and it could be that this additional process is the only place in which moral considerations have a real impact.

Still, it isn't enough just to point out that there might be some other way to explain the findings. What one wants is an alternative model, a specific hypothesis about how an intervening process might be shaping our use of the word 'intentionally' in a way that is more or less unrelated to our underlying competencies. Then we can check to see whether this alternative model gives us a better account of the data than the straightforward hypothesis that moral considerations are playing some role in the competencies themselves.

Of course, it will never be possible to assess all conceivable alternative models. We therefore proceed by considering three models that have actually been proposed.

1. Mele (2001) suggests that the effect might be due, not to people's (largely tacit) concept of intentional action, but rather to certain explicit beliefs they hold about the relation between intentional action and moral blame. Specifically, he suggests that people hold an explicit belief that an agent can be blameworthy for performing a behavior only if that agent performed the behavior intentionally. This explicit belief might be more or less unrelated to the purely tacit mechanisms that normally direct people's application of the concept of intentional action. Indeed, the content of the belief might directly contradict the contents of the non-conscious states that make these mechanisms possible.

Still, the content of people's explicit beliefs could be having a large impact on their responses to specific cases. When they encounter a case like that of the executive harming the environment, their tacit competence might spit out the conclusion: 'This behavior is unintentional.' But then they might think: 'Wait! The agent is clearly to blame for his behavior, and agents can only be blameworthy for performing intentional actions. So the behavior in question just *must* be intentional after all.'

It certainly does seem possible, as Mele suggests, that people hold various explicit beliefs about the relation between intentional action and moral blame. The question is simply whether these explicit beliefs alone can explain all of the ways in which moral considerations appear to be influencing people's application of the concept of intentional action. Suppose, for example, that people somehow ceased to believe that all blameworthy behaviors were intentional. Would moral considerations still continue to have an impact on their application of the concept of intentional action?

To address this question, I tried to create a situation in which people would come to believe that a behavior can be blameworthy even if it is not intentional. Subjects were given a story about an agent who performed a behavior unintentionally but seemed clearly to be deserving of blame. (The story concerned an agent who harms other people while driving drunk.) Subjects were then asked (a) whether or not the agent acted intentionally and (b) whether or not the agent was to blame for his behavior. As expected, almost all subjects answered no to the first question and yes to the second. Immediately after answering this question, subjects were presented with a case in which moral considerations usually have an impact on people's intentional action intuitions.

Consider the position of a subject answering this second question. Presumably, she does not believe that all blameworthy behaviors have to be intentional. (After all, in her answer to the previous question, she said explicitly that the agent acted unintentionally but was blameworthy nonetheless.) She now faces a story about an agent who performed an immoral behavior. The key question is whether the moral status of the agent's behavior will have any impact on her judgment as to whether or not it was performed intentionally.

The answer is that the moral status of the behavior continues to have an impact even in this situation. As in previous studies, subjects were far more likely to classify the behavior as intentional when it was morally bad. Faced with this new result, Mele (2003) has retracted his previous view. He now claims that moral considerations do indeed play a role in people's concept of intentional action.

2. Adams and Steadman (2004a) suggest that the effect might be due entirely to conversational pragmatics. The basic idea is that people are describing blameworthy behaviors as 'intentional' because they want to avoid certain unwanted implicatures. When a person utters the sentence 'He didn't do that intentionally,' there is often a clear implicature that the agent is not to blame for what he has done. Thus, when people are asked whether the chairman harmed the environment intentionally or unintentionally, they may be understandably reluctant to respond that his behavior was entirely unintentional.

The alleged problem here lies in the specific method by which we have been trying to figure out whether people regard a given behavior as intentional. Our method has been to look at people's application of the word 'intentional' and, from that, to make inferences about which behaviors they truly believe to have been performed intentionally. But, as Adams and Steadman rightly point out, people's use of this word is no sure guide to their application of the corresponding concept. Factors like conversational pragmatics may influence people's use of words even if they play no role at all in the fundamental competencies underlying folk psychology.

What we need here, ideally, is some independent method for figuring out whether people regard a given behavior as intentional—a method that makes no use of the word 'intentionally.' Then we can check our earlier results against the results obtained using this independent method. If the independent method yields results that differ in some important respect from those obtained when we simply asked people whether a given behavior was performed intentionally, we might suspect that our earlier results were due in part to pragmatic factors and did not truly reveal people's underlying concept of intentional action. If, however, the alternative method yields the very same results we obtained using the original method, we would have good reason to believe that those earlier results were telling us something important about which behaviors people truly regard as intentional.

As it happens, there is such an independent method. We can determine whether or not people regard a given behavior as intentional by looking at their use of the phrase 'in order to.' It seems that people are generally unwilling to say that an agent performed a behavior 'in order to' attain a particular goal unless they believe that the agent performed that behavior intentionally. Thus, if a speaker utters a sentence of the form 'She *A*-ed in order to *B*,' we would normally assume that the speaker takes the agent to have *A*-ed intentionally.

Using this alternative method, we can retest our original hypothesis. Do people genuinely regard the harming of the environment as an intentional action, or are they only labeling it 'intentional' because they want to avoid certain pragmatic implicatures? One way to find out would be to ask whether people are willing to say that the chairman harmed the environment 'in order to' attain a particular goal. In actual fact, it appears that they regard some sentences of this form as perfectly acceptable. Faced with the harm vignette, people generally think it sounds right to say: 'The chairman harmed the environment in order to increase profits.'

But, surprisingly enough, people who have been given the help vignette do not generally think it sounds right to say: 'The chairman helped the environment in order to increase profits.'

Presumably, this asymmetry in people's use of the phrase 'in order to' reflects an asymmetry in people's views about which behaviors were performed intentionally (Knobe 2004). Since people regard the harming of the environment as intentional and the helping of the environment as unintentional, they are willing to use the phrase 'in order to' for harming but not for helping.

Adams and Steadman (2004b) are not convinced by this response. They argue that the effect for 'in order to' can be understood in terms of the very same pragmatic processes they had originally posited to explain the effect for 'intentionally.' The idea is that people see immediately that no agent can perform a behavior 'in order to' attain a goal unless that agent performs the behavior intentionally. Any factor that has an impact on the pragmatics of 'intentionally' should therefore have an impact on the pragmatics of 'in order to' as well.

Although Adams and Steadman may ultimately turn out to be right on this score, their pragmatic explanation for the use of 'in order to' definitely lacks the intuitive plausibility of the explanation they originally offered for the use of 'intentionally.' It is common practice to deny that an agent deserves blame by saying 'He didn't do that intentionally,' but we do not normally deny that an agent is blameworthy by using a sentence like 'It doesn't sound right to say that he did that "in order to" attain a goal.' In fact, if someone used such a sentence in an ordinary conversation, we would probably have no idea what she was trying to say. There seems not to be any direct connection between being blameless and not performing an action in order to attain a goal. The only way to recover the alleged implicature here would be to first (a) infer that the use of 'in order to' was sounding wrong because the behavior itself was unintentional, then (b) determine that classifying a behavior as unintentional indicates that the behavior is not deserving of blame, and finally (c) conclude that the sentence therefore implicates that the agent is not blameworthy. Such a complex chain of reasoning could hardly take place in the few seconds it normally takes people to answer these questions.

3. Nadelhoffer (2004b) and Malle and Nelson (2003; cf. Malle 2004) suggest that the data are best explained in terms of the distorting effects of people's feelings of *blame*. The key idea here is that moral considerations play no role at all in the fundamental competence underlying people's concept of intentional action. However, when people classify an agent's behavior as immoral, they may quickly come to feel that the agent is deserving of blame. This feeling then distorts their reasoning, leaving them with a strong motivation to declare the agent's behavior intentional and thereby justify the blame they have already assigned.

Before evaluating this hypothesis in more detail, we need to make a few preliminary comments about the notion of moral blame itself. Then we can compare a number of competing models of the relationship between judgments of blame and the concept of intentional action. The aim will be to see which of these models best explains people's intuitions about specific cases.

To begin with, we need to make a clear distinction between the judgment that a behavior is *bad* and the judgment that an agent is *blameworthy*. Consider the agent who hurts his wife's feelings. Here we might say that the agent's behavior itself is bad. That is to say, when we ignore every other aspect of the situation, we might classify the hurting of the wife's feelings as a bad thing. Still, we will be unlikely to blame the agent if he has a good excuse (ignorance, mental illness, provocation, etc.) or if his behavior is in some way justified (e.g., because hurting his wife's feelings leads to some good consequence in the long run).

These two kinds of judgments seem to result from two distinct stages in the process of moral assessment. First we make a judgment as to whether or not the behavior itself is bad and then—depending on the outcome of this first stage—we may end up making a judgment as to whether or not the agent deserves blame. Where in this whole process does the concept of intentional action appear?

The commonsense view works something like this:

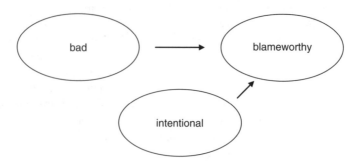

On this model, people determine whether the behavior itself is bad without making any use of the concept of intentional action. However, they do use the concept of intentional action when they are trying to determine whether or not the agent deserves blame.

One problem with this commonsense view is that it offers no explanation for the fact that people's moral judgments sometimes influence their intuitions as to whether or not a behavior was performed intentionally. Nadelhoffer, Malle, and Nelson therefore propose that the process sometimes works more like this:

On this model, people do not use the concept of intentional action to determine whether or not the agent is blameworthy. Instead, they assign blame *before* they have even applied the concept. Then they apply the concept in such a way as to justify the blame they have already assigned.

If the process really does work like this, it would be reasonable to infer that people were making some kind of error. This model does not posit a role for moral considerations in the fundamental competence underlying people's concept of intentional action. Rather, it seems to be describing a kind of bias that can infect people's thought processes and lead them astray.

There is, however, another plausible way to make sense of the data reported thus far. Perhaps the process actually works like this:

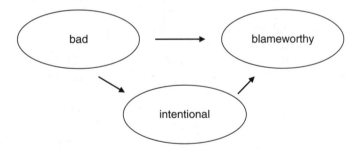

This third model can make sense of the fact that people's moral judgments sometimes influence their intuitions as to whether or not a behavior was performed intentionally, but it also retains the commonsense view that people use the concept of intentional action when they are trying to determine whether or not the agent deserves blame. The basic idea is that people's judgment that the behavior itself is bad can influence their intuitions as to whether the behavior was performed intentionally and that these intuitions can, in turn, play an important role in the process by which people determine whether or not to assign blame.

In the cases we have been discussing thus far, these competing models make identical predictions. Take the case of the corporate executive who harms the environment. Here we find that people both (a) classify the agent's behavior as bad and (b) blame the agent for that behavior. Since people judge the case to be both bad and blameworthy, there is no obvious way to figure out which of these two judgments is influencing their intuitions.

To decide between the competing models, we therefore need to find a case in which an agent brings about a bad side effect but is *not* considered blameworthy. In such a case, the different models will yield different predictions. If the badness of the side effect only impacts people's intuitions by first leading to feelings of blame, people should be inclined to regard the side effect as unintentional. But if people's intuitions can be directly influenced by judgments of badness—without any mediation of feelings of blame—they should be inclined to regard the side effect as intentional.

For a simple test case, let us modify our vignette about the corporate executive trying to decide whether or not to implement a new program. This time, we will not suppose that the program leads to environmental harm or any other morally significant consequence. Instead, we can suppose that the program has only two important effects: it increases sales in Massachusetts but decreases sales in New Jersey. The executive knows that the gain in Massachusetts will be far larger than the loss in New Jersey, and she therefore decides to implement the program.

Now consider the status of the behavior *decreasing sales in New Jersey*. Here it seems that the agent has done something bad without being in any way blameworthy. When we say that the agent's behavior is bad, we simply mean that decreasing sales in New Jersey is, taken in itself, a bad thing. Of course, it isn't *morally* bad to decrease sales, and it might even be helpful on the whole, given its consequences. Still, there is a straightforward sense in which one might say: 'It's *too bad* that she had to decrease sales in New Jersey.' At the same time, though, it is clear that the agent is in no way deserving of blame for her behavior. If anything, she deserves praise for finding a policy that increases sales on the whole.

And yet people generally say that the executive intentionally decreased sales in New Jersey (Knobe and Mendlow 2004). This result spells trouble for any theory that tries to account for the role of moral considerations in terms of blame alone. What we have here is a case in which the agent is not considered blameworthy but in which people's beliefs about good and bad are nonetheless influencing their intentional action intuitions. This kind of result cannot plausibly be explained in terms of people's efforts to justify a prior judgment of blame. (After all, there is no blame here to justify!) The most plausible hypothesis seems to be that people's judgments of good and bad are actually playing a role in the fundamental competencies underlying their concept of intentional action.[1]

Thus far, we have been considering the evidence for and against specific alternative models. Ultimately, though, it may not be enough merely to consider the various alternative models that are already available in the literature.

No matter how many alternative models one eliminates, it will always be possible for future researchers to devise new ones. Indeed, even in the absence of any specific alternative model, one may be tempted to suppose that *some* alternative model can adequately explain the data. What we need to address, then, is the widespread sense—never explicitly defended but deeply felt nonetheless—that an alternative model is needed. That is to say, we need to address the widespread sense that moral considerations just *couldn't* be playing any role in the fundamental competencies underlying folk psychology.

This sense is never fully articulated by any of the authors cited above. Instead of arguing explicitly against the view that moral considerations play some fundamental role in folk psychology, these authors simply propose alternative models and then try to show that their models provide plausible explanations of the data. The presumption seems to be that, if any alternative model can provide a plausible explanation, that model is to be preferred over the hypothesis that moral considerations really are playing a role in folk psychology. But what is the source of this presumption?

The answer lies, I think, in a particular view about the nature of folk psychology. This view says that the basic purpose of folk psychology is to enable people to predict each other's behavior or to offer them some other form of quasi-scientific, purely naturalistic understanding. When folk psychology is understood in this way, it seems that it would be *pointless* for moral considerations to play any real role. Thus, if moral considerations appear to be influencing people's use of words like 'intentional,' one is naturally led to search for some alternative to the view that these considerations are actually having an impact in the fundamental competencies underlying folk psychology. The goal then becomes to find some way in which people's fundamental competencies can be overridden, corrupted, or otherwise shielded from view.

But, of course, there is another possible approach. Instead of starting out with certain preconceptions about the nature of folk psychology and then trying to square the data with those preconceptions, we can start out with the data and try to figure out what the data might be telling us about the nature of folk psychology. The use of moral considerations may not facilitate the process of predicting behavior, but perhaps we can find some other activity in which the use of moral considerations would prove genuinely helpful.

IV

In particular, let us focus on the process by which people assign praise and blame. It seems clear that the concept of intentional action plays an important role in this process. Specifically, it seems that people are generally inclined to give an agent more praise and blame for behaviors they regard as intentional than for those they regard as unintentional.

Now suppose that we think of the concept of intentional action in terms of this second use. Suppose, in other words, that we think of it as a tool used for determining how much praise or blame an agent deserves for her behaviors

(Bratman 1984, 1987). Then we can check to see whether the criteria according to which people apply the concept seem to make more sense under this construal than they did when we tried to understand every aspect of the concept solely in terms of its 'scientific' use.

First of all, we should note that the three features we encountered in our discussion of intentional action—trying, foresight, and skill—play a crucial role in the process by which people normally assign praise and blame. Thus, when people are wondering how much praise or blame an agent deserves, their conclusion will sometimes depend on whether or not the person was *trying* to perform a given behavior, whether she chose to do something that she *foresaw* would involve performing that behavior, whether she had the *skill* to perform that behavior reliably.

A question now arises as to how people employ information about these various features in making an overall judgment about how much praise or blame the agent deserves. One sees immediately that this process must be extremely complex. It is not as though, for example, the presence of foresight always increases praise or blame by a constant amount. Rather, different features will be relevant to different behaviors—with a single feature sometimes making a big difference in how much praise or blame an agent gets for one type of behavior yet having almost no impact on the amount of praise or blame that an agent gets for some other type of behavior.

This phenomenon has important implications for the study of praise and blame. It indicates that there is no single way of combining information about psychological features that can be used to determine praise and blame for all possible behaviors. So, for example, suppose we had a concept *shmintentional* that could be given some simple definition like:

> A behavior is shmintentional if and only if the agent had skill
> and either trying or foresight.

We could not make praise and blame judgments by simply checking to see whether a given behavior was shmintentional. The problem is that different features are relevant to different behaviors and that shmintentionality is therefore more relevant to praise and blame judgments for some behaviors than for others.

For a simple example, we can return to the environmental cases that we presented above. Suppose that an agent decides to perform a given behavior because he wants to increase profits. The agent knows that his behavior will have some impact on the environment. But he does not care at all about the impact he is having on the environment—he is only performing the behavior as a way of increasing profits. Will people feel that this agent deserves any praise or blame for what he has done? Clearly, people's views will depend on the particular type of impact that the agent is having on the environment. If the agent is *harming* the environment, they may feel that he deserves a considerable amount of blame. But if he is *helping* the environment, they will probably feel that he deserves almost no praise.

What we see here is a remarkable convergence between the conditions under which people assign praise and blame and the conditions under which they regard a behavior as intentional. We noted above that there is a puzzling asymmetry in people's intuitions about intentional action in side-effects cases. People seem to be far more inclined to say that an agent brought about a side effect intentionally when they regard that side effect as bad than when they regard it as good. And now we see an analogous asymmetry in people's judgments about praise and blame—namely, that people are far more inclined to give the agent praise or blame for a side effect when they regard that side effect as bad than when they regard it as good.

Interestingly, a similar effect emerges for the various cases we described in which the agent lacks the skill to reliably perform the behavior. First, consider the 'achievement' case, where the agent is shooting at a bull's-eye target. There, the amount of praise we give the agent appears to depend on skill, with the agent getting very little praise if his success is due almost entirely to luck. (Our concern here is not with *moral* praise—but we are dealing with a form of praise all the same.) But suppose we consider cases in which the hitting of the target is either immoral or morally good. Then people will tend to give the agent a large amount of praise and blame even when the agent has almost no skill and only manages to hit the target through luck.

Once again, we find a surprising convergence between people's judgments of praise and blame and their intentional action intuitions. We showed above that people are considerably more likely to say that the hitting of the target is intentional when they regard it either as immoral or as morally good than when they regard it as an achievement. Now we find that this same pattern emerges in people's judgments of praise and blame: people generally give the agent considerably more praise and blame for 'lucky successes' when they regard those successes as immoral or morally good than when they regard them as achievements.

Seen in this light, the pattern of people's intentional action intuitions no longer seems so incoherent or pointless. We have been assuming that people sometimes use the concept of intentional action as a tool for determining how much praise or blame an agent deserves—with people generally giving the agent more praise and blame for behaviors that they regard as intentional than for behaviors that they regard as unintentional. But we also found that there is no fixed list of features that people always regard as necessary and sufficient for the agent to receive praise or blame for a given behavior. Rather, a given feature may be highly relevant to the praise or blame an agent receives for one behavior while remaining almost entirely irrelevant to the praise or blame the agent receives for another, somewhat different behavior. Thus, if the concept of intentional action is to be helpful in the process of assessing praise and blame, people cannot go about determining whether or not a behavior is intentional by simply checking to see whether it has all the features on some fixed list. People would have to look for different features when confronted with different behaviors. And that seems to be exactly what people do. People's intentional action intuitions seem to exhibit a certain flexibility, such that they look for different features when confronted with different behaviors, and they tend to consider in each case the specific features that would be relevant to determining whether the agent is deserving of praise or blame.

We are now in a position to offer a new hypothesis about the role of moral considerations in people's concept of intentional action. The key claim will be that people's intentional action intuitions tend to track the psychological features that are most relevant to praise and blame judgments. But—and this is where moral considerations come in—different psychological features will be relevant depending on whether the behavior itself is good or bad. That is to say, we use different psychological features when we are (a) trying to determine whether or not an agent deserves blame for her bad behaviors from the ones we use when we are (b) trying to determine whether or not an agent deserves praise for her good behaviors.

We can now offer a somewhat more detailed model than the one presented above.

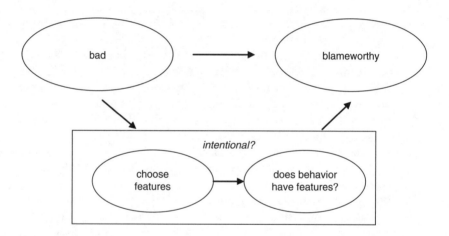

Here the overall process of determining whether or not the behavior was performed intentionally is broken down into two sub-processes. The first sub-process takes in information about whether the behavior itself is good or bad and uses this information to determine which features are relevant. The second sub-process then checks to see whether the behavior in question actually has these features and thereby generates an intentional action intuition.

Thus, suppose that the person is confronted with the behavior *harming the environment*. The first sub-process might determine that, since the behavior itself is bad, it should be considered intentional if the agent showed either trying or foresight. Then the second sub-process might determine that the agent actually did show foresight and that his behavior is therefore rightly considered intentional.

The chief contribution of this new model is the distinctive status it accords to moral considerations. Gone is the idea that moral considerations are "distorting" or "biasing" a process whose real purpose lies elsewhere. Instead, the claim is that moral considerations are playing a helpful role in people's underlying competence itself. They make it possible for people to generate intentional action intuitions that prove helpful in the subsequent process of assessing praise and blame.

V

Folk psychology is widely regarded as a tool for the prediction and explanation of behavior. Since people's concept of intentional action appears to be an integral part of folk psychology, one might be tempted to draw the conclusion that the concept of intentional action should be understood primarily in terms of this "scientific" use. We have been sketching a theory according to which this conclusion is false. The theory emphasizes instead that the concept of intentional action is used in the process by which people assign praise and blame.

In saying this, we in no way deny that the concept of intentional action is often *used* in the tasks of prediction and explanation. Nor do we deny that it is *adequate* for these tasks—that it can do a decent job of fulfilling various scientific purposes. What we are denying is that the concept is in any sense *specialized* for these tasks.

Instead, it appears that people's concept of intentional action should be understood as something like a multipurpose tool. If we want to understand why the concept works the way it does, it is not enough to examine its use in the tasks of prediction and explanation. Many important facts about the concept can be correctly understood only when we see that it also plays an important role in the process by which people determine how much praise or blame an agent deserves for his or her behavior.

A question now arises as to how this finding about people's concept of intentional action should affect our views about the nature of folk psychology as a whole. One possibility would be that people's concept of intentional action is simply an exception. That is, it might turn out that all the rest of folk psychology truly is best understood as a collection of tools for predicting and explaining behavior and that the concept of intentional action just happens to be one case in which this otherwise accurate theory breaks down. A second possibility, however, would be that many aspects of folk psychology are susceptible to an analysis like the one we have provided here for the concept of intentional action. In other words, it might turn out that many other aspects of folk psychology are shaped in some important respect by a concern for issues of praise and blame. Such an analysis might be correct for certain trait concepts; it might be correct for our practice of giving reason explanations; it might even be correct for ordinary causal attributions. But these questions lie outside the scope of the present essay. With any luck, they will be addressed in future research.

NOTES

I am grateful to Gilbert Harman, Bertram Malle, Alfred Mele, and Shaun Nichols for comments on an earlier draft.

1. [*Note added in 2007*] The hypothesis offered in this early essay is that the only type of moral judgment that influences people's intentional action intuitions is the judgment that a behavior is *bad*. In the years since I first put forward this hypothesis, it has been put to the test in a number of carefully designed empirical studies (Cushman 2007; Phelan and Sarkissian 2008; Tannenbaum et al. 2007; Sinnott-Armstrong et al. 2007; Wright and Bengson 2007). Sadly, those studies have conclusively demonstrated that my hypothesis was false. The collapse of this original hypothesis has led to a profusion of new models which aim to accommodate all of the recent data while also evading the problems that beset the models I discuss here (e.g., Alicke 2006; Knobe 2007; Machery 2008; Malle 2006; Nadelhoffer 2006; Nichols and Ulatowski 2007).

REFERENCES

Adams, F. (1986). Intention and Intentional Action: The Simple View. *Mind and Language* 1, 281–301.

Adams, F., and Steadman, A. (2004a). Intentional Action in Ordinary Language: Core Concept or Pragmatic Understanding? *Analysis* 64, 173–181.

Adams, F., and Steadman, A. (2004b). Intentional Actions and Moral Considerations: Still Pragmatic. *Analysis* 64, 268–276.

Alicke, M. (2006). Blaming Badly. *Journal of Cognition and Culture*.

Brand, M. (1984). *Intending and Acting*. Cambridge, MA: MIT Press.

Bratman, M. (1984). Two Faces of Intention. *Philosophical Review* 93, 375–405.

Bratman, M. (1987). *Intention, Plans, and Practical Reason*. Cambridge, MA: Harvard University Press.

Cushman, F. (2007). The Effect of Moral Judgment on Causal and Intentional Attribution: What We Say, or How We Think? Unpublished manuscript. Harvard University.

Feltz, A., and Cokely, E. (2007). An Anomaly in Intentional Action Ascription: More Evidence of Folk Diversity. *Proceedings of the Cognitive Science Society*.

Ginet, C. (1990). *On Action*. Cambridge: Cambridge University Press.

Harman, G. (1976). Practical Reasoning. *Review of Metaphysics* 29, 431–463.

Knobe, J. (2003a). Intentional Action and Side Effects in Ordinary Language. *Analysis* 63, 190–193.

Knobe, J. (2003b). Intentional Action in Folk Psychology: An Experimental Investigation. *Philosophical Psychology* 16, 309–324.

Knobe, J. (2004). Intention, Intentional Action and Moral Considerations. *Analysis* 64, 181–187.

Knobe, J. (2007). Reason Explanation in Folk Psychology. *Midwest Studies in Philosophy*.

Knobe, J., and Burra, A. (2006). Intention and Intentional Action: A Cross-Cultural Study. *Journal of Culture and Cognition* 6, 113–132.

Knobe, J., and Mendlow, G. (2004). The Good, the Bad, and the Blameworthy: Understanding the Role of Evaluative Considerations in Folk Psychology. *Journal of Theoretical and Philosophical Psychology* 24, 252–258.

Leslie, A., Knobe, J., and Cohen, A. (2006). Acting Intentionally and the Side-Effect Effect: 'Theory of Mind' and Moral Judgment. *Psychological Science* 17, 421–427.

Lowe, E. J. (1978). Neither Intentional nor Unintentional. *Analysis* 38, 117–118.

Machery, E. (2008). The Folk Concept of Intentional Action: Philosophical and Experimental Issues. *Mind and Language* 23: 165–189.

Malle, B. (2006). Intentionality, Morality, and Their Relationship in Human Judgment. *Journal of Cognition and Culture* 6, 87–113.

Malle, B. F. (2004). *How the Mind Explains Behavior: Folk Explanations, Meaning, and Social Interaction.* Cambridge, MA: MIT Press.

Malle, B. F., and Nelson, S. E. (2003). Judging Mens Rea: The Tension between Folk Concepts and Legal Concepts of Intentionality. *Behavioral Sciences and the Law* 21, 563–580.

McCann, H. (1986). Rationality and the Range of Intention. *Midwest Studies in Philosophy* 10, 191–211.

McCann, H. (2005). Intentional Action and Intending: Recent Empirical Studies. *Philosophical Psychology* 18, 737–748.

Mele, A. (1992). Recent Work on Intentional Action. *American Philosophical Quarterly* 29, 199–217.

Mele, A. (2001). Acting Intentionally: Probing Folk Notions. In B. F. Malle, L. J. Moses, and D. Baldwin (Eds.), *Intentions and Intentionality: Foundations of Social Cognition.* Cambridge, MA: MIT Press.

Mele, A. (2003). Intentional Action: Controversies, Data, and Core Hypotheses. *Philosophical Psychology* 16, 325–340.

Mele, A. R., and Moser, P. K. (1994). Intentional Action. *Noûs* 28, 39–68.

Nadelhoffer, T. (2004a). The Butler Problem Revisited. *Analysis* 64, 277–284.

Nadelhoffer, T. (2004b). Praise, Side Effects, and Intentional Action. *Journal of Theoretical and Philosophical Psychology* 24, 196–213.

Nadelhoffer, T. (2005). Skill, Luck, Control, and Folk Ascriptions of Intentional Action. *Philosophical Psychology* 18, 343–354.

Nadelhoffer, T. (2006). Bad Acts, Blameworthy Agents, and Intentional Actions: Some Problems for Jury Impartiality. *Philosophical Explorations* 9, 203–220.

Nichols, S., and Ulatowski, J. (2007). Intuitions and Individual Differences: The Knobe Effect Revisited. *Mind and Language.*

Phelan, M., and Sarkissian, H. (2008). The Folk Strike Back; Or, Why You Didn't Do It Intentionally, Though It Was Bad and You Knew It. *Philosophical Studies.*

Pizarro, D., Knobe, J., and Bloom, P. (2007). College Students Implicitly Judge Interracial Sex and Gay Sex to Be Morally Wrong. Unpublished manuscript. Cornell University.

Sinnott-Armstrong, W., Mallon, R., McCoy, T., and Hull, J. (2007). Intention, Temporal Order, and Moral Judgments. Unpublished manuscript. Dartmouth College.

Sverdlik, S. (2004). Intentionality and Moral Judgments in Commonsense Thought about Action. *Journal of Theoretical and Philosophical Psychology* 24, 224–236.

Tannenbaum, D., Ditto, P. H., and Pizarro, D. A. (2007). Different Moral Values Produce Different Judgments of Intentional Action. Unpublished manuscript. University of California–Irvine.

Wright, J., and Bengson, J. (2007). Asymmetries in Folk Judgments of Responsibility and Intentional Action. Unpublished manuscript. University of Wyoming.

Young, L., Cushman, F., Adolphs, R., Tranel, D., and Hauser, M. (2006). Does Emotion Mediate the Effect of an Action's Moral Status on Its Intentional Status? Neuropsychological Evidence. *Journal of Cognition and Culture* 6, 291–304.

8

Bad Acts, Blameworthy Agents, and Intentional Actions

Some Problems for Juror Impartiality

Thomas Nadelhoffer

1. INTRODUCTION

In the landmark *Smith* case of 1961, jurors in England had to determine the guilt of a man named Smith who had driven a car containing stolen goods in a zigzag course in order to shake off a policeman who had been clinging to the side of the car. When the policeman was finally shaken off, he rolled into oncoming traffic and sustained fatal injuries (*D. P. P. v. Smith* [1961] A. C. 290). Imagine that you are on that jury and your task is to decide whether Smith intentionally killed the policeman. In addition to considerations about Smith's relevant mental states and the relationship between these mental states and his actions—e.g., did Smith foresee that his actions would bring about the policeman's death—what other factors would affect your verdict? Would your decision concerning whether Smith killed the policeman intentionally be influenced by your evaluative belief that Smith brought about bad consequences? On the surface, it seems that the goodness or badness of Smith's actions should be completely *irrelevant* to the question of whether he performed them *intentionally*, but there is growing evidence that ascriptions of intentional actions are often influenced by evaluative considerations.

In this essay, I first briefly review some of the recent empirical work on the relationship between moral judgments and folk ascriptions of intentional action. Then, I shed light on the nature of this relationship by discussing Mark Alicke's affective model of blame attribution (2000). Next, I argue that Alicke's research—when coupled with recent data concerning folk ascriptions of intentional action—gives us reason to worry that jury deliberations in criminal trials involving serious crimes may be partial or biased in a fundamental way. And while psychologists long ago identified how the appearance, gender, race, occupation, or sexual preference of the defendant and the victim may sometimes bias jury deliberations, the main point of this essay is to suggest that perhaps there is an even more basic sort of partiality that occurs when jurors are asked to make judgments concerning a defendant's mental states—especially when the crime in question is a serious one. After all, if the *immorality* of an action or side effect biases folk ascriptions of intentionality, and all serious criminal offenses such as murder and rape are immoral in addition to being illegal, then a juror's ability to determine the relevant *mens rea* (i.e., guilty mind) of someone like Smith in an unbiased way may be seriously undermined.[1] After considering some possible solutions to the particular type of juror partiality I have identified, I conclude that philosophers, psychologists, and legal theorists will need to continue to work together if we are to minimize the biasing effect that moral judgments have on jurors' judgments concerning the *mens rea* of defendants.

2. SETTING THE STAGE

There is growing empirical evidence that people are more likely to judge that a morally negative action or side effect was brought about intentionally than they are to judge that a structurally similar nonmoral action or side effect was brought about intentionally (e.g., Knobe 2003a, 2003b, 2004a; Nadelhoffer 2004a, 2004b, 2004c, 2005). So, for instance, if two individuals A and B place a single bullet in a six shooter, spin the chamber, aim the gun, and pull the trigger, but A shoots a person and B shoots a target, people are more likely to say that A shot the person intentionally than they are to say that B shot the target intentionally—even though their respective chances of success (one-in-six) and their control over the outcome are identical in both cases.

This goes right to the heart of a long-standing debate in the philosophy of action concerning the nature and proper role of ascriptions of intentionality. One of the central issues of this debate is whether moral considerations do—or *should*—affect our application of the concept of intentional action. While some scholars suggest that our use of this concept is often affected by moral considerations (e.g., Bratman 1987; Duff 1982, 1990; Harman 1997), others claim that moral considerations either do not or should not have an effect (e.g., Butler 1978; Katz 1987; Mele and Sverdlik 1996). On this latter view, while we may correctly appeal to the intentionality of an action in our attempt to determine someone's moral or legal responsibility, the converse is not the case—i.e., attributions of blame and praise should not affect our ascriptions of intentional action.[2]

For now, I want to provide a brief sketch of the recent debate concerning the relationship between moral judgments and judgments of intentionality. The most natural place to start such an investigation is with the work of Joshua Knobe—one of the first philosophers to bring data about folk intuitions to bear on issues in the philosophy of action. In a series of novel experiments, Knobe set out to determine whether folk intuitions about the intentionality of foreseeable yet undesired side effects are influenced by moral considerations (Knobe 2003a, 2003b). Each of the 78 participants in the first of these side-effect experiments were presented with a vignette involving either a 'harm condition' or a 'help condition.' Those who received the harm condition read the following vignette:

> The vice-president of a company went to the chairman of the board and said, "We are thinking of starting a new program. It will help us increase profits, but it will also harm the environment." The chairman of the board answered, "I don't care at all about harming the environment. I just want to make as much profit as I can. Let's start the new program." They started the new program. Sure enough, the environment was harmed. (Knobe 2003a, 191)

They were then asked to judge how much blame the chairman deserved for harming the environment (on a scale from 0 to 6) and to say whether they thought the chairman harmed the environment intentionally; 82 percent of the participants claimed that the chairman harmed the environment intentionally.

Participants in the help condition, on the other hand, read the same scenario except that the word 'harm' was replaced by the word 'help.' They were then asked to judge how much praise the chairman deserved for helping the environment (on a scale from 0 to 6) and to say whether they thought the chairman helped the environment intentionally. Only 23 percent of the participants claimed that the chairman intentionally helped the environment (Knobe 2003a, 192). When Knobe first published these surprising results he concluded that people do—and presumably should—rely on their judgments concerning the badness of an action in determining whether the action was performed intentionally, and then they use these intentionality judgments to determine whether the agent deserves blame for having performed the action in question (Knobe 2003a, 2003b, 2004). However, according to Knobe's original analysis of the data, moral goodness does not have a similar influence on folk ascriptions of intentional action.

I have subsequently argued that not only can the moral goodness of an action or side effect influence our judgments of intentionality (Nadelhoffer 2005)—albeit to a lesser degree than badness—but also that judgments concerning the moral blameworthiness or praiseworthiness of agents can have a similar influence on our ascriptions of intentional action (Nadelhoffer 2004b).[3] For present purposes, I am going to simply assume that my arguments for the latter claim are correct—although for the problem of juror partiality that I will be examining in this essay, not a lot will hinge on the issue. Keep in mind that if any negative moral considerations influence our judgments concerning the intentionality of an action or side effect, then we have reason to worry that jurors may not be able to make impartial judgments about a defendant's mental state in cases involving bad acts or blameworthy agents. Indeed, it appears that the more negative a case is—morally speaking—the less likely it becomes that jurors will be impartial. But I am getting ahead of myself. Before I discuss the particular problem of jury partiality that I have purportedly identified, I first want to examine a recent model of the psychology of blame that lends additional support to my own view concerning the relationship between blame attribution and ascriptions of intentional action.

3. MARK ALICKE'S CULPABLE CONTROL MODEL
OF BLAME ATTRIBUTION

One of the key notions underlying much of the recent research on moral psy-chology is 'automaticity'—i.e., "the mind's ability to solve many problems, including high-level social ones, unconsciously and automatically" (Greene and Haidt 2002, 517). The seeming ubiquity of these automatic mental processes has led some researchers to reject rationalist models of moral psychology in favor of nonrationalist affective models. According to these affective models, "moral judgment is more a matter of emotion and affective intuition than delibera-tive reasoning" (Greene and Haidt 2002, 517). And while these new explana-tory models make room for certain types of higher cognition, they nevertheless suggest that emotional and nonrational processes, rather than deliberative and rational ones, are primarily responsible for our moral judgments. One affective model of moral psychology that is particularly salient for our present purposes is Mark Alicke's model of the psychology of blame.

Alicke develops what he calls the Culpable Control Model (CCM) of blame attribution—a model that purportedly explains, "the conditions that increase as well as mitigate blame and analyzes the process by which blame and mitiga-tion decisions are made" (Alicke 2000, 557). Unlike other theoretical perspec-tives on blame and responsibility that focus on *normative* questions concerning how ascriptions of blame and responsibility should be made, the CCM focuses on the cognitive factors that actually influence these ascriptions, i.e., rather than discussing how judgments concerning blameworthiness should *properly* be made in *ideal* circumstances, he examines how they are *actually* made in *ordinary* circumstances.

According to the CCM, the primary factor in ascriptions of blame is the per-sonal control—i.e., "the freedom to effect desired behaviors and outcomes or to avoid undesired ones" (Alicke 2000, 557)—of the agent who has performed the morally inappropriate act. Alicke identifies three different aspects of per-sonal control: (a) the mental element (e.g., mental states such as desires, plans, motives, etc.), (b) the behavioral element (e.g., actions and omissions), (c) the consequential element (e.g., immediate and extended 'behavioral outcomes'). And these three aspects in turn coincide with the following structural links: "a link between mind and behavior, one between behavior and consequence, and one between mind and consequence" (Alicke 2000, 557).[4] On this view, structural links designate the different factors of personal control that affect ascriptions of blame and responsibility. Whenever these factors of personal control are firmly established, ascriptions of blame intensify, whereas if these factors are somehow constrained, blame is mitigated.

While the CCM is similar to traditional rationalist models of blame and responsibility in acknowledging that "people are socialized to predicate blame on criteria such as intention, causation, and foresight" (Alicke 2000, 557), it differs from these other models in the emphasis it places on the claim that "personal control judgments and blame attributions are influenced by relatively unconscious, spontaneous evaluations of the mental, behavioral, and consequence elements. Spontaneous evaluations are affective reactions to the harmful event and the people involved" (Alicke 2000, 558). According to Alicke, these spontaneous and relatively unconscious responses can be triggered by both the 'evidential structural linkage information' concerning the three aforementioned factors of personal control and other 'extra-evidential factors' such as a person's appearance, reputation, social status, etc. As he says:

> When blame-validation mode is engaged, observers review structural linkage evidence in a biased manner by exaggerating the actor's volitional or causal control, by lowering their evidential standards for blame, or by seeking information to support their blame attribution. In addition to spontaneous evaluation influences, blame-validation processing is facilitated by factors such as the tendencies to over ascribe control to human agency and to confirm unfavorable expectations. (Alicke 2000, 558)

Thus, the CCM suggests that judgments concerning personal control—and hence of moral blameworthiness—are unwittingly influenced by spontaneous affective reactions to the agents and actions involved. This influence can be both direct and indirect.

One way that spontaneous reactions influence structural linkage assessments is by altering perceptions of the evidence itself. When this happens, "observers who spontaneously evaluate the actor's behavior unfavorably may exaggerate evidence that established her causal or volitional control and de-emphasize exculpatory evidence" (Alicke 2000, 566). Another way that these reactions affect observers' judgments is by engendering blame-validation processing that subsequently increases the observer's "proclivity to favor blame versus non-blame explanations for harmful events and to de-emphasize mitigating circumstances" (Alicke 2000, 568–69). To the extent that the observer believes that the action in question is immoral, she will be inclined to look for explanations of the action that favor ascriptions of blame while at the same time over-looking explanations that do not. Thus, as a result of both spontaneous evaluations and blame-validation processing, observers tend to "over ascribe control of human agency and to confirm unfavorable expectations" (Alicke 2000, 558).

To see how these kinds of biases operate, consider the following three studies: the participants in the first study were told that a homeowner shot someone in an upstairs bedroom who was presumed to be an intruder (Alicke, Davis, and Pezzo 1994). In the positive outcome version, the victim was described as a violent criminal who was responsible for other burglaries in the neighborhood. In the negative outcome version, the victim was the boyfriend of the homeowner's daughter who had been packing clothes for a trip. Participants were then asked to rate the causal relevance of a variety of factors, e.g., the fact that the homeowner had two beers to drink shortly before the shooting. Participants who received the negative outcome version found that the beer played a greater causal role in the shooting than participants who received the positive outcome version. This suggests that "spontaneous evaluations of the outcome directly affected blame ascriptions, which participants then buttressed by altering their causal control assessments" (Alicke 2000, 565).

In the second study, participants received a vignette that contained an ambiguous story about a subway passenger who was approached by four teenagers asking for money. Feeling threatened, the passenger nervously fired two shots thereby killing one of the teenagers. Upon reading the story, some participants were told that the teenagers were gang members with criminal records whereas others learned that the teenagers were star athletes trying to collect money for their football team. Not surprisingly, the blame ratings from the two respective pools of participants showed the same sort of 'outcome bias effect' that has been found in other studies (e.g., Alicke and Davis 1989)—i.e., the shooter was blamed more in the case involving the star athletes than in the case involving the gang members. Moreover, participants also learned that there were four eyewitness accounts—two for the prosecution and two for the defense—and they were told that owing to time limitations they would each only be able to read the testimony of three of the four. Interestingly, 75 percent of the participants in the star athlete group preferred to read more pro-prosecution testimony whereas 60 percent of the participants in the gang member group preferred to read pro-defense testimony. Alicke concludes that studies such as these show that participants "who reacted more negatively to the actor for killing innocent victims favored information that supported a blame attribution" (Alicke 2000, 567).

Finally, in the third study, participants read about a driver who got into an accident while speeding (Alicke 1992). Participants learned that the driver was speeding either to hide an anniversary present or a vial of cocaine. Moreover, they learned that the driver encountered a number of environmental obstacles—slippery road, poor visibility, etc. Participants were then asked to say whether the driver's speeding or the environmental factors played a greater role in causing the accident. The results showed that participants were more inclined to attribute the accident to the driver rather than the environmental conditions when the driver was hiding the cocaine than they were when he was hiding an anniversary gift. Once again, it appears that "spontaneous evaluations of the actor's motives led participants to exaggerate his causal control over the accident" (Alicke 2000, 567).

Given the results of these kinds of experiments, Alicke concludes that "cognitive shortcomings and motivational biases are endemic to blame" (2000, 557)—an admittedly disheartening finding. But as disturbing as it is that spontaneous moral intuitions and judgments often have such a negative effect on our ability to impartially consider the evidence surrounding a case, Alicke's CCM of blame attribution nevertheless helps shed light on the aforementioned biasing effect that moral considerations have on folk ascriptions of intentional action.

4. ASCRIPTIONS OF INTENTIONAL ACTION AND THE PARTIALITY OF JURY DELIBERATION

In fleshing out the implications of the aforementioned research on moral psychology and folk ascriptions of intentional action for the problem of jury partiality, I will be primarily concerned with serious crimes that are *mala in se* (i.e., both illegal and immoral) such as murder and rape. In order for an agent to be held responsible for these types of crimes, the prosecution must prove two things: first, the agent has to be guilty of having performed the physical element of the offense—i.e., the *actus reus* or guilty act; second, the agent must have acted with the relevant mental or subjective element of the offense—i.e., the *mens rea* or adequately culpable state of mind. And for the types of crimes we are presently concerned with, *mens rea* usually implies that the agent performed the action either purposely, intentionally, designedly, consciously, or knowingly. In its narrowest interpretation—sometimes referred to as the elemental meaning—*mens rea* simply refers to the mental state explicitly required in the definition of the offense in question.[5]

Having briefly discussed the *mens rea* requirement of criminal law, we should now examine the problem that recent research into folk ascriptions of intentional action poses for juror impartiality. After all, to the extent that moral considerations affect folk ascriptions of intentional action, the ability of a defendant who is being prosecuted for a serious crime to receive a fair and unbiased assessment by the jurors is undermined. If the folk—in this case the jurors—are more likely to say that an action was performed *intentionally* if the action was *immoral*, and the defendant whose guilt the jurors are being asked to determine is accused of performing an act that is immoral in addition to being illegal, then the jurors will naturally be more inclined to say that the defendant's act was intentional. This problem is especially pressing in cases where jurors must judge whether the offense was committed with a sufficiently culpable mind.

In first-degree murder trials, for example, jurors are informed that in order for the defendant to be guilty as charged, he must have either (a) committed a murder that involved deliberate meditation, (b) committed a murder that involved extreme atrocity or cruelty, or (c) committed a murder during the commission of a felony (Model Jury Instructions on Homicide).[6] For our present purposes, the jury instructions for deliberate meditation should suffice. The three elements are (a) that the defendant committed an unlawful killing (i.e., a killing that was not an accident or was not committed in selfdefense), (b) that the killing was committed with malice (i.e., the defendant either had an intent to cause death or caused the death intentionally), and (c) that the killing was committed with deliberate premeditation (i.e., the defendant thought before he acted and decided to kill after deliberation).

Based on these instructions, a juror must believe that the defendant's crime meets all three of these conditions if he is to be found guilty of first-degree murder with deliberate meditation. But if moral considerations—such as the immorality of the *actus reus*—influence juror ascriptions of intentionality, then these considerations will likewise influence whether the jurors judge that the defendant committed the crime with the requisite amount of malice and deliberation, *especially when acting with malice is simply taken to mean acting intentionally*. Similarly, if folk ascriptions of the intentionality of the *side effects* of actions are affected by the immorality of the action, then in the *Smith* case mentioned earlier, the jurors' verdict may have been affected by the *immoral nature of the outcome* of Smith's actions.

To see whether the moral badness of the policeman's death may have affected the juror's decisions in the Smith case, I ran a preliminary study that involved vignettes based on the case. Participants were 126 undergraduates—half of whom received the following vignette:

> *Case 1 (C1):* Imagine that a thief is driving a car full of recently stolen goods. While he is waiting at a red light, a police officer comes up to the window of the car while brandishing a gun. When he sees the officer, the thief speeds off through the intersection. Amazingly, the officer manages to hold on to the side of the car as it speeds off. The thief swerves in a zigzag fashion in the hope of escaping—knowing full well that doing so places the officer in grave danger. But the thief doesn't care; he just wants to get away. Unfortunately for the officer, the thief's attempt to shake him off is successful. As a result, the officer rolls into oncoming traffic and sustains fatal injuries. He dies minutes later.

They were then asked the following questions. First, did the thief knowingly bring about the officer's death? Second, did the thief intentionally bring about the officer's death? Third, how much blame does the thief deserve for the death of the officer (on a scale from 0 to 6, 0 being no blame and 6 being a lot of blame)? The results were as follows:

> Q1. 75 percent said that the thief knowingly brought about the officer's death.
> Q2. 37 percent said that the thief intentionally brought about the officer's death.
> Q3. The average blame rating was 5.11 on a 6-point scale.

In order to see whether the badness of the death of the officer and/or the perceived moral culpability of Smith was acting expansively on participants' ascriptions of knowledge and intentionality, I gave the other participants a case that is structurally identical to the first case—only this time it is an innocent driver whose actions bring about the death of an attempted carjacker. This case runs as follows:

> *Case 2 (C2):* Imagine that a man is waiting in his car at a red light. Suddenly, a car thief approaches his window while brandishing a gun. When he sees the thief, the driver panics and speeds off through the intersection. Amazingly, the thief manages to hold on to the side of the car as it speeds off. The driver swerves in a zigzag fashion in the hope of

escaping—knowing full well that doing so places the thief in grave danger. But the driver doesn't care; he just wants to get away. Unfortunately for the thief, the driver's attempt to shake him off is successful. As a result, the thief rolls into oncoming traffic and sustains fatal injuries. He dies minutes later.

The participants were then asked the following questions. First, did the driver knowingly bring about the thief's death? Second, did the driver intentionally bring about the thief's death? Third, how much blame does the driver deserve for the death of the thief (on a scale from 0 to 6, 0 being no blame and 6 being a lot of blame)? The results were as follows:

Q1. 51 percent said that the driver knowingly brought about the car thief's death.
Q2. 10 percent said that the driver intentionally brought about the car thief's death.
Q3. The average blame rating was 2.01 on a 6-point scale.

If we compare the results of C1 and C2, we see that even though the cases are identical in terms of the cognitive and conative considerations of the thief and the driver, the participants in C1 were more likely to say that the thief *knowingly* brought about the officer's death (75 percent) than the participants in C2 were to say that the driver knowingly brought about the death of the car thief (51 percent)—a statistically significant difference [χ^2 (1, N = 126) = 7.62, $p < 0.01$]. Moreover, the participants in C1 were also much more likely to say that the thief intentionally brought about the death of the officer (37 percent) than the participants in C2 were to say that the driver intentionally brought about the death of the car thief (10 percent)—a statistically significant difference [χ^2 (1, N = 126) = 12.94, $p < 0.001$]. And given the difference in the respective blame ratings from the two groups of participants (5.11 versus 2.01), we find *prima facie* evidence that moral considerations do explain the asymmetry of the participants' judgments.

My main goal in this study was to use a scenario based on a famous criminal trial to see whether moral judgments might influence jurors' judgments concerning whether a defendant acted either knowingly or intentionally. And while the results are mostly in line with earlier studies (Knobe 2003a, 2003b, 2004; Nadelhoffer 2004a), there are at least two noteworthy features of my *Smith* study. First, the results suggest that people's judgments concerning whether an agent knowingly brought about a result may also be affected by moral considerations. This is particularly important since for most criminal offenses, a defendant is maximally culpable as long as she either purposely (i.e., intentionally) or knowingly performed the prohibited action (or brought about the prohibited side effects). Hence, if moral judgments affect jurors' deliberations concerning both the intentionality and the foreseeability of a prohibited action or side effect, then the particular type of juror partiality I have identified in this essay is wider in scope than I had originally envisioned. Second, the results suggest that judgments concerning the moral character of either the victim or the defendant (or perhaps both) seem to have had an influence on participants' intuitions as well. However, more studies would admittedly need to be run that tested specifically for these two effects.

If further studies confirm these preliminary results, then the 'cards' were likely stacked against Smith before the trial even began given the moral gravity of the consequences of his actions—which is to say, because his actions brought about bad side effects, the jurors were more inclined to judge that the policeman's death was foreseeable and that Smith brought about his death intentionally. Thus, the influence that moral considerations have on folk ascriptions of intentional action may often undermine a juror's ability to make impartial judgments concerning whether the defendant satisfies the requisite subjective or mental element of the crime he is being accused of having committed.[7]

Consider, for instance, the following three cases: first, in the frequently quoted *Desmond* case of 1868, a group of Fenian conspirators blew up a prison wall with dynamite in a failed attempt to free some of their imprisoned comrades. Even though their plot failed, the explosion killed a number of people living nearby. The conspirators were subsequently charged and convicted of murder (*Desmond, Barret & Others* [1868] 11 Cox C. C. 146). Second, in the *Hyam* case of 1975, a woman was jealous of a rival who had supplanted her in the affections of a mutual lover. As a result, the defendant went to her rival's house in the middle of the night, poured gasoline through her letterbox, and lit the door of her house on fire. Although the defendant's intention was merely to scare her rival away, the fire got out of hand and killed two of her rival's children. The defendant was subsequently charged and convicted of murder (*Hyam* [1975] A. C. 55). Finally, in *Regina v. Cunningham*, the defendant—who was desperate for money at the time—went into the cellar of the duplex he was renting and illegally removed the gas meter from the gas pipes in order to sell it. Although the switch for the gas was only two feet away from the meter, the defendant did not shut it off. Consequently, a considerable amount of gas filled the cellar and the duplex, partially asphyxiating another tenant (*Regina v. Cunningham*, Court of Criminal Appeal, 1957, 41 Crim. App. 155, [1957] 3 *Weekly L.R.* 76). The defendant was subsequently convicted of unlawfully and maliciously endangering the life of the tenant.[8]

If Alicke's CCM is correct, the ability of jurors to pass impartial judgments about the intentionality of a defendant's actions is greatly undermined in cases where they are being presented with a defendant who is charged with having committed an overtly immoral act. According to CCM, the immoral nature of the act can *spontaneously* trigger jurors to go into the default mode of blame attribution—a mode that causes them to be affected by negative and relatively unconscious reactions that prejudice both their assessment of the crime and their assessment of the structural linkages relative to establishing the defendant's guilt. This problem is compounded even further if Alicke is right that these spontaneous blame-validation biases are not "exceptions to rational norms," but rather "inherent aspects of blame ascription" (Alicke 2000, 558).

In this case, the mere fact that the defendant is accused of having committed a heinous crime increases the changes that jurors will view the evidence in a biased or impartial way. After all, once a juror's blame-validation mode has been triggered, she will be more likely to exaggerate the defendants's volitional or causal control and more inclined to lower the evidential standards of blame upon which the verdict is supposed to be based. Moreover, this spontaneous presumption of blame can cause the juror to *selectively look for evidence that supports blame attribution* while at the same time causing her to *overlook factors that might otherwise mitigate or exculpate blame or guilt.*[9]

This sobering possibility suggests that perhaps folk ascriptions of intentional action *should not* be affected by evaluative considerations, even if the evidence suggests that they frequently are. Minimally, to the extent that the sixth Amendment of the U.S. Constitution guarantees that "the accused shall enjoy the right to a speedy and public trial, by an *impartial* jury" (my emphasis), judges should consider taking more direct measures to inform jurors of the genuine risk each of them runs of allowing moral considerations to lead them to pass partial verdicts. Perhaps, if jurors were made aware of the various—and seemingly predictable—ways that their judgments can be unwittingly affected by evaluative considerations and blame-validation biasing, they would be better able to live up to their legal duty to base their decisions solely on the material facts of the case. But as we are about to see, there is reason to suspect that not even heavy-handedness on the part of judges would help secure an impartial jury for the accused.

5. SOME POSSIBLE SOLUTIONS

Some scholars have suggested that one way of minimizing the influence that moral considerations have on our ascriptions of intentionality would involve making sure that the criminal law defines mental states in a way that clearly distinguishes culpability from intentionality. According to Bertram Malle and Sara Nelson, for instance, even if legal scholars are correct in pointing out that "in criminal law, attributions of *mens rea* simply are (at least provisionally) attributions of culpability" (Lacey 1993, 625), it does not follow that we cannot take steps to ensure that moral judgments and judgments of intentionality remain separate in the minds of jurors. On their view, "to the extent that judgments of intentionality have important implications for verdicts and sentencing and do not just foreshadow them, every effort should be made to dissociate intentionality judgments from evaluative feelings or culpability assignments" (Malle and Nelson 2003, 576). In short, Malle and Nelson suggest that we should do everything we can to separate the *mens* from the *rea* in the criminal law.

One dissociative strategy put forward by Malle and Nelson for separating the *mens* from the *rea* would involve asking jurors to make intentionality judgments while at the same time "exhorting them to leave their evaluative feelings aside" (Malle and Nelson 2003, 576). Indeed, this is precisely the kind of possibility I entertained at the end of the last section when I suggested that perhaps the biasing effect that moral considerations have on jurors' ascriptions of intentional action could be minimized if jurors were informed of the potential for bias. And while this is certainly something that we should do more of than we currently do, it is unclear whether taking these kinds of measures would be very effective.

In an interesting paper on what they call 'mental contamination'—i.e., "cases whereby a judgment, emotion, or behavior is biased by unconscious or uncontrollable mental processes"—Timothy Wilson and Nancy Brekke suggest that in order for individuals to be able to avoid cognitive biases, the four following conditions would need to be met (Wilson and Brekke 1994, 118). First, they must be made aware of the unwanted mental processes in question. Second, they must be motivated to correct the error. Third, in addition to being motivated to correct for the error, they must be "aware of the direction and the magnitude of the bias" (Wilson and Brekke 1994, 118). Finally, they must have sufficient control over their mental processes to be able to correct for the biases in question. For present purposes, I am going to assume that in order for Malle and Nelson's jury instruction dissociative strategy to work, jurors would minimally need to be able to satisfy these four conditions as well. Unfortunately, the empirical data from social and cognitive psychology suggest that attempts on the part of jurors to keep judgments of intentionality separate from judgments of culpability will be unsuccessful.

First, there is gathering evidence that many (if not most) of our cognitive processes are inaccessible to conscious processing (see, e.g., Erikson and Simon 1980; Jacoby, Lindsay, and Toth 1992; Kihltstrom 1987; Nisbett and Wilson 1977; Posner and Rothbart 1989). Second, recent research has suggested that even if people are made aware of the occurrence and magnitude of a cognitive bias, their ability to subsequently control their thoughts and feelings is often very limited (Bargh 1989; Logan 1989; Wegner 1989, 1992; Wegner and Pennebaker 1993). To get a sense for the relevance of this kind of research for our present concern, consider the research that has been carried out specifically on mental contamination and legal proceedings. For example, rules of evidence and other procedural rules have been put in place to prevent biases from affecting jurors' judgments concerning the evidence. One assumption that underlies a number of these rules is that jurors are able to discount or ignore testimony and evidence that turns out to be inadmissible. However, there is considerable evidence that people are unable to discount information very effectively (see, e.g., Sue, Smith, and Caldwell 1973; Thompson, Fong, and Rosenhan 1981; Wrightsman 1991).

Yet another problem for Malle and Nelson's suggestion concerning jury instruction is that people often underestimate their own susceptibility to mental contamination even once they are made aware of the general ubiquity of the underlying biases, while at the same time overestimating their own ability to control their mental processes. Consider, for example, the problem of prejudice and stereotyping. Even once people are made aware of the fact that stereotypes are usually learned at an early age and are often invoked automatically when we encounter members of certain groups (see, e.g., Billing 1985; Brewer 1989), people nevertheless underestimate their own tendencies to stereotype—which thereby undermines their ability to prevent prejudices and stereotypes from biasing their judgments (Devine 1989; Wegner 1994). Worse yet, it appears that under certain circumstances, the "very act of trying to suppress stereotypic responses can increase their frequency" (Wilson and Brekke 1994, 133).

When we look at data on mental contamination and cognitive biases collectively, we have good reason to suspect that instructing jurors not to allow their culpability judgments to affect their intentionality judgments will be rather ineffectual. And for present purposes it makes little difference whether this is because (a) the biases in question are inaccessible to the jurors, (b) the jurors themselves underestimate their susceptibility to the biases, (c) the jurors overestimate their ability to control their mental processes, or (d) some combination thereof. Minimally, more studies would need to be run that specifically address people's ability to dissociate their judgments concerning the intentionality of an agent's action and their judgments concerning the culpability of the agent. And while I am doubtful that instructing jurors to dissociate intentionality and culpability will be effective—especially in cases involving serious crimes such as assault or murder—the issue is straight-forwardly empirical. So, the verdict on Malle and Nelson's dissociative strategy will be out until the relevant studies are run.

In the meantime, I want to reconsider the aforementioned possibility that perhaps the entire way I have framed the issue concerning the relationship between moral judgments and ascriptions of intentional action is itself misguided or incorrect. One of the basic assumptions of my treatment of this relationship is that the former judgments often *distort* the latter ones. On this view, the folk concept of intentional action is ordinarily applied roughly along the lines of the five-component model put forward by Malle and Knobe—whereby performing an action intentionally "requires the presence of five components: a desire for an outcome; beliefs about an action that leads to that outcome; an intention to perform the action; skill to perform the action; and awareness of fulfilling the intention while performing the action" (Malle and Knobe 1997, 12). However, once morally loaded features are built into scenarios, these features often trump or override the standard application of the concept of intentional action—thereby distorting our judgments about intentionality. According to the moral biasing model I have put forward in this essay, affective responses often undermine our ability to apply the concept of intentional action in an unbiased way.

Indeed, the very fact that I have called this a 'biasing effect' indicates that I think that even though moral considerations surely do act expansively on folk ascriptions of intentional action, I nevertheless follow Mele and Sverdlik (1996) in believing that ideally they ought not have this effect—i.e., that whereas our ascriptions of intentional action should affect our judgments concerning an agent's responsibility, the converse should not be the case. Nichols and Knobe have called the kind of model I have been developing—whereby affective or emotional responses sometimes *inappropriately* bias our otherwise rational judgments—a "performance error model" (Nichols and Knobe 2007). And while they are mainly interested in models of folk morality rather than models of folk psychology, I think the notion of a performance error is helpful in the present context—especially given that not everyone agrees that what I have been calling a 'biasing effect' represents a performance error at all.

Knobe, for instance, has suggested that folk psychology cannot be properly understood if we assume that its sole purpose is to predict and explain behavior—rather it is best understood as a multipurpose tool (Knobe 2003b; Knobe and Burra 2006). While allowing that folk psychology plays an important role in the prediction and explanation of other people's behavior, Knobe insists that it plays other important roles in our daily lives as well. On his view, some folk psychological concepts—such as intentional action—are "bound up in a fundamental way with evaluative questions—questions about good and bad, right and wrong, praise and blame" (Knobe 2003b, 309–10). Given the intimate relationship between judgments of intentionality and moral judgments, it purportedly does not make sense to talk about moral judgments having a biasing effect on ascriptions of intentional action. After all, according to Knobe's view, moral considerations "really do play a role in the very concept of intentional action" (Knobe and Burra 2006).

While I wholeheartedly agree with both Knobe's claim that folk psychology is best viewed as a multifaceted tool and his claim that judgments of intentionality and moral judgments are intimately related, his view nevertheless fails to allay my present worries concerning jury partiality. After all, the problem I have been concerned with in this essay is that people are more likely to judge that a morally bad action or side effect is intentional than they are to judge that a structurally similar morally good or neutral action or side effect is intentional. Hence, while it may be true that the concept of intentional action cannot be fully understood lest we appreciate the role it plays in our moral deliberations, it nevertheless appears that people sometimes put the moral cart before the intentional horse. Consequently, even if the concept of intentional action is intimately bound up with moral considerations—which I entirely accept—there is still a question concerning the proper direction of fit.

If the concept of intentional action were not relevant to issues of moral responsibility, then it is unlikely that it would play such a central role in criminal proceedings in the first place. But the role it is supposed to play in the criminal law is as follows: judges and jurors are first supposed to determine whether the defendant is responsible for having performed the *actus reus* as well as whether she satisfied the relevant *mens rea* requirement for the crime of *x-ing*.[10] Having made a decision concerning whether the defendant did *x* purposely, knowingly, recklessly, etc., judges and jurors can then determine whether the defendant is legally culpable for *x-ing*. However, in cases where the crime with which the defendant has been charged is particularly bad—or the defendant is a particularly immoral or sordid individual—the empirical data suggest that there is a real risk that these moral features may distort the judgments of judges and jurors concerning whether the defendant purposely, knowingly, or recklessly committed the crime in question.

In this respect, the moral cart once again ends up ahead of the intentional horse. Surely, we don't want the very fact that a defendant is charged with having committed an immoral act to make it more likely that jurors will find her to be guilty of the crime in question. Hence, it looks like we have a performance error after all even if we accept Knobe's view of folk psychology—unless, of course, he thinks that not only should our ascriptions of intentional action inform our moral judgments, but also that the latter should sometimes inform the former. Surprisingly, Knobe suggests something along precisely these lines when he says that even though the blameworthiness or praiseworthiness of an individual cannot (or should not?) affect our ascriptions of intentional action, the intrinsic badness or goodness of an action often can (and presumably should) influence people's judgments of intentionality (Knobe and Burra 2006).

But even if Knobe's 'badness not blame' hypothesis were correct—and as I have already suggested, there is evidence that it is not—this would at best only solve half of the problem with juror partiality that I am presently addressing. After all, if jurors in a trial involving a gruesome death are more likely to say that the defendant intentionally brought the death about because the death is perceived to be intrinsically bad, then in most cases involving serious crimes, the cards really are stacked against the defendants from the start. This problem persists even if the blameworthiness of the defendant is not similarly affecting jurors' judgments of intentionality.

Ultimately, the issue with which I am presently concerned is not whether ascriptions of intentional action are relevant to our moral considerations—something few people would deny—but whether the gathering data on the relationship between the two give us reason to worry that *mens rea* concepts such as intentional action are likely to be used impartially in criminal proceedings. By my lights at least, Knobe's preferred account of the relationship between folk psychology and folk morality does not help allay this doubt. After all, if the main worry is that negative moral judgments concerning either the badness of the crime or the blameworthiness of the defendant are actually influencing the judgments of intentionality that jurors are supposed to rely on in determining the defendant's culpability, then it is a small consolation to be told that these two kinds of judgments are intimately related. But if, on the other hand, the influence that moral considerations have on ascriptions of intentional action really does amount to a performance error—at least as far as the criminal law is concerned—and if we have reason to doubt whether jurors can successfully avoid making the error even if they are made aware of it, then where does that leave us when it comes to intentionality and the criminal law?

If *mens rea* concepts such as knowingly, purposely, and intentionally are going to continue to play a role in legal proceedings, we need to do everything within our power to ensure that they are used impartially. Figuring out how best to accomplish this goal will require more of the kind of empirical research I have already examined. Presumably, leaving judges and jurors to their own devices will continue to be inadequate. But until we have a better understanding of both the nature and depth of the problem, we will be unable to devise any viable solutions. One important step involves taking a closer look at the relationship between folk psychology and folk morality. Another step involves a close examination of the role that *mens rea* concepts play in ordinary language and the criminal law. This is an investigation that will require philosophers, psychologists, and legal scholars to work hand in hand. If my own project serves to motivate further research along these lines, then it will have been a success even if I admittedly left a number of important questions unanswered.

NOTES

I would like to thank Alfred Mele, Joshua Knobe, Joel Anderson, George Rainbolt, Virginia Tice, and two anonymous referees for their helpful comments and suggestions on earlier drafts of this essay.

1. While the main focus in this essay is on the potential partiality of jury deliberations, the problems I discuss concerning the biased application of *mens rea* concepts would presumably arise in trials that only involve judges—although more studies would need to be run that tested whether judges were immune to the sort of biases at issue in a way that jurors are not. Given the data I discuss in section 3, 1 doubt that judges are any better at avoiding these biases than the folk—but it is admittedly a hunch on my part.

2. My own view on this matter has evolved. Whereas I originally agreed with Knobe that moral considerations both do *and* should influence our ascriptions of intentional action, I now think the normative claim that the former should affect the latter is incorrect for the reasons I discuss in section 4.

3. For the purposes of this essay, whenever I discuss intentionality, I am only talking about the question of whether an agent's actions are intentional. This sort of intentionality is to be distinguished from discussions of intentionality that one finds in the literature on the philosophy of mind. When philosophers talk about intentionality in this latter context, they are usually interested in the question of how some of our mental states can be *about* things in the world.

4. These three structural links are called 'volitional behavioral control,' 'volitional outcome control,' and 'causal control,' respectively (Alicke 2000, 560).

5. While the Model Penal Code does not define what it means for an action to be done intentionally, it gives the following guidelines for deciding whether an action is done purposely or knowingly (Section 2.02): (a) A person acts purposely with respect to a material element of an offense when: (i) if the element involves the nature of his conduct or a result thereof, it is his conscious object to engage in conduct of that nature or to cause such a result; and (ii) if the element involves the attendant circumstances, he is aware of the existence of such circumstances or he believes or hopes that they exist. (b) A person acts knowingly with respect to a material element of an offense when: (i) if the element involves the nature of his conduct or the attendant circumstances, he is aware that his conduct is of that nature or that such circumstances exist; and (ii) if the element involves a result of his conduct, he is aware that it is practically certain that his conduct will cause such a result. In cases involving the types of serious crimes we have been discussing, the requisite *mens rea* is usually either purposely or knowingly. For a more thorough discussion of *mens rea*, see Duff (1990), Hart (1968), and Kenny (1968).

6. For a complete version of Model Jury Instructions on Homicide go to: www.sociallaw.com.

7. That such biasing occurs has been shown in other psychological experiments as well. For example, Fischoff's research on 'hindsight bias' suggests that the actual outcome of an action may alter an observer's judgment concerning how foreseeable the risks were to the agent before the action was performed (Fischoff 1975). As a result of hindsight bias, events that have *already occurred*—which is the case in *all criminal trials*—are judged to have been more likely to occur than they would have been judged *before their occurrence*. In these studies, two groups of subjects were given the very same set of antecedent conditions leading up to an accident—the only difference being that some subjects were told that the accident in question had already taken place, whereas others were not. Interestingly, the subjects who were told that the accident actually occurred were much more likely to say that the agent could have foreseen the accident than those who were not told the accident occurred, even though all of the antecedent conditions were the same in both groups. These studies also suggested that in addition to causing observers to overestimate the degree to which decision makers foresaw the accidents before the accidents occurred, hindsight bias may cause observers to distort the level of uncertainty facing the decision maker. And in cases where juries are asked to determine whether the consequences of a defendant's actions were either foreseeable, foreseen, or intentionally brought about, the potential for hindsight bias is particularly problematic.

8. The conviction was later overturned due to the way the judge had defined 'maliciously' when giving the jury their instructions.

9. And while the possibility that jurors' verdicts are consistently being affected by blame-validation biasing is problematic in and of itself, it becomes even more troublesome when jurors are further affected by other arbitrary factors such as the race of the defendant or the victims. As Alicke says, "Racially prejudiced observers...who respond more negatively to a minority group member's harmful actions, require less evidence of intention, negligence, foresight, or causal influence than unbiased observers" (Alicke 2000, 566). In addition to race, psychologists have also shown that other factors can produce these kinds of negative spontaneous reactions as well, such as the appearance, personality, and demographics of the observers, perpetrators, or victims. Of course, the idea that the race, appearance, or character of the defendant might prejudice the jury is neither novel nor surprising, but when considered in light of the other factors I have already examined that may bias jurors' ascriptions of intentional action and blame, it certainly deepens the fear that getting a fair trial by jury is neither as common nor as easy as we had previously hoped.

10. It is worth highlighting the fact that before the problem of juror partiality I have been discussing could arise in a criminal proceeding, the jurors would have already decided that the defendant is responsible for committing the prohibited act in question. So, for instance, in the Smith case no one questioned the fact that his actions ultimately led to the officer's death. The issue was whether he was guilty of homicide or some lesser offense such as manslaughter—an issue that can only be resolved by making judgments about Smith's mental states.

REFERENCES

Alicke, M. D. 1992. Culpable causation. *Journal of Personality and Social Psychology* 63: 368–78.

———. 2000. Culpable control and the psychology of blame. *Psychological Bulletin* 126: 556–74.

Alicke, M. D., and T. L. Davis. 1989. The role of a posteriori victim information in judgments of blame and sanction. *Journal of Experimental Social Psychology* 25: 362–77.

Alicke, M. D., T. L. Davis, and M. V. Pezzo. 1994. *A posteriori* adjustment of *a priori* decision criteria. *Social Cognition* 8: 286–305.

Bargh, J. A. 1989. Conditional automaticity: Varieties of automatic influence in social perception and cognition. In *Unintended thought: Limits of awareness, intention, and control,* edited by J. S. Uleman and J. A. Bargh. New York: Guilford Press.

Billing, M. 1985. Prejudice, categorization, and particularization: From a perceptual to a rhetorical approach. *European Journal of Social Psychology* 15: 79–103.

Bratman, M. 1987. *Intention, plans, and practical reason.* Cambridge, Mass.: Harvard University Press.

Brewer, M. B. 1989. A dual process model of impression formation. In *Advances in social cognition,* edited by R. S. Wyer and T. K. Srull. Hillsdale, N.J.: Erlbaum.

Butler, R. 1978. Report on *Analysis* 'problem' no. 6. *Analysis* 38: 113–14.

Devine, P. G. 1989. Stereotypes and prejudice: Their automatic and controlled components. *Journal of Personality and Social Psychology* 56: 5–18.

Duff, R. A. 1982. Intention, responsibility, and double effect. *Philosophical Quarterly* 32 (126): 1–16.

———. 1990. *Intention, agency, and criminal liability.* Oxford: Basil Blackwell.

Erikson, K. A., and H. A. Simon. 1980. Verbal reports as data. *Psychological Review* 87: 215–51.

Fischoff, B. 1975. Hindsight does not equal foresight: The effect of outcome knowledge on judgment under uncertainty. *Journal of Experimental Psychology: Human Perception and Performance* 1: 288–99.

Greene, J., and J. Haidt. 2002. How (and where) does moral judgment work? *Trends in Cognitive Science* 6: 517–23.

Harman, G. 1997. Practical reasoning. In *The philosophy of action,* edited by A. Mele. Oxford: Oxford University Press. First published in 1976 in *Review of Metaphysics* 79: 431–63.

Hart, H. L. A. 1968. *Punishment and responsibility.* Oxford: Oxford University Press.

Jacoby, L., S. D. Lindsay, and J. P. Toth. 1992. Unconscious influences revealed: Attention, awareness, and control. *American Psychologist* 47: 802–9.

Katz, L. 1987. *Bad acts and guilty minds.* Chicago: University of Chicago Press.

Kenny, A. 1968. Intention and purpose in law. In *Essays in legal philosophy,* edited by R. Summers. Oxford: Basil Blackwell.

Knobe, J. 2003a. Intentional action and side effects in ordinary language. *Analysis* 63: 190–94.

———. 2003b. Intentional action in folk psychology: An experimental investigation. *Philosophical Psychology* 16 (2): 309–24.

———. 2004. Intention, intentional action, and moral considerations. *Analysis* 64: 181–87.

Knobe, J., and A. Burra. 2006. What is the relation between intention and intentional action? *Journal of Cognition and Culture.*

Lacey, N. 1993. A clear concept of intention: Elusive or illusory? *Modern Law Review* 56: 621–42.

Logan, G. D. 1989. Automaticity and cognitive control. In *Unintended thought: Limits of awareness, intention, and control,* edited by J. S. Uleman and J. A. Bargh. New York: Guilford Press.

Malle, B., and J. Knobe. 1997. The folk concept of intentional action. *Journal of Experimental Social Psychology* 33: 101–21.

Malle, B., and S. Nelson. 2003. Judging *mens rea*: The tension between folk concepts and legal concepts of intentionality. *Behavioral Sciences and the Law* 21: 563–80.

Mele, A., and S. Sverdlik. 1996. Intention, intentional action, and moral responsibility. *Philosophical Studies* 82: 265–87.

Nadelhoffer, T. 2004a. The Butler problem revisited. *Analysis* 64: 277–84.

———. 2004b. Praise, side effects, and intentional action. *Journal of Theoretical and Philosophical Psychology* 24: 196–213.

———. 2004c. Blame, badness, and intentional action: A reply to Knobe and Mendlow. *Journal of Theoretical and Philosophical Psychology* 24: 259–69.

———. 2005. Skill, luck, and intentional action. *Philosophical Psychology* 18: 343–54.

Nichols, S., and J. Knobe. 2007. Moral responsibility and determinism: The cognitive science of folk intuitions. *Noûs.*

Nisbett, R. E., and T. D. Wilson. 1977. Telling more than we can know: Verbal reports on mental processes. *Psychological Review* 84: 231–59.

Posner, M., and M. K. Rothbart. 1989. Intentional chapters on unintentional thoughts. In *Unintended thought: Limits of awareness, intention, and control,* edited by J. S. Uleman and J. A. Bargh. New York: Guilford Press.

Sue, S., R. E. Smith, and C. Caldwell. 1973. Effects of inadmissible evidence on the decisions of simulated jurors: A moral dilemma. *Journal of Applied Social Psychology* 3: 345–53.

Thompson, W. C., G. T. Fong, and D. Rosenhan. 1981. Inadmissible evidence and juror verdicts. *Journal of Personality and Social Psychology* 40: 453–63.

Wegner, D. M. 1989. *White bears and other unwanted thoughts.* New York: Viking Press.

———. 1992. You can't always think what you want: Problems in the suppression of unwanted thoughts. In *Advances in experimental social psychology.* Vol. 25, edited by M. P. Zanna. San Diego, Calif.: Academic Press.

———. 1994. Ironic processes of mental control. *Psychological Review* 101: 34–52.

Wegner, D. M., and J. W. Pennebaker, eds. 1993. *The handbook of mental control.* Englewood Cliffs, N.J.: Prentice Hall.

Wilson, T. D., and N. Brekke. 1994. Mental contamination and mental correction of unwanted influences on judgments and evaluations. *Psychological Bulletin* 116 (1): 117–42.

Wrightsman, L. S. 1991. *Psychology and the legal system.* Pacific Grove, Calif.: Brooks/Cole.

PART IV

THE FUTURE OF
EXPERIMENTAL PHILOSOPHY

This final section presents a series of essays, most of them published here for the first time, that offer further theoretical reflection on key issues in experimental philosophy. Some of the essays are concerned with metaphilosophical questions, others with specific philosophical issues that can be addressed using experimental methods. All of the essays mix philosophical reflection with in-depth discussions of particular empirical results.

Cushman and Mele return to the topic of intentional action, taking up an interesting new perspective on the issue. Instead of discussing the ways in which different cases lead to different intuitions, they focus on the ways in which different people can have different intuitions about the very same case. Their essay reports results from a new experiment that yields a variety of surprising new findings about these differences. For example, they demonstrate a consistent pattern such that people become progressively more likely to regard certain kinds of immoral behavior as unintentional as they consider more and more cases of a given type.

Prinz explores the complex conceptual geography of recent work on the intersection of philosophy and psychology. He begins by drawing a distinction between *experimental philosophy* and *empirical philosophy*. Both of these subfields of philosophy can then be distinguished, in turn, from the discipline of experimental psychology. Although experimental philosophy and experimental psychology share a common methodology, Prinz argues that these two intellectual enterprises actually seek quite different ends. Specifically, work in experimental philosophy tends to be focused on people's intuitions regarding some particular subject matter—free will, causation, or whatever—whereas work in experimental psychology usually looks for more general processing mechanisms that people use in thinking about a broad variety of different subject matters.

Sinnott-Armstrong suggests that there is a pervasive asymmetry between the sorts of intuitions people display in *concrete* contexts and those they display in *abstract* contexts. Marshalling a broad array of different sorts of empirical data, he argues that this asymmetry can be found in people's intuitions about epistemology, moral responsibility, and many other fields of philosophical inquiry. He then explores the difficult question as to how we ought to proceed when we find our intuitions conflicting in this way.

Sosa begins by distinguishing between truly substantive disagreement and merely verbal disagreement. He then argues that much of the 'disagreement' uncovered by experimental philosophers is not really substantive at all. Instead, he suggests, the findings might simply be an artifact of people's tendency to use the same words in rather different ways. Hence, some of the more surprising results from recent experimental philosophy might merely be reflecting ambiguities in particular English words—'intentional,' 'responsible,' etc.—rather than genuine disagreements in philosophical intuition.

9

Intentional Action

Two-and-a-Half Folk Concepts?

Fiery Cushman & Alfred Mele

What are the criteria people use when they judge that other people did something *intentionally?* This question has motivated a large and growing literature both in philosophy and in psychology. It has become a topic of particular concern to the nascent field of experimental philosophy, which uses empirical techniques to understand folk concepts. We present new data that hint at some of the underlying psychological complexities of folk ascriptions of intentional action and at distinctions both between diverse concepts and between associated mechanisms.

In section 1, we provide some background, introduce a new study of ours (study 1), and discuss some rules that lay folk may employ in making judgments about whether or not actions are intentional. On the basis of some new data and some studies of moral judgment, we suggest that there may be two folk concepts of intentional action. In most work in this area, it is assumed that majority judgments about what is or is not done intentionally in vignettes provide evidence about *the* folk concept of intentional action. But what about minority judgments? Do folk minorities display interesting patterns of judgment across a wide array of cases? Our study 1 was designed to generate evidence about this.

In section 2, we consider the hypothesis that there may be distinct folk concepts of *intention* and that these concepts may be associated with differences in judgments about whether "side-effect actions" are intentional. We discuss a study by Hugh McCann (2005) that was designed to provide evidence about whether folk judgments about vignettes accord with the "Simple View" of intentional action—the thesis that agents perform an action *A* intentionally only if they have an intention to *A*. We also discuss a new study of ours (study 2) that was motivated by the worry that it is not clear to some subjects that what experimenters regard as side effects in certain stories are, in fact, side effects. We show that modifying a certain well-known story so as to make it clear that harm is produced as a side effect has a significant effect.

In section 3, we explore necessary background conditions for intentional action. We discuss some pertinent results of our study 1 and a study by Thomas Nadelhoffer (2004). The vignettes at issue here feature either seriously deviant causal connections between agents' desires to do something and their doing it or "lucky" connections between these two things (for example, someone who wants to throw an eleven with a single toss of a pair of dice in order to win a game may luckily succeed in throwing an eleven and winning the game.)

In section 4, our final section, we formulate a trio of hypotheses that call for further testing. We also raise a pair of associated questions for investigation.

1. BACKGROUND AND DATA

In a well-known study, Joshua Knobe (2003) compares reactions to two business chairmen. One knowingly *harms* the environment by starting a profit-making venture and does not "care at all" about harming it; the other knowingly *helps* the environment by starting a profit-making venture and does not "care at all" about helping it. A substantial majority of people asked about the first chairman say that he *does* intentionally harm the environment, and a substantial majority asked about the second chairman say that he *does not* intentionally help the environment.

A body of work in philosophy and psychology has been targeted at the question why people make asymmetrical judgments about intentionality in cases such as these. However, we will begin by focusing on a different puzzle in the data: Why do some people deem *both* the harming and the helping intentional while others deem *neither* intentional? In doing so, we follow Shaun Nichols and Joseph Ulatowski (2007), who report some interesting findings about folk responses to Knobe's "chairman" vignettes. They get very similar results to Knobe. But unlike Knobe, they ask respondents why they answered as they did; and in another study all respondents are asked about both chairmen. Nichols and Ulatowski found that people who give the majority response in the "harm" scenario typically explain their answers by appealing to the chairman's *belief* that he would harm the environment, and those giving the majority response in the "help" scenario typically appealed to the chairman's lacking an *intention* or *motive* to help the environment. When they ask other people about both scenarios, an interesting pattern emerges. Of the 44 respondents, 16 say that both the harming and the helping are intentional (the *double intentional response*), 14 say that neither is intentional (the *double nonintentional response*), and 14 say that the harming but not the helping is intentional (the *asymmetrical response*). Notably, no subjects give the mirror-image asymmetrical response, saying that helping but not harming is intentional. This pattern of results leads Nichols and Ulatowski to suggest that there are two distinct folk concepts of intentional action, one featuring belief and the other desire, and that something about the moral assessment of good and bad outcomes biases responses systematically toward one concept or the other.

We will have much to say about the evidence for multiple folk concepts of intentional action. For the moment, we wish simply to sketch the appropriate logical space in which to test Nichols and Ulatowski's theory. Focusing our attention on the particular roles of belief and desire as conditions for the ascription of intentional action, there are four possible cases: belief present, desire present (B+D+); belief present, desire absent (B+D−); belief absent, desire present (B−D+); and belief absent, desire absent (B−D−). By "belief" we mean agents' *justified* beliefs that *they will perform those actions* when they are *very confident* that this is so. By "desire" we mean agents' desires *to perform those actions* (either as ends or as means to ends).

According to definitions of intentional action that make both belief and desire necessary conditions for intentional action, the only case of intentional action is B+D+ (reviewed in Malle & Knobe 1997). Given such a definition, neither the chairman's helping the environment nor his harming it is an intentional action. Based on their study of the CEO cases, Nichols and Ulatowski propose two concepts of intentional action—one centered on the concept of belief and the other centered on the concept of desire. More specifically, as we interpret Nichols and Ulatowski, they propose that one concept treats belief as both necessary and sufficient for intentional action and admits both B+D+ and B+D− as cases of intentional action while the other concept treats desire as both necessary and sufficient and admits both B+D+ and B−D+.[1] Nichols and Ulatowski's two folk concepts do not generate contrasting predictions for B+D+, or for B−D−, nor do their cases distinguish belief- or desire-based concepts from concepts requiring both belief and desire. The cases that are diagnostic, therefore, are B+D− and B−D+.

A limitation of Nichols and Ulatowski's study is that by focusing strictly on the CEO cases, which are of type B+D−, they restrict their analysis to only one of the two logical pairs that are diagnostic of the belief- and desire-based concepts of intentional action. The fact that certain people judge both CEOs to have intentionally performed the actions asked about (call these people "type YY," indicating a pair of "yes" responses to the questions) whereas other people judge both CEOs to have unintentionally performed those actions ("type NN," indicating a pair of no answers) is evidence that people hold differing views about the sufficiency of belief for intentional action and the necessity of desire. But Nichols and Ulatowski suppose that these groups also hold differing views about the necessity of belief and the sufficiency of desire—and therefore that group YY should deem cases of type B−D+ unintentional while group NN deems such cases intentional. This supposition is derived from the explicit justifications offered by subjects, which generally appealed *either* to belief *or* to desire. An alternative possibility is that the two groups agree about cases of type B−D+. To decide between these possibilities, it is necessary to test cases of that type.

Study 1 was designed to provide precisely that test. One hundred fifty subjects were presented with both CEO cases, along with six additional cases of type B+D− and six cases of type B−D+ (two additional scenarios were presented;

they will be discussed below).[2] The order in which the scenarios were presented was counterbalanced between subjects. The full text of all sixteen scenarios is printed in our Appendix. Respondents answered questions of the form "Did S intentionally A?" on a seven-point scale for all sixteen vignettes: 1 was a strong "no" and 7 a strong "yes."

Of the 150 respondents, some (the NN respondents) gave answers in the 1 to 3 range to both "chairman" questions, some (the YY respondents) gave answers in the 5 to 7 range to both questions, and some (the YN respondents) gave answers in the 1 to 3 range in the "help" scenario and in the 5 to 7 range in the "harm" scenario. We discuss the relative sizes of these three groups later.

According to the view that there are two folk concepts of intentional action, one that treats belief as a necessary and sufficient condition and another that treats desire as a necessary and sufficient condition, subjects in group YY should judge cases of type B+D− as more intentional than cases of type B−D+, while subjects in group NN should exhibit exactly the reverse pattern, judging cases of type B+D− as less intentional than cases of type B−D+. This was not the observed pattern of results, however (see chart 9.1).

An analysis of variance revealed that intentionality ratings were determined by a significant interaction between case type (B+D− vs B−D+) and subject type (YY vs NN) ($F(1,10) = 30.17$, $p < .001$).[3] But while groups YY and NN differed

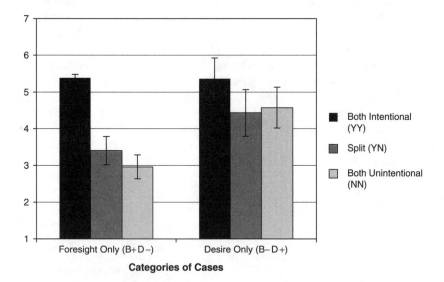

Chart 9.1. Mean intentionality rating for cases of type B+D− and B−D+, comparing across subjects of type YY, YN, and NN. The means and standard errors are calculated using cases as the unit of measurement, rather than using individual responses as the unit of analysis, in order to ensure that the observed effects generalize across diverse cases.

substantially in their judgments of intentionality in cases of type B+D− (which mirror the CEO cases), these groups were in much closer agreement regarding cases of type B−D+. Moreover, far from group YY rating cases of type B−D+ as less intentional than group NN, as would be predicted by Nichols and Ulatowski's model, there was in fact a significant effect in the opposite direction ($t(5) = 7.06, p < .01$).

These results suggest that the primary factor that distinguishes group YY from NN is whether belief is considered to be a sufficient condition for intentional action (or whether desire is considered a necessary condition). By contrast, there is not strong evidence that the groups differ substantially in their treatment of desire as a sufficient condition for intentional action. As we will explain, our data are consistent with the following propositions:

1. Groups NN and YY assess vignettes as though they employ rule *D*: An action is intentional if it is performed with desire, given the necessary background conditions (which do not include belief).
2. Group YY assesses vignettes as though it *also* employs rule *B*: An action is intentional if it is performed with belief. (That is, this group assesses vignettes as though it uses rule *D* + *B*.)

We turn now to the subjects who made asymmetrical judgments about the chairmen—that is, to the YN group, nearly two-thirds of the subjects in the present sample. One may attempt to account for the effect of moral judgment on the YN group's attribution of intentional actions in at least two ways:

3. Group YN assesses vignettes similarly to group NN but with a new rule, *MB*: Belief is a sufficient condition for intentional action in and only in cases of *morally bad* actions. (Thus, individuals who ordinarily deem B+D− cases unintentional switch and treat them as intentional when the pertinent action is morally bad.)
4. Group YN assesses vignettes similarly to group YY but with a new rule, *MG*: Desire is a necessary condition for intentional action in cases in which the action is characterized in terms of a *morally good* outcome. (Thus, individuals who ordinarily deem B+D− cases intentional switch and treat the pertinent actions as unintentional when those actions are characterized in terms of morally good outcomes.)[4]

Notice that rule *MB* would only affect the judgments of subjects who do not regularly employ rule *B*: For subjects who regularly employ rule *B*, belief is a sufficient condition for intentional action in all cases, not just in cases of morally bad action. Likewise, rule *MG* would only affect the judgments of subjects who sometimes employ a rule like *B*: For subjects who never employ a rule like *B*, belief is never a sufficient condition for intentional action and desire is always a necessary condition (whether or not the action is characterized in terms of a morally good outcome).

As can be seen in chart 9.1, groups YN and NN gave virtually identical mean ratings of intentionality, while both groups differed substantially from group YY on cases of type B+D−. This suggests that subjects in group YN generally view belief to be insufficient for the ascription of intentional action but make a specific exception for cases of morally bad actions—that is, it suggests that (in addition to rule *D*) they use rule *MB*.

Further evidence that the effect of moral judgment is attributable to a rule like *MB* as opposed to *MG* comes from an analysis of the minority responses to each case as a function of the order of presentation of test items. Subjects were presented with a total of sixteen scenarios to judge, counterbalanced for order. Roughly half of the subjects responded to the CEO harm case within the first four scenarios, while the remainder responded to that case within the final five scenarios. Strikingly, subjects were five times as likely to judge that the CEO did not intentionally harm the environment when responding toward the end of the test, compared to subjects who responded to CEO harm toward the beginning. Specifically, 27% of subjects who saw CEO harm toward the end made the minority judgment that the CEO did not intentionally harm the environment, while only 5% of subjects who saw CEO harm toward the begin-ning made that judgment. Chi-square analysis revealed this pattern of results to differ significantly from chance (Pearson $\chi^2 = 12.53$, N = 142, p < .001). Recall that the subjects who judged that the chairman did not intentionally harm the environment (group NN) showed a virtually identical profile of judgment on our nonmoral cases to those who made split judgments about CEO help and harm (group YN). Taken together, these data suggest that subjects who might otherwise have deemed CEO harm intentional on the basis of rule *MB* were influenced not to rely on rule *MB* when judging CEO harm by the experience of repeatedly treating belief as insufficient for intentional action. That is, hav-ing repeatedly treated belief as insufficient for intentional action in nonmoral cases, subjects were unwilling to judge that the chairman intentionally harmed the environment.

By contrast, the proportion of subjects who judged that the CEO inten-tionally *helped* the environment was nearly identical for those who saw CEO help toward the beginning of the test (16%) and toward the end of the test (19%), and chi-square analysis revealed no significant difference between these groups (Pearson $\chi^2 = 0.12$, N = 142, p = .73). Recall that subjects who judged that the chairman intentionally helped the environment (group YY) produced a markedly different pattern of judgments than subjects who gave asymmetri-cal responses to the help and harm cases (group YN). Specifically, group YY frequently judged nonmoral cases to be intentional when belief was present without desire, and group YN did not. These data suggest that individuals who judge the CEO help case to be intentional do so not because of the moral good-ness of the environment's being helped, but rather because of a unique concept of intentional action consonant with rule *B*.

A brief summary of the preceding discussion is in order. We have suggested that a large majority considers belief to be sufficient specifically for
a *morally bad* action's being intentional (rule *MB*) while only a minority
considers belief to be sufficient for intentional action without regard to the
moral status of the action (rule *B*). Based on this combination of factors,
we would expect a majority of subjects to judge CEO harm intentional, a
majority to judge CEO help unintentional, and only a minority to judge both
CEO cases intentional. Furthermore, as we see it, the experience of treating
belief as insufficient for intentional action in a range of relevant stories leads
some subjects to reject the influence of moral badness and abandon rule *MB*
(and a few subjects deem the chairman's harming the environment unintentional even though they see the story early). Therefore, an additional minority judges both CEO cases unintentional. In this way, we can account for all
three groups of subjects: YY, YN, and NN. Also, our study of nonmoral cases
of type B−D+ leads us to conclude that all subjects consider desire to be sufficient for intentional action given necessary background conditions that do
not include belief (rule *D*).

The tendency of some subjects to reject rule *MB* in favor of uniformly treating belief as insufficient for intentional action is noteworthy. A neighboring
field of research may shed light on this tendency. Studies of moral judgment
have demonstrated the influence of competing systems, one characterized by
conscious reasoning and the other by intuition (Greene et al. 2001; Pizarro
& Bloom 2003; Greene et al. 2004; Cushman et al. 2006; Koenigs et al. 2007).
The evidence suggests that people sometimes override or reject their intuitive
responses when they fail to align with their consciously held views, especially
when the contradiction is made apparent (Pizarro & Bloom 2003; Cushman
et al. 2006). Analogously, it may be that some implicit mechanism is responsible
for the effect of moral judgment on the attribution of intentional action (leading to patterns of judgment consonant with *MB*), but that the explicit rules for
assigning intentionality do not include moral judgment and rely instead on
factors such as belief and desire. An important direction for future research is
to query subjects on their explicit principles for decisions about whether or not
actions are intentional and to compare these explicit principles to the actual
pattern of judgments produced.

The responses of groups NN, YY, and YN may seem to be the product of
three distinct concepts of intentional action—roughly, *one that makes desire a
necessary condition for intentional action, one that makes belief a sufficient condition for intentional action,* and *one that includes rule MB*. However, it may be
that, in fact, there are just two concepts of intentional action at work and rule
MB captures a qualitatively different implicit effect of moral judgment. Now,
one of us is less confident than the other about the nature of concepts and
more willing not to stop at two folk concepts of intentional action and to go all
the way to three (the third being a concept of intentional action that includes
MB). Splitting the difference, we get two-and-a-half folk concepts. Hence, this
article's subtitle.

2. INTENTIONS, INTENTIONAL ACTIONS, AND SIDE EFFECTS

Some readers may be inclined to think that what really separates the YY, NN, and YN groups is a difference of opinion about what the agents *intend* to do. The thought about the "chairman" scenarios in particular is that the YY group understands "intention" in such a way that the two chairmen intend, respectively, to harm and to help the environment, the NN group understands "intention" in such a way that the chairmen lack these intentions, and the YN group understands "intention" in such a way that the chairman who harms the environment intends to harm it whereas the chairman who helps it does not intend to help it. (It might even be said that the YY group has a "foresight"-centered concept of *intention*, whereas the NN group has a "desire"-centered concept of it.)

There is evidence that different concepts of intention are not doing all this work. Hugh McCann (2005) reports the results of two relevant studies. In the first, about one-fourth of the 106 respondents answered the first question below, another such group answered the second, and the remaining respondents answered both questions (counterbalanced):

Did the chairman harm the environment intentionally?
Was it the chairman's intention to harm the environment?

The results appear in table 9.1. "The design of the second experiment was the same as the first, except that the second question asked what the chair had intended, not what had been his intention" (McCann 2005, p. 741). There were 99 respondents. See table 9.2 for the results.

Obviously, in both experiments, of the people who answered both questions, the majority of those who said that the chairman intentionally harmed the environment did not give the matching answer about his intention or what he intended. Although the differences in the NN, YY, and YN groups' answers to the "intentionally" questions about the chairman may be explained partly by differences in how they understand such words as "intention" and "intend," it is safe to conclude that these differences do not provide the whole explanation.

Table 9.1

	One question	Two questions
"Intentionally"	63%	80%
"Intention"	27%	12%

Table 9.2

	One question	Two questions
"Intentionally"	64%	75%
"Intend"	42%	31%

A technical term—*side-effect actions*—will prove useful here. We set the stage for our definition of it by observing that actions have effects, and an agent's *bringing about* such an effect is an action. For example, unbeknownst to Don, his turning on a light when he entered his house frightened an intruder. That is, at least one effect of his turning on the light was the intruder's fright. His bringing about this effect—something describable as "Don's frightening the intruder"—is an action. "Side-effect actions," as we understand this expression, are defined in terms of the effects of actions that the agent seeks to perform and succeeds in performing. The following will do as a definition: *X* is a side-effect action performed by an agent *S* if and only if *S* successfully seeks to perform an action *A*, *E* is an effect of his so doing, *X* is his bringing about *E*, and *X* has the following properties: *S* is not at the relevant time seeking to *X* either as an end or as a means to an end, and *X* is not in fact a means to an end that *S* is seeking at the relevant time. (Some things we do are means to ends we are seeking at the time even if we do not conceive of them as such then. For example, Ed, who has no concept of calories, is running in order to lose weight. Because his bringing it about that he burns more calories than usual is a means to his losing weight, we do not count it as a side-effect action—even though Ed has no idea that his bringing this about is a means to his end. Hence, the final clause in our definition of *side-effect action*.) Given this definition, Don's frightening the intruder is a side-effect action. Don successfully seeks to turn on the light, the intruder's fright is an effect of his so doing, his frightening the intruder is his bringing about that effect, and his frightening the intruder is neither something that he was seeking to do at the time (either as an end or as a means to an end) nor a means to an end that he was seeking in acting.

Some side-effect actions are *anticipated* by the agent, as in Knobe's "chairman" stories, on a natural reading of them. In Knobe's story, on our reading of it, the chairman's harming the environment is a side-effect action. Now, as we mentioned, some of McCann's respondents say that it was the chairman's intention to harm the environment or that the chairman intended to harm the environment. Some of them may impute to the chairman motives that are not attributed to him in the story. And some may understand "intend" in such a way that what we count as side-effect actions can be intended.

Here is Knobe's "harm" story:

> The vice-president of a company went to the chairman of the board and said, "We are thinking of starting a new program. It will help us increase profits, but it will also harm the environment." The chairman ... answered, "I don't care at all about harming the environment. I just want to make as much profit as I can. Let's start the new program." They started the new program. Sure enough, the environment was harmed. (2003, p. 191)

As we read the story, the chairman's harming the environment is a side-effect action. But we can see how someone may read it differently. As we read it, the chairman is told that starting the program will have two effects that are *independent* of one another: increased profits and a harmed environment. But

Table 9.3

	Harm mean	Help Mean
Harm alone (N = 55)	4.51	—
Harm first (N = 48)	4.14	2.48
Help first (N = 54)	3.59	2.20

someone might suppose that the program will harm the environment before profits are increased, that the harm is part of the causal process that results in increased profits, that the chairman knows this, and, accordingly, that he seeks to harm the environment as a means to increasing profits. (Example: The new program is to cut down a beautiful forest and build a large airport; profits are made long after the forest is destroyed.)

Testing a less ambiguous version of the story seems advisable. In the following version, it is clear that the harm is a side-effect:

> NEW CHAIRMAN (HARM). The vice-president of a company went to the chairman of the board and said, "We are thinking of starting a new program. It will help us increase profits for this year's balance sheet, but in ten years it will start to harm the environment." The chairman answered, "I don't care at all about harming the environment. I just want to make as much profit for this year's balance sheet as I can. Let's start the new program." They started the new program. Sure enough, ten years later, the environment started to be harmed.
>
> Did the chairman intentionally harm the environment?

In Study 2, we tested this story under three different conditions. Some respondents were presented with this story alone, others with this story and then a parallel "help" story, and a third group with the parallel "help" story and then our "harm" story. Respondents to a pair of stories were instructed to circle their answer (1 to 7) to the question about the first story, to turn the sheet over and answer the question about the second story, and not to revise their first answer. All respondents were undergraduates at Florida State University who had not taken any philosophy courses. The results are shown in table 9.3.

3. OTHER NECESSARY CONDITIONS?

When we stated rule *D* in section 1, we alluded to necessary background conditions. We turn now to these conditions. In section 2, we defined *side-effect actions*. What we call *seek-type actions*—actions that an agent seeks to perform and succeeds in performing—are very different. We found remarkable agreement among the NN, YY, and YN groups regarding actions of this kind. Their responses are consistent with the hypothesis that although they treat desire as a necessary condition for intentional seek-type action, they do not treat it as a sufficient condition for this. This was predictable in light of the philosophical literature on causal deviance and lucky success (see Mele 1992).

Study 1 included two stories featuring causal deviance, BEE (based on Mele 1987) and WEEDS:

> BEE. Mark wants to provide the right answer to a multiple choice question. He thinks that the right answer is "bee," which is option "c." But he is rushing, and he circles the letter "b" instead of the letter "c" next to the word "bee." As it happens, "bee" was not the right answer, but "b" ("ant") was. Luckily for Mark, the answer he circled was correct.
>
> Did Mark intentionally provide the right answer?

> WEEDS. Jen sees some bothersome weeds growing next to her driveway and wants to eliminate them. She decides to go to the hardware store to buy weed spray. As she pulls out of her garage, the wheel slips in her hand and she drives off to the side of the driveway. All the weeds are crushed and killed under the car. With the weeds eliminated, Jen doesn't need to go to the hardware store.
>
> Did Jen intentionally eliminate the weeds?

Our results are shown in table 9.4.

All three groups count both of the featured actions as not intentional—perhaps because of the extreme causal deviance. Morally valenced counterparts of these stories might generate significant disagreement, an issue that definitely merits study. In any case, one candidate for a necessary background condition in rule D is the absence of relevant extreme causal deviance.

We turn to lucky success. One of the seek-type stories in study 1 is about a person who wanted to win a dice game, knew that he would do so if and only if he rolled an eleven on his next toss of a pair of dice, and rolled an eleven. The results for the question whether he intentionally rolled an eleven were NN = 2.41, YY = 3.08, YN = 2.21. Another candidate for a necessary background condition in rule D is that the agent's success is not largely a matter of luck.

Table 9.4

	NN (22)	YY (25)	YN (95)
Bee	1.27	1.60	1.27
Weeds	2.36	1.84	1.46

Naturally, one wants to ask what counts as "largely" here. Thomas Nadelhoffer (2004, p. 281) tested the following morally loaded story about a die toss (based on Mele and Sverdlik 1996, p. 279):

> Brown wants to kill Smith now. Smith is in another building.
> There is a bomb in that building and Brown can detonate it only
> by producing a six-dotted image on the lens of a camera that is
> focused on the top of a table in Brown's room and wired to the
> bomb. So, Brown takes out a normal, fair, six-sided die and tosses
> it onto the table, hoping that it will land six-up. By throwing a six,
> Brown detonates the bomb, thereby killing Smith.

Of his 40 respondents, 87.5% answered "yes" to the question "Did Brown intentionally kill Smith?"; and 55% of another group of 40 respondents answered "yes" to the question "Did Brown intentionally roll a six?"

The results for the following morally neutral version of the story were different:

> Brown is playing a simple game of dice. The game requires that
> Brown roll a six to win. So, hoping to get a six, Brown throws a die
> onto the table. Unluckily for the other players, the die lands six-up
> and Brown wins the game. (Nadelhoffer 2004, p. 279)

Sixty-two percent of Nadelhoffer's 40 respondents answered "yes" to the question "Did Brown intentionally win the game?"; and 10% of another group of 40 respondents answered "yes" to the question "Did Brown intentionally roll a six?"

Including some stories falling into what we think of as the "killing die" genre in a battery of stories that yields NN, YY, and YN groups may turn up differences among these groups regarding the bearing of moral considerations on "intentionally" judgments about lucky seek-type actions. We hope that such an effect will be investigated in future research.

4. CONCLUSION

As things stand now, we believe that the hypotheses below merit further testing. They are framed in terms of propositions that we repeat for the reader's convenience:

> Rule B. An action is intentional if it is performed with belief.
> (Recall that by "belief" here we mean agents' justified beliefs
> that they will perform the action when they are very confident
> that this is so.)
> Rule D. An action is intentional if it is performed with desire,
> given the necessary background conditions (which do not include
> belief). (Recall that by "desire" here we mean agents' desires
> to perform the action, either as a means or as an end.)

Rule *MB*. Belief is a sufficient condition for intentional action in and only in cases of morally bad actions.

Here are the hypotheses:

1. Everybody uses rule *D* (though people may diverge on how much deviance or luck is too much).
2. Only about 20% of people use rule *B*.
3. Many people use rule *MB*, but perhaps in some qualitatively different way than rules *D* and *B* that is less likely to be explicitly endorsed.

These hypotheses suggest at least two areas for future investigation. First, if there are two concepts of intentional action—one that features an augmented version of *D* that also makes desire a *necessary* condition for intentional action, and one that features a rule like *B*—what are their origins, and how can we account for the observed pattern of conceptual diversity? Perhaps there is a regular developmental sequence whereby individuals begin with one concept of intentional action and move toward another, or perhaps these concepts are stable across the lifetime but differ between individuals. Second, how are rules like *B* and *D* (or an augmented version of *D*) applied differently from rule *MB* such that (as in Nichols and Ulatowski's study) the former appear to be explicitly endorsed as criteria for the assignment of intentionality whereas the latter often is not? We have suggested that this has something to do with a division between explicit and implicit systems of judgment, but this hypothesis requires further mechanistic detail as well as further experimental validation. Also relevant is the conceptual question whether explicit systems of judgment are linked to *concepts* in ways that implicit systems of judgment are not.

As new stories are added to our mix, we may find that the "rules" in terms of which our hypotheses are formulated should be refined. However, we predict that the general idea that there are significantly different conceptions of intentional action in our respondents and that they diverge in roughly the ways identified (perhaps among other ways) will be sustained. Some people may prefer the word "concept" to our "conceptions." But, to quote Knobe's chairmen, we "don't care at all about" which of the two words is chosen.[5]

APPENDIX: THE SIXTEEN VIGNETTES

MUSIC. Louis goes to the concert hall to hear two of his favorite pieces, one by Beethoven and one by Mozart. In between the Beethoven and the Mozart, however, the orchestra is performing a piece by Bartok that Louis really dislikes hearing. Louis knows that he won't be able to leave during the Bartok piece, but he buys tickets to the concert anyway just so he can hear the Beethoven and Mozart.

Did Louis intentionally listen to the piece by Bartok?

BARK. George is a mailman who hates barking dogs. There is an old house at the end of Bellows Lane where there is always a dog tied up out front. Whenever George takes the shortest route by the front of the house, the dog barks at him. Whenever George takes the longer route by the side of the house, the dog doesn't see him and doesn't bark. Today George's legs are tired and he wants to take the shortest route even though he will have to endure the barking. George walks up to the front of the house, and the dog barks.

Did George intentionally cause the dog to bark?

BIRDS. Stacey is very fond of cardinals—she thinks they are a particularly lovely bird. She goes to the garden center and gets a bird feeder that is designed to attract lots of cardinals. An employee at the garden center tells Stacey that the feeder is also sure to attract blue jays. "I don't care about the blue jays," says Stacey. "As long as it attracts cardinals, I am happy." Stacey sets up the feeder, and it attracts cardinals and blue jays.

Did Stacey intentionally attract blue jays to her back yard?

FATTY. Susan's friend works as a chef in a diner. Her friend is sick and asks Susan to take over for a few days. Susan is disgusted by all the grease and fatty foods in the diner. In fact, she is so disgusted that she decides to stop eating fatty foods. When she tells this to her nutritionist, he replies that the change in diet will be perfectly healthy, but will cause Susan to lose some weight. Susan replies that losing weight doesn't matter one way or the other to her. She just thinks fat and grease are disgusting. Susan stops eating fatty foods, and she loses some weight.

Did Susan intentionally lose some weight?

POOL. Tom is on a first date at a pool hall. He wants to impress his date by hitting a difficult shot, the red striped ball in the side pocket. He takes a close look and aligns the cue stick for the necessary shot. But Tom knows that he is not a very good pool player. His hand is shaking and he does not guide the cue stick properly. Nevertheless, the cue stick hits the ball just right and the shot is a success: The red striped ball goes in the side pocket. Tom's date is very impressed.

Did Tom intentionally hit the red striped ball into the side pocket?

RIFLE. Lydia desperately wants to win the rifle contest. She has taken one class on shooting, and the instructor told her again and again how she had a natural talent that was as good as any expert. Therefore, Lydia is just as confident that she will hit the bull's-eye as experts are about their own chances of hitting bull's-eyes. Of course, without any experience, she is not very good at using a rifle—her instructor was just trying to be nice. She raises the rifle, gets the bull's-eye in the sights, and pulls the trigger. Her hand slips on the barrel of the gun, and the shot goes wild. Nonetheless, the bullet hits the bull's-eye. Lydia wins the contest.

Did Lydia intentionally hit the bull's-eye?

BOWL. Earl is an excellent and powerful bowler. His friends tell him that the bowling pins on lane 12 are special 200-pound metal pins disguised to look like normal pins for the purposes of a certain practical joke. They also tell him that it is very unlikely that a bowled ball can knock over such pins. Apparently as an afterthought, they challenge Earl to knock over the pins on lane 12 with a bowled ball and offer him ten dollars for doing so. Earl believes that his chance of knocking over the pins on lane 12 is very slim, but he wants to knock them down very much. He rolls an old bowling ball as hard as he can at the pins, hoping that he will knock down at least one. To his great surprise, he knocks them all down! The joke, it turns out, was on Earl: The pins on lane 12 were normal wooden ones.

Did Earl intentionally knock down the pins?

STOCK. Laura is a Wall Street stock trader. She goes into a local deli for lunch and orders alphabet soup. As she lifts the spoon to her mouth, the noodles read "ABD UP." ABD is the stock symbol for the company Associated Blicket Detectors. Everybody knows that ABD is an overpriced and failing stock, but Laura believes that the noodles are a supernatural sign that she will make a huge profit on ABD. She puts all her available money into ABD, and the stock takes off. Laura makes a huge profit.

Did Laura intentionally make a huge profit?

POND. Al said to Ann: "You know, if you fill in that pond in the empty lot next to your house, you're going to make the kids who look for frogs there sad." Ann replied: "I know that I'll make those kids sad. I like those kids, and I'll definitely regret making them sad. But the pond is a breeding ground for mosquitoes; and because I own the lot, I am responsible for it. It must be filled in." Ann filled in the pond, and, sure enough, the kids were sad.

Did Ann intentionally make the kids sad?

COACH. Coach Don decided during midseason that his son Donnie should become a starting player on their high-school baseball team: Donnie had become one of the best players on the team. Don knows that Donnie's being a starting player would make both Donnie and himself happy. Like anyone, Don likes to be happy, and he likes his son to be happy. But Don takes his responsibility as a coach very seriously. He does not allow himself to consider personal happiness when making decisions about his ball team. Don starts Donnie in the next game, and they both feel happy.

Did Don intentionally make Donnie happy?

CEO HARM. The vice-president of a company went to the chairman of the board and said, "We are thinking of starting a new program. It will help us increase profits, and it will also harm the environment." The chairman of the board answered, "I don't care at all about harming the environment. I just want to make as much profit as I can. Let's start the new program." They started the new program. Sure enough, the environment was harmed.

Did the chairman intentionally harm the environment?

CEO HELP. The vice-president of a company went to the chairman of the board and said, "We are thinking of starting a new program. It will help us increase profits, and it will also help the environment." The chairman of the board answered, "I don't care at all about helping the environment. I just want to make as much profit as I can. Let's start the new program." They started the new program. Sure enough, the environment was helped.

Did the chairman intentionally help the environment?

BEE. Mark wants to provide the right answer to a multiple choice question. He thinks that the right answer is "bee," which is option "c." But he is rushing, and he circles the letter "b" instead of the letter "c" next to the word "bee." As it happens, "bee" was not the right answer, but "b" ("ant") was. Luckily for Mark, the answer he circled was correct.

Did Mark intentionally provide the right answer?

WEEDS. Jen sees some bothersome weeds growing next to her driveway and wants to eliminate them. She decides to go to the hardware store to buy weed spray. As she pulls out of her garage, the wheel slips in her hand and she drives off to the side of the driveway. All the weeds are crushed and killed under the car. With the weeds eliminated, Jen doesn't need to go to the hardware store.

Did Jen intentionally eliminate the weeds?

SNIPE. Harry is a nature photographer who has been trying to catch a snapshot of the rare blue-billed snipe for many years. Harry is also very superstitious. When he receives a piece of mail delivered to the wrong address, he takes it as a sign. The letter's return address is from a house on the outskirts of a remote town in the back country of North Carolina. Harry is sure that if he finds the house, he will find the blue-billed snipe. Of course, the probability of finding the snipe at the house is very small, since the snipe is so rare. Harry visits the town, walks out to the house, and sure enough he sees a snipe there. He takes the picture he has long been hoping for.

Did Harry intentionally find the snipe?

DICE. Milt wanted to win the dice game. He knew that only an 11 on his next toss of the dice would make him the winner, and he wants very much to roll an 11. The chances of rolling an 11 are one out of thirty-six. Milt rolls the dice, they come up 11, and he wins the game.

Did Milt intentionally roll an 11?[6]

NOTES

1. Obviously, when people are asked why they judge that the chairman intentionally harmed the environment, they should offer what they take to be a *sufficient* condition for intentional action; and when they are asked why they judge that he did not inten-

tionally help the environment, they should offer what they take to be an unsatisfied *necessary* condition. But Nichols and Ulatowski write as though both groups are doing more than that. For example, they write: "The data provide support for the view that there are two different interpretations of 'intentional action' available....In the CEO cases, we found that one minority seems to consistently interpret it as foreknowledge and another minority seems to interpret it as motive." This suggests neither sufficiency nor necessity alone, but both together.

2. Subjects logged in voluntarily to the Moral Sense Test Website, which has been used in previous studies of moral judgment (Cushman et al. 2006; Hauser et al. 2007). After filling out a brief demographic questionnaire, subjects judged the degree of intentional action for each of 16 vignettes. A sample version of the task is available at moral. wjh.harvard.edu/~methods. All tests were conducted in accordance with the policies of the Committee on the Use of Human Subjects at Harvard University.

3. The statistics for this section are all computed taking mean responses to individual cases as the unit of analysis, rather than individual responses. This is a more conservative statistical approach that ensures that the observed effects generalize across different types of scenarios and are not driven by any single item tested.

4. It is no part of our aim in these propositions to provide complete accounts of the rules each group may use. For example, group NN also assesses vignettes as though it employs a rule stating that desire is a necessary condition for intentional action, and we mention no such rule in our proposition about that group.

5. We are grateful to Adam Feltz and Jeremy Johnson for assistance with the administration of the FSU surveys and data management.

6. Readers will notice that we misstated the probability of rolling an eleven. (When we said "11," we meant to say "double ones," and our "one out of thirty-six" was for that.) We doubt that the misinformation had a significant effect.

REFERENCES

Cushman, F. A., Young, L., & Hauser, M. D. 2006. "The Role of Reasoning and Intuition in Moral Judgment: Testing Three Principles of Harm." *Psychological Science* 17: 1082–89.

Greene, J. D., Nystrom, L. E., Engell, A. D., Darley, J. M., & Cohen, J. D. 2004. "The Neural Bases of Cognitive Conflict and Control in Moral Judgment." *Neuron* 44: 389–400.

Greene, J. D., Sommerville, R. B., Nystrom, L. E., Darley, J. M., & Cohen, J. D. 2001. "An fMRI Investigation of Emotional Engagement in Moral Judgment." *Science* 293: 2105–8.

Hauser, M. D., Cushman, F. A., Young, L., Jin, R., & Mikhail, J. 2007. "A Dissociation between Moral Judgment and Justification." *Mind and Language* 22: 1–21.

Knobe, J. 2003. "Intentional Action and Side-Effects in Ordinary Language." *Analysis* 63: 190–94.

Koenigs, M., Young, L., Adolphs, R., Tranel, D., Cushman, F. A., Hauser, M. D., & Damasio, A. 2007. "Damage to the Prefrontal Cortex Increases Utilitarian Moral Judgments." *Nature* 446: 908–11.

Malle, B., & Knobe, J. 1997. "The Folk Concept of Intentionality." *Journal of Experimental Social Psychology* 33: 101–21.

McCann, H. 2005. "Intentional Action and Intending: Recent Empirical Studies." *Philosophical Psychology* 18: 737–48.

Mele, A. 1987. "Intentional Action and Wayward Causal Chains: The Problem of Tertiary Waywardness." *Philosophical Studies* 51: 55–60.

Mele, A. 1992. "Acting for Reasons and Acting Intentionally." *Pacific Philosophical Quarterly* 73: 355–74.

Mele, A., & Sverdlik, S. 1996. "Intention, Intentional Action, and Moral Responsibility." *Philosophical Studies* 82: 265–87.

Nadelhoffer, T. 2004. "The Butler Problem Revisited." *Analysis* 64: 277–84.

Nichols, S., & Ulatowski, J. 2007. "Intuitions and Individual Differences: The Knobe Effect Revisited." *Mind and Language.*

Pizarro, D. A., Uhlmann, E., & Bloom, P. 2003. "Causal Deviance and the Attribution of Moral Responsibility." *Journal of Experimental Social Psychology* 39: 653–60.

10

Empirical Philosophy and Experimental Philosophy

Jesse J. Prinz

There seems to be a methodological revolution taking place in philosophy. In some corners of the field, it's business as usual, but in others, philosophers have become resolutely impure: integrating lessons from various branches of psychology (cognitive, developmental, social, and cross-cultural), neuroscience (cognitive, molecular, and clinical), evolutionary theory, experimental economics, and other "scientific" fields. The trend has been especially widespread in philosophy of mind and moral philosophy, but methodological perturbations can be felt in other areas as well. To use a trite metaphor, philosophers have been rolling up their sleeves and getting their hands dirty. The latest development in this trend takes this slogan even more seriously. Rather than just reporting scientific findings, philosophers are contributing to science by designing and conducting experiments. As with any revolution, it can be a bit hard to make sense of what's happening while the battles are still taking place. In this chapter, I will attempt to describe and defend some of the methodological changes. I will distinguish two different approaches, which I will call experimental and empirical philosophy respectively. I will also argue that neither approach can function without some armchair methods, and neither collapses into psychology. The borders in this area are blurry, but even rough distinctions can help expose a methodological division of labor. Like many divisions of labor, the different methods I will discuss are best construed as components of a collective process rather than isolated intellectual fiefdoms.

1. WHAT USE PHILOSOPHY?

1.1. Philosophy as Observation

Philosophy is notoriously difficult to define. It is sometimes identified by its subject matter. For example, philosophy is said to address questions that are highly abstract, or general. But that definition is hard to sustain, because philosophical questions range from the abstract (what is existence?) to the highly specific (is infanticide permissible?). Sometimes philosophy is characterized not by its subject matter, but by the comparative intractability of the questions it addresses. Philosophical questions are said to be enduring in a way that questions in some other fields are not. But this also seems unpromising. Some philosophical questions might be answered with the right insight (is justified true belief sufficient for knowledge?), and some scientific questions are extremely difficult to resolve without being recognized as philosophical (how many dimensions are there in the universe?). There are certain kinds of questions that philosophy has traditionally not been interested in, such as practical questions that are neither normative or too specific to be revelatory about human nature (how can we cure tuberculosis? how can we build a semi-conductor?), as well as descriptive questions that can be resolved without clarifying any concepts (is magnesium heavier than gold?). Philosophy is not always directly concerned with conceptual clarification (are there innate ideas?), but philosophical theories typically turn at some point on conceptual issues that are difficult to resolve (what is innateness?).

I don't intend this as a definition. Professional philosophers have certainly written extensively about topics that are quite distant from thorny conceptual questions (Is Christianity a reaction against Roman oppression? Can we have an image of a triangle that is not isosceles, scalene, or equilateral?). But I do think that, in Western thought since Plato, conceptual issues have had a kind of centrality in philosophy, and we often identify a problem as philosophical in virtue of recognizing a link to such issues. I am content to say that a highly significant proportion of work that we call "philosophical" turns on conceptual clarification. It is no surprise, therefore, that one of the most dominant philosophical methods is conceptual analysis. The centrality of conceptual analysis is clear in Plato's dialogues, as well as much twentieth-century Anglophone philosophy, which tends to equate conceptual analysis with the analysis of linguistic meanings. In the intervening centuries, conceptual analysis is not always as overt. Descartes, for example, is trying to find a foundation for knowledge in his most famous philosophical works, and Locke is inquiring into the origin of ideas. But Descartes' central arguments hinge on conceivability claims, which are often construed as conceptual, and Locke's project can be described as a theory of the nature of concepts, and proposed analyses can be found throughout his *Essay*. Likewise, modern normative theories have typically depended on analyses of moral concepts.

In sum, philosophical projects often centrally involve resolution of difficult conceptual questions, and conceptual analysis is, thus, a central tool of philosophy. And this raises a question. Can these features be used to draw a sharp distinction between philosophy and fields that we refer to as "empirical"? An empirical field is one that relies centrally on observation, especially observations that are repeatable, sharable, and used to develop accurate theories of various aspects of the world. Philosophers sometimes suppose that conceptual analysis is not empirical, because it does not use the most familiar instruments of observation: the senses and artifacts designed for observation and measurement. Rather, philosophers conduct their analyses from the armchair, but reflecting on things, conducting thought experiments, and engaging in dialogue. These methods are designed to elicit "intuitions," and intuitions are presumed to be a direct reflection of conceptual truths.

Notice, however, that armchair elicitation of intuitions qualifies as a form of observation in a broad sense of the term. How do we discover what our intuitions are? Presumably, we introspect. Intuitions are presented to us as mental states that become accessible to consciousness and available for reporting. An idea comes before the mind, along with a felt sense of confidence in that idea, and we report the result. Introspection can be described as a kind of observation. Through introspection, we pick up on information stored in our mind-brains. We can introspect on the same topic twice, and we can compare our own introspective observations to those of others. The fact that we don't use sensory transducers isn't very interesting. The key point is that we are picking up on something that is there to be detected (concepts that have been stored in memory). Moreover, when we introspect on our concepts, we are often engaged in sensory observation one step removed. We got our concepts through observations of the external world and perceptual mediated interactions with other human beings. Plato thought concepts were memories of encounters with ideal objects prior to birth. He was wrong about this, but many of our concepts are memories of ordinary objects experienced in life. Others involve networks of words that have been inferentially linked by observing the behaviors of members of our linguistic communities.

In sum, armchair conceptual analysis can be characterized as an introspective memory retrieval process. As such, it can be regarded as a form of observation. And this leads to the question, how good a form of observation is it? I don't think it's a bad method. Introspection does give us access to something. But introspection is not the only or necessarily the best method of observation. First, introspection, like all memory retrieval, is a constructive process. What we recall often depends on beliefs, expectations, norms, context, and other factors. It is prone to confabulation and distortion. It can be heavily influence by our theories, by social pressures, and by background knowledge. Second, conceptual information is often stored in the form of exemplars or paradigm cases. Philosophers often use conceptual analysis to identify necessary and sufficient conditions. If this is done on the basis of stored exemplars, it will inevitably require the addition and subtraction of information. We might assume that introspection reveals a rule that is already present in the mind, when in fact we are actually drawing inferences from specific cases in the course of what appears to be an innocent retrieval process. Third, the results of introspection are often variable across individuals. Introspective psychology failed because different labs reported different results under the same test conditions. In philosophy, debates often collapse into intuition mongering because defenders of opposing views are equally confident about conflicting intuitions. People in different cultural settings may have conflicting intuitions, but this variation is missed by contemporary Anglophone philosophers who are predominantly Western, highly educated, politically liberal, white, and male. Fourth, introspection provides access to only a limited portion of stored knowledge. Conceptual structure (like the structure of syntactic rules) can be inaccessible to consciousness.

This does not entail that we should give up on introspection. Far from it. Introspective reports, we will see, are even essential for certain experiments. But it does follow that we need to be cautious about philosophical intuitions, and we should be open to the use of other methods that help reveal the content of our concepts.

In this section, I have argued that philosophical methodology is observation in a broad sense of the term. For clarity of exposition, I will often use the word "empirical" in a narrower sense, to refer to research that calls on controlled experiments and statistical analyses. In this terminology, traditional philosophical methods contrast with empirical methods, but both are observational, and, in that sense, there is not sharp distinction.

1.2. Are There Distinctively Philosophical Questions?

I just suggested that philosophy would benefit if traditional philosophical methods were combined with other methods of observation. But a purist might respond that such supplementation is impossible in some cases. It might be asserted that certain kinds of questions can only be answered using traditional philosophical methods. In this section, I will consider three kinds of questions that might appear to transcend empirical methods. First, there are foundational epistemological questions concerning the justification of empirical methods. Descartes argued that we cannot trust the results of observation until we have proven that such results are reliable, and we can't prove that by observation, on pain of circularity. Second, there are conceptual questions. It is often suggested that conceptual truths cannot be scientifically revealed but are instead prior to scientific inquiry. If so, then, to the extent that philosophy is concerned with projects that have a conceptual dimension, methodological purism might be justified. Finally, it is widely believed that philosophical methods are the only ones suitable for addressing normative questions. Other methods are descriptive—they reveal how things are, not how they should be. I will address each of these suggestions in turn.

Consider first the Cartesian idea that only pure philosophical reflection can provide epistemic foundations for observation. Given what I have said already, there is something a bit odd about this idea. If pure philosophical reflection is introspection, then philosophical reflection is just as vulnerable to skeptical doubts as anything else. Consider Descartes *cogito*. "I think therefore I am" can be interpreted in different ways. For example, it might be regarded as a conceptual truth (there is not thought without a thinker), or as a truth that can be directly recognized as true. Both options are dubious. The concept of thinking can be characterized, it would seem, without mentioning a thinker, and it has been questioned for centuries whether we have direct introspective access to a self. Few agree on what the self is, let alone self-awareness. Introspection cannot settle such issues. And since introspection is an observational method, it is prone to errors of the kind that infect outward perception. The assumption that armchair reflection can provide privileged foundations is based on a questionable (perhaps magical) view of how introspection works. Moreover, the entire Cartesian project may be called into question. Descartes thinks that we need foundations to justify observation, but he may be wrong. Empiricists traditionally argued that observations don't need independent justification, because they are given to us noninferentially and incorrigibly. If, however, I am right about the fallibility of introspection, this is an unpromising strategy. A better strategy is to say we don't need foundations for observation because we don't need foundations at all. This has been a very popular view in twentieth-century thought, as in the case of Quine's coherentism, according to which every claim is, in principle, revisable. Empirical observation, on this view, is potentially relevant for any claim. I cannot undertake a defense of this view here. I merely want to point out that Descartes' effort to identify a role for pure philosophy may be doubly flawed: philosophy is itself a form of observation, so it cannot provide a noncircular justification for observation, and observation may not need a foundation in the first place. If so, we must look beyond Descartes to find distinctively philosophical questions.

Let's turn from epistemic foundations to the assumption that philosophical methods have a privileged role to play in answering conceptual questions. This strikes me as seriously confused. There is considerable controversy about what concepts are, but, whatever they are, philosophical methods are neither the best nor the only tools for studying them. According to many theories, concepts are mental representations. If the primary philosophical method is armchair reflection, and reflection involves introspective memory access, then reflection can play some role in discovering the structure of our concepts, but other tools can as well. As with syntax, many facts about the structure of concepts may be unavailable to consciousness. For example, research in psychology suggests that concepts are constituted in part by prototypes: representations of typical category instances. Introspection might have played a role in coming up with this idea, but it took other methods (measuring reaction times, error rates, developmental sequences, word frequency, etc.) to provide strong evidence for the claim that prototypes are ubiquitous features of psychological life. The fact that we can readily imagine typical instances of categories and access images of these in consciousness does not prove that prototype representations are regularly at work during conceptual tasks. Introspection rarely reveals how we solve problems but delivers instead some information about the end result (Nisbett and Wilson, 1977). If concepts are mental representations, we should not expect that they are readily available to consciousness.

Now suppose that concepts are not mental representations. What might they be? They could supervene on patterns of behavior in the linguistic community. But, if so, introspective methods will be poorly suited to reveal their structure. Even dialogue with a community of philosophers will be insufficient. Instead, one would need to survey a broader range of language users, and one would need to observe how words are used in ordinary conversational contexts.

If concepts are something outside the head, an armchair method will be of limited value in the study of their structure.

One might argue that concepts are neither mental representations nor summaries of linguistic behaviors, but rather norms. A concept might be defined as norm-governed inferential roles, and one might think that norms cannot be discovered by scientific methods. This would follow only if norms cannot be studied scientifically—the topic I will turn to next. But before taking up that issue, I want to make a remark about the concept expressed by "concept." I have been suggesting that whatever concepts are, they can and should be studied using a range of methods that extend beyond armchair reflection. But how do we decide what concepts are in the first place? Isn't that a matter for philosophy to resolve?

The question can be put more pointedly by showing that each competing theory of concepts seems to beg various questions of the others. Suppose I say that concepts are mental representations. How can I prove that? Well, I could look to see how we mentally represent the word "concept." But this method of proof would beg the question against those who say concepts supervene on linguistic behavior. They would say we should investigate the concept *concept* by seeing how the word "concept" is used. Perhaps these methods would converge on similar results, but suppose they didn't. Then it seems there would be no single way to determine the concept expressed by "concept." Theorists might agree about what entities exist (linguistic behavior and mental representations) while disagreeing about what the word "concept" should designate. No empirical test can resolve this kind of conflict. But I don't think that proves that philosophical methods have a special role to play, because introspecting intuitions can do nothing to get us out of this quagmire. Instead, we must simply choose a use of the term "concept" and see what mileage we can get out of the resulting theory. There is an element of fiat and of pragmatic confirmation in theory construction. That element is not philosophical in any traditional sense, lest philosophy be construed as the method of making arbitrary terminological choices. So even if the concept expressed by "concept," and hence the best approach to conceptual investigation, cannot itself be resolved using purely empirical methods, it doesn't follow that philosophy plays a foundational role in investigating concepts.

I've been trying to suggest that questions pertaining to concepts are amenable to methods other than the armchair approach associated with traditional philosophy. In making this point, I left one argument untouched: the proposal that concepts have a normative nature might be used to support the conclusion that concepts must be investigated using philosophical methods, because normative questions cannot be investigated any other way. I now want to ask whether normative questions are distinctively philosophical.

Let me first observe that the questions about normativity are often linked to conceptual questions. For example, Kant's normative theory makes use of conceptual claims about freedom, the good, duty, and humanity. If conceptual claims can be empirically tested, then Kant's theory can be empirically tested.

Likewise, Mill's defense of utilitarianism begins with the claim that happiness has intrinsic value. This can be interpreted as a conceptual truth (something would not count as happiness if it were not valuable). If it's not a conceptual claim, then it is presumably an empirical claim as well—a claim about whether happiness is, as a matter of fact, always experienced as good.

Normative claims are also linked to conceptual claims more directly. Normative claims take the form of "ought" statements, and the validity of those statements depends on what concept is expressed by the word "ought." For this reason, there is a sense in which one can derive an ought from an is (Prinz 2007a, 2007b). I have developed this argument elsewhere, but a summary may suffice for present purposes. Suppose "ought" is a referring expression. Reference is a relation that can be empirically investigated. We can see what people mean by "reference," we can see how people try to relate words to world, we can see what natural relations exist between words and world, and so on. Our best empirically informed theory of reference will identify some relation, R, that is the reference relation. R may be a causal relation, a nomic relation, a historical relation, a function from verbal behavior, an abstract resemblance relation, and so on. Once we know what R is, we can investigate the word "ought" or the underlying concept and determine what it bears R to. And when we discover what "ought" refers to, we will have thereby discovered what users of that word ought to do.

My own view is that "ought" expresses certain kinds of emotions and those emotions refer to response-dependent properties (powers to cause those emotions). If something has the power to cause these emotions in me, then I ought to do it. This rough sketch illustrates a method of deriving normative claims from empirical methods. I may be entirely wrong about what "ought" refers to, because I may have the wrong theory of reference or I may be wrong about what bears the reference relation to "ought." The crucial point, for present purposes, is that there is a way to investigate norms empirically.

Against this, one might point out that a lot of normative discourse is actually an expression of our values, rather than an inquiry into what our values are. When I say, "You ought to keep your promises," I am telling you what you should do, not (just) describing how things are. But this observation about the function of moral discourse does not prove that philosophy has a privileged role. Why should philosophers have a special authority when recommending action? It seems that any authority we have as philosophers stems from our training in conceptual analysis, and hence our ability to determine what we mean by moral terms. But this, I have already suggested, is a project that can be pursued using any observational method, philosophical and otherwise. Once we have figured out what we mean by moral terms, we can use those terms to make recommendations, but making recommendations can be done by anyone who grasps those terms. So the distinctively normative character of moral discourse is not the aspect of moral discourse that makes morality seem more philosophical than scientific. Philosophers' contribution to morality qua philosophers is descriptive.

I conclude that the empirical sciences can contribute to normative theories. Philosophical methods (introspective memory retrieval) are a legitimate way to investigate what we mean by moral terms, but not the only way, nor necessarily the best. Empirical methods can be used to determine what people mean by "ought," "good," "person," "right," and so on. And empirical methods can be used to determine what falls under these terms once their meanings are fixed. Empirical methods can also make other contributions to normative theory. For example, if ought implies can (an empirically testable claim), it can be empirically shown that there are certain things we are not obligated to do, because we can't do them. Or, to take another example, we can use empirical methods to expose the origins of deeply held values, as Nietzsche does in his genealogy of morals. When we discover that a value has an ignoble origin, we may decide to abandon it, and thereby undercut the normative force that it once had on us. Of course, the normative force in this case is psychological: genealogy can undercut the *feeling* or *belief* that we ought to act in accordance with a particular value. But that psychological sense of normativity may be the only meaningful sense of the term. We may discover, empirically, that norms are dependent on our psychological states, and, if so, psychological changes of the kind Nietzsche seeks to provoke can be normative changes.

These considerations lead me to think that empirical methods can make a contribution to all questions that philosophers have traditionally posed. Philosophers should welcome any method that can shed light on traditional philosophical questions. Philosophical methods may be informative for answering certain kinds of questions, but there is reason to doubt that there are any questions for which philosophical methodology is the only option. Indeed, if philosophical methods are observational, that suggestion hardly makes sense. As Quine taught, philosophy is continuous with science. I would even say it is a form of science. And it is not a form that has exclusive jurisdiction over any class of questions.

2. DATA MINING AND DATA COLLECTING

2.1. Two Approaches to Naturalized Philosophy

Once it is established that philosophical questions can be illuminated by empirical inquiry, the next question is, how should philosophers avail themselves of empirical research? There are two basic approaches that can be easily found in the literature. Some philosophers make use of empirical results that have been acquired by professional scientists. Most typically, these philosophers cite neuroscientists and psychologists, but they also call on linguists, evolutionary biologists, roboticists, and anthropologists, among others. These results are used to support or refute philosophical theories. I will call this approach "empirical philosophy." Other philosophers also conduct their own psychological experiments, an approach known as "experimental philosophy." Some philosophers mine the data of others, and some collect data themselves. In principle, the distinction between empirical and experimental philosophy need not be very significant. The experiments that philosophers perform could be performed by behavioral scientists, and any philosopher with the right tools and training could perform any kind of study that a behavioral scientist might perform. Moreover, most philosophers who conduct experiments are also empirical philosophers, calling on empirical findings by behavioral scientists. There are, nevertheless, some differences between the ways empirical and experimental philosophy have been approached in the recent literature. The kinds of studies that philosophers conduct are often different in kind than the ones they cite, and this has some bearing on the kind of questions that experimental philosophers often take themselves to be answering. I will try to offer a rough characterization of the difference. In so doing, I am not trying to suggest that experimental and empirical philosophy *must* differ along the lines I suggest; only that they often do, and that there are reasons for these differences.

Empirical philosophers have taken on a wide range of issues, but most fall squarely in the philosophy of mind. Most typically, philosophers who use empirical work are attempting to establish the nature of a particular class of mental states or processes. For example, they want to know the nature of consciousness, concepts, language, mental imagery, perception, dreaming, pain, emotion, desire, or moral judgment. Sometimes they are interested in broad questions about cognitive architecture, such as modularity, the format of mental representations, the boundaries of the mind, or mental plasticity. Sometimes they are interested in questions of where mental capacities come from, and they call on such fields as developmental psychology, machine learning, or evolutionary theory.

Empirical philosophers are often best described as what Dennett calls reverse engineers. They are trying to figure out how the mind works. They postulate various representations and processes. The questions tend to be of a general character: the nature of emotions, not of fear; the nature of concepts, not of any particular concept; the nature of character traits, not of courage; and so on. Disputes in this area are often first-order. They are disagreements about mental ontology (what exists in the mind). Philosophers disagree about the physical basis of consciousness, about whether emotions can exist without judgments, about whether imagery uses the same representational resources as perception.

It should be clear from this sketch that empirical philosophers are often not overtly concerned with conceptual questions. They are not trying to figure out what people mean by "concept" or "pain" or "wrong." Rather, they are taking these as natural kind terms that can be used to pick out some uncontroversial paradigm cases, and they then seek to determine the underlying nature of those cases. Conceptual questions sometimes arise (Can "pain" apply to an unconscious state? Do we consider the feelings induced by facial feedback to be genuine emotions even if they lack intentional objects?). But these questions are often settled by determining the essence of paradigm cases, not by investigating how people think of the relevant categories. On in some cases, concepts are analyzed in order to pursue first-order questions, rather than as an end in itself (Are there several concepts of consciousness? Cf. Block 1995). When this is done, the expectation tends to be that the conceptual analyses will accurately portray their referents (since there are several concepts of consciousness, there are probably several neural correlates). It is also noteworthy that when empirical philosophers make conceptual claims, they rarely make them by appeal to empirical results. Rather, they do armchair conceptual analysis to guide or interpret first-order empirical results.

Experimental philosophy is often different in this respect. Experimental philosophers have been especially concerned to understand how ordinary concept users understand certain categories (see chapters 2–9, this volume). Often they focus on mental categories, and, in this respect, much experimental philosophy concerns itself with trying to understand folk psychology (How do we understand intentions? Do we believe in free will? Are we moral objectivists?). The philosophers who ask these questions are often not primarily concerned with investigating the capacities that these constructs represent (What are intentions? Is there free will? Are there moral facts?). And they do not assume that folk psychology is correct (if people believe in libertarianism, it doesn't follow that free will exists). The questions asked by experimental philosophers tend to be more specific then questions asked by empirical philosophers, focusing on specific concepts, for example, rather than concepts in general.

I just said that experimental philosophers have an interest in folk psychology, but, to be clear, their interest in this topic differs significantly from the interest reflected in the work of philosophers and psychologists who have contributed to the so-called theory of mind debate. That debate concerns a general question about the processes underlying our capacity to attribute mental states. Experimental philosophers focus on specific mental states, such as intention, not our general mentalizing abilities. Experimental philosophers are also often neutral about the underlying mechanisms. For example, they tend not to take sides on the question of whether people attribute mental states on the basis of folk theories or by processes of simulation (though I will note an exception below). Once again, experimental philosophers tend to be somewhat more interested in specific folk concepts than in underlying mechanisms and processes.

In this respect, experimental philosophy bears a resemblance to traditional conceptual analysis in philosophy. Traditional philosophers, since Plato, focus on specific concepts and offer analyses. It is usually assumed that the concepts being investigated should be analyzed in accordance with how ordinary language users understand concepts. Both experimental philosophers and traditional conceptual analysis share this interest in common. There are also two further links between experimental philosophy and traditional conceptual analysis. First, methods used by experimental philosophers usually involve asking subjects to report semantic knowledge by introspection; subjects are given vignettes, which serve a role comparable to philosophical thought experiments, and these elicit intuitions, which subjects record on questionnaires. Thus, the most typical experiments conducted by philosophers ask ordinary people to do what philosophers have traditionally done when reflecting on concepts.

Traditional methods of philosophy are not eliminated; they are simply democratized. Elsewhere I have called this the *a posteriori priori* method, because it combines *a priori* reflection with data analysis (Prinz 2007a). Each subject knows her or his own intuition by armchair reflection, but the experimenter gains knowledge of the most typical responses (or other statistical facts) only by calculating how a group of subjects responds.

This brings me to the second way in which experimental philosophy is related to traditional conceptual analysis. By analyzing the intuitions of multiple untrained respondents, experimental philosophers can determine whether the intuitions reported by professional philosophers align with ordinary language users. Traditional philosophers build their theories on intuitions, and they often assume these intuitions are shared. But, in actuality, philosophers' intuitions are often biased. For example, they are often theory-laden and culturally specific. Experimental philosophers have used their studies to expose these biases by showing that philosophers' intuitions are not universally shared (chapters 2 and 3, this volume). Thus, experimental philosophy uses the traditional philosophical method of reporting intuitions together with statistical analysis to criticize philosophers' claims about what the authoritative intuitions should be. Sometimes they also try to show that philosophical intuitions are ephemeral by introducing small differences how thought experiments are presented (such as presentation order, or vivid language) can influence the resulting intuitions (e.g., Swain et al. 2008).

When experimental philosophy is used to criticize traditional philosophy, it potentially severs the link between conceptual claims and ontological claims. Since Plato, traditional philosophers have often assumed that we can figure out the nature of some first-order thing (love, truth, the good, etc.) by figuring out how people understand the concepts. Concepts are presumed to be a window onto ontology. As remarked already, experimental philosophers do not typically assume that our concepts are accurate. When they show variation in subjects' conceptual intuitions, they raise questions about whose concepts, if any, are correct. If conceptual intuitions are highly variable, then building a first-order theory of the basis of intuitions may be a mistake. In this way, experimental philosophy can be seen as justifying empirical philosophy. If intuitions are unreliable, then perhaps other methods should be used in developing first-order theories. Experiments that directly measure mental processes, for example, can be used to determine whether our intuitions about those processes are correct.

In summary, empirical philosophy and experimental philosophy are both trends that relate empirical evidence to philosophical questions, but they have tended to differ in certain respects. Empirical philosophers tend to be interested in relatively general, first-order questions, and, when they analyze concepts, they typically do so from the armchair in order to guide and systematize empirically informed investigations of how the mind works. Experimental philosophers have more often been interested in second-order questions about specific concepts, and they offer conceptual analyses by doing statistical analyses on untrained subjects' armchair intuitions. Empirical philosophers often aim to support traditional philosophical theories, and when they criticize traditional theories, they tend to do so by showing that those theories make false first-order predictions. Experimental philosophers are somewhat more concerned with casting doubt on traditional theories, and they tend to do so by challenging the conceptual intuitions on which those theories are based.

This distinction between experimental and empirical philosophy is very rough. As we will see in a moment, there are counter-examples in the literature, and the distinction is likely to blur even more in the years to come. But, I will now also suggest that there is a reason for the distinction that I have been discussing here.

2.2. Why the Difference?

Empirical philosophy works by citation. Philosophers cite relevant empirical research and use it to argue for philosophical conclusions (e.g., in defense of theories that have been traditionally defended by philosophers). Experimental philosophers conduct their own research. This difference bears on the kinds of questions that practitioners of the two approaches have been able to ask.

Few philosophers have extensive training in experimental design or statistics, and even fewer have access to extensive laboratory resources, such as measurement devices, computer terminals for conducting experiments, money for paying subjects, or institutional infrastructure to list experiments along with psychological studies that large introductory classes can take for course credit. As a result, philosophers usually run simple questionnaire studies that can be done on a voluntary basis as brief exercises in undergraduate classrooms, usually just after a class has been conducted. Some philosophers recruit subjects using online experiments or poll pedestrians on the street corners or collaborate with researchers at non-Western universities. The studies increase the subject pool, but they still use questionnaires. Measuring reaction times or physiological responses, for example, requires tools and training that most philosophers don't have.

Questionnaire studies work by asking people to report their intuitions. The easiest studies to conduct are ones that do not causally influence those intuitions during the course of the experiment. It is possible to affect intuitions by, say, manipulating presentation order, word choice, and accompanying images. But experiments that manipulate intuitions are harder to design and to conduct using questionnaires. For example, if an experimenter wants to influence intuitions by presenting photographs, it is difficult to control the duration of the presentation using questionnaires. Philosophical training also tends to focus on enduring intuitions rather than the processes that generate them, so the idea that intuitions can be altered is less salient, and perhaps less interesting, for many philosophers who embark on experimental research. The easiest experiments to design (which are still, by no means, easy) involve adapting standard philosophical thought experiments to a questionnaire format so they can be tried on untrained respondents.

These contingent facts have two related implications. First, if a philosopher is going to conduct experiments, the experiments are likely to be questionnaire studies. Second, since questionnaire studies are especially useful for collecting lay intuitions, the philosophers who conduct experiments will tend to do work that focuses on lay intuitions rather than, say, underlying psychological processes that are not accessible to consciousness. The interest in lay intuitions is hardly surprising. Throughout the history of philosophy, there has been a tendency to rely on intuitions, and experimental philosophers are people who have training in that tradition and interest in intuitions. Questionnaire methods happen to be ideally suited for testing intuitions, because intuitions can be elicited by vignettes and consciously accessed and reported. Thus, given an interest in this topic and the ability to run questionnaire studies without extensive training, it is not surprising that there is now a community of philosophers applying these techniques. Philosophers in this community often construct questionnaires that use thought experiments similar to ones that have been used by armchair philosophers, and these experiments are explicitly designed to determine whether the intuitions of armchair philosophers are correct. Experimental philosophers have been able to challenge the intuitions driving philosophical theories in epistemology, theory of reference, the free will debate, and other areas (see especially the research conducted by Steve Stich and his collaborators or former students).

Suppose, however, one wants to contribute to a research area that has been less intuition based. For example, consider the task of developing a positive theory of consciousness. If you want to know the conditions under which consciousness arises, intuitions will be of only limited use. We can recall cases from the armchair in which consciousness can wax and wane (e.g., long-distance truck drivers), but when we do this, we are recalling prior experiences, not analyzing the concept expressed by "conscious." Sometimes conceptual analyses play a role in theory construction in this area, as when philosophers distinguish between consciousness and awareness, between state consciousness and creature consciousness, or between access consciousness and phenomenal consciousness. But philosophers in this area are largely concerned with trying to explain how different kinds of consciousness can arise in a physical brain, so the conceptual analyses are only a first-step in theory construction. One then needs to postulate processes that account for the defensible conceptual distinctions, and those processes are not simply read off our concepts but instead take the form of empirical conjectures. Intuitions about who is conscious when, or about where consciousness comes from, are not believed to be sufficient. Indeed, it is widely assumed that, if consciousness is a physical or functional process, that fact is not intuitively obvious; on the contrary, it is a deeply surprising fact. This is not to say the intuitions about consciousness are uninteresting or irrelevant to the study of consciousness (Knobe and Prinz 2008). Intuitions may help us reveal whether there are multiple concepts of consciousness, and studies of how people attribute consciousness can be used to diagnose philosophical arguments that have been used to support various first-order theories.

There are many other areas where research extends beyond intuitions. If you are interested in the nature of concepts, and you believe that conceptual structure is not consciously available, you will probably want to call on experiments that measure reaction times, developmental trajectories, and semantic priming. I don't mean to suggest that intuitions have played no role in research on the nature of concepts. For example, research on concept combination has used intuitions to show that some conceptual compounds have emergent features (features that come readily to mind for the compound, but not for the parts). Questions about typicality have been used to reveal that category instances can be ranked in order of similarity to paradigm instances. Research on intuitions about unusual transformations has shown that subjects intuitively recognize that natural kind concepts have hidden essences. And so on. But two things should be noticed about these studies. First, the intuitions are not the main object of inquiry in their own right, but rather they reveal facts about the underlying structure of concepts in general; the intuitions are regarded as evidence for something unconscious, just as intuitions about grammaticality might reveal the components of syntax. Second, as a result, collection of intuitions is not the only method used in this domain, and, ideally, conclusions drawn from intuitions are confirmed in other ways. The first observation may help to explain why such research methods have not been obvious to people with training in philosophy, and the second observation explains why limitations in resources have had an impact on the extent to which philosophers can contribute experimentally in this domain. In other words, philosophers could easily conduct experimental research on the nature of concepts, but facts about philosophical training have made this possibility less salient and less inviting than, say, the prospect of doing experimental research on folk intuitions about knowledge.

It is an interesting question how empirical and experimental philosophy are related, given the difference in research interests. The relationship may be partially historical. One possible scenario goes like this: a few philosophers who were interested in first-order problems, like the nature of consciousness or cognitive architecture, began citing empirical results, because those results were obviously relevant to theory construction. Then the next generation of philosophers began to use empirical results more broadly, and the desire for empirical confirmation of philosophical theories became commonplace. This may have had two effects. First, excitement about empirical results got some philosophers thinking that it would be rewarding to partake in experimentation. Some early experimental efforts were directed at first-order problems, because that's what empirical philosophers had been focusing on, but the practical issues mentioned a moment ago restricted many philosophers to use of questionnaire studies, which are often not the optimal tools for tackling first-order questions. Second, upon adopting the mantra, "Go empirical!" some philosophers began to notice that traditional philosophy was rife with claims that could be empirically tested, including claims about philosophical intuitions. These two factors (the observation that intuitions can be tested and an urge to experiment combined with limitations in tools and training) may have each played a role in fueling the rise of experimental philosophy, and the characteristic focus on lay intuitions. The pioneering efforts proved to be so interesting that the earlier focus on first-order problems that triggered an interest in experimentation was pushed to the back burner, and a cottage industry emerged around the investigation of lay intuitions.

If this speculative history is right, there is a historical link between empirical philosophy and experimental philosophy, even though the two approaches tend to tackle different kinds of problems. That said, I don't want to suggest that the connection is merely historical and that experimental and empirical philosophers always investigate different things. Like empirical philosophers, some experimental philosophers have conducted questionnaire studies in an effort to reveal facts about underlying processes. For example, Stich and Nichols (1992) conducted an ingenious and elegant study to cast doubt on the simulation theory of mental state attribution. If people make predictions about another person's preferences using the same mechanisms by which they would make decisions for themselves, then certain reasoning errors that arise in first-person decision making should also appear when making third-person attributions. Stich and Nichols showed that a classic first-person error does not occur in third-person attribution, suggesting that at least some attributions are not driven by simulation. They used questionnaires to conduct the study, but they were not primarily interested in lay intuitions as an object of investigation. Obviously, philosophers can do this sort of thing, and, when they do, it qualifies as experimental philosophy. My point is that studies of lay intuitions have been more prominent in recent research. So much so that one might reserve the term "Experimental Philosophy" with capital letters for studies conducted by philosophers designed to examine such intuitions. One might say Experimental Philosophy investigates folk intuitions and concepts, whereas experimental philosophy is a more encompassing category.

In this context, it is important to note that the use of questionnaires is not essential to capital letter Experimental Philosophy. Questionnaires are very well suited for exploring folk intuitions, but they may not be the only method for doing so. For example, one could investigate conceptual connections within folk theories by measuring reaction times. If two concepts are semantically linked in our minds, then the activation of one should prime the other, and reaction times should be affected. Thus, the questionnaire method used by most Experimental Philosophers and the research objective of investigating folk concepts can come apart. Questionnaires can be used to test for underlying processes and other methods can be used for testing hypotheses about folk concepts.

So far, I have been suggesting that there are two kinds of questions: questions about folk conceptual analyses and questions about underlying representations and processes in the mind. This distinction helps to explain the division of labor between experimental philosophy and empirical philosophy. But there are also areas in which the distinction is hard to sustain. Sometimes the investigation of lay intuitions reveals facts about underlying processes, even when the intuitions are taken as an interesting object of investigation in their own right. In other words, sometimes Experimental Philosophy with capital letters bears directly on questions about how the mind works (as opposed to merely bearing on questions about the content of folk concepts or theories). For a nice example of this, consider Knobe's studies of the relationship between evaluative judgments and attributions of intentional action (chapter 8, this volume). Knobe has shown that our ordinary intuitions about whether a side effect has been brought about intentionally depends on whether or not that side effect violates a rule. This is a fascinating discovery about the folk concept of intentional action, and it stands alone, in this respect, as a nice piece of empirically informed conceptual analysis. In other words, the result would be interesting even if it didn't reveal anything about how the mind works in general, but only something about the content of one specific concept. On the other hand, the result suggests that there is no sharp separation between the way we ascribe mental states and our values, and that suggests that two mental capacities (theory of mind and moral cognition) may interact in interesting ways. It shows that something normative (how should people act) influences something descriptive (did someone act with intention). There are many interpretations of what is going on here, but many of them take the form of information processing models. The claim is not simply that the concept expressed by "intentionally" has a moral feature, but rather that values, desires, or other nondescriptive attitudes are causally linked to cognitive mechanisms that may have been regarded as purely descriptive prior to this discovery. Fact and value are not processes independent in folk psychology. That is a discovery about cognitive architecture.

In this section, I have tried to do two things. I offered a diagnosis of why experimental philosophy and empirical philosophy have differed, and I also tried to underscore that the differences are not sharp: philosophers can conduct experiments that contribute to the understanding of mental processes in addition to shedding light on the content of folk concepts. If philosophers begin doing experiments that are designed to discover underlying mental processes, their work will begin to look more like what professional psychologists do. Therefore, I will conclude this meditation on methodology with a final question: do the recent trends in philosophy undermine the distinction between philosophy and other fields?

3. THE END OF DISCIPLINES?

Traditionally, one might have tried to draw the distinction between philosophy and psychology by methodology: laboratory research vs. armchair. But that is no longer tenable, given the rise of empirical and experimental philosophy. Both make extensive use of lab results. Moreover, laboratory work often makes extensive use of armchair reflection: scientists must pose questions, generate hypotheses, design study methods, and draw conclusions from data. Empirical findings can influence any of these stages, but they can also be performed from the armchair. If science and philosophy refer to methods, then these methods work in concert and are anemic when performed in isolation. Data without theory is empty, and theory without data is blind. Perhaps one can do a better job of differentiating philosophy and psychology by drawing on the distinction that I have been discussing in section 2.

If the characterizations I have offered are correct, then both empirical philosophers and experimental philosophers are doing something different from what experimental psychologists typically do. Like empirical philosophers, experimental psychologists tend to be interested in first-order questions about how the mind works, and when they perform a study on a particular folk concept, they are typically using that study to learn about concepts more generally. But unlike empirical philosophers, experimental psychologists conduct experiments, and their published papers are usually research reports. Experimental psychologists tend to write few theoretical papers, and when they do, those papers often take the form of literature reviews. Empirical philosophers are theoreticians. They are not collecting data but rather constructing arguments and theories, trying to figure out the implications of empirical studies. Empirical philosophers often integrate a range of different studies, from different branches of science, rather than reviewing work that has been done using similar techniques and paradigms. Philosophers tend not to write mere literature reviews (they would be accused of scientific journalism—a pejorative—if they did that). Instead they try to find clever ways of using empirical findings in the service of developing original arguments for or against existing philosophical theories. For example, Doris (2002) and Harman (1999) survey research that shows strong situational influences on behavior, but they also use the empirical findings to argue against prevailing versions of virtue ethics. In my own work, I have tried to use empirical research to support the empiricist theory of concepts (Prinz, 2002), William James's theory of emotion (Prinz, 2004), and the sensibility theory of moral judgment (Prinz, 2007). Very philosophical aims!

One might put the point by saying that empirical philosophy is a form of theoretical psychology, which tries to systematize empirical results, draw implications, guide research, and relate laboratory findings to broad overarching issues that have been of traditional concern in philosophy. Philosophers sometimes also reinterpret the results of psychologists and criticize both experimental designs and the inferences that experimental psychologists draw from their own studies. Psychologists do those things too, of course, but, in psychology departments, tenure and promotion depend on data collections, not just theoretical reflection, and publications without new results are not highly valued. Empirical philosophers often allow themselves to be much more speculative than their colleagues in psychology, and they are, in this sense, less data driven.

At first glance, experimental philosophy might appear more similar to experimental psychology. Like psychologists, experimental philosophers conduct experiments. But there are also differences. Like empirical philosophers, experimental philosophers tend to have a theoretical orientation. Even when writing up results, they tend to dedicate more space to theoretical reflection than they do to reporting research methods and results. In addition, as noted already, experimental philosophers tend to focus on questions about specific lay concepts rather than general questions about underlying psychological processes. In this respect, their interests differ from experimental psychologists. A psychologist might ask a general question such as, "what kinds of rules and representations are used in attributing mental states," whereas an experimental philosopher might ask, "how do ordinary people think about mental states of type M?"

In sum, it seems that empirical philosophy, experimental philosophy, and experimental psychology all differ as they are most frequently practiced. This difference could be tested by, for example, asking people to sort publications into these three categories. I think the differences are noticeable. But, I also think the differences are contingent. Experimental philosophers sometimes investigate first-order problems, and experimental psychologists sometimes write theoretical papers. Experimental philosophers also collaborate with experimental psychologists and cognitive neuroscientists. When either occurs, the distinction between the two becomes harder to discern.

It is becoming increasingly common to find papers that are difficult to classify, and the division of labor between fields is becoming less and less fixed. I think that is a good thing. Some philosophers are good at doing psychology (i.e., conducting experiments to discover underlying mechanisms and processes), and some psychologists are good at doing philosophy (i.e., constructing theories in response to the kinds of questions that philosophers have traditionally asked). I think training in philosophy is valuable when doing cognitive science. The questions that philosophers have traditionally asked have enduring interest, and the theories that philosophers have proposed are often both testable and worth testing. Philosophers bring an incredibly rich historical legacy to the lab, and that legacy covers topics that psychologists have hardly begun to investigate. Philosophers are also trained in argumentation, and this is an asset in experimental design and discussion; philosophers are good at seeing what follows from what. Psychologists, for their part, know a lot about how the mind works, and they know how to test hypotheses. They are skilled at converting speculative theories into carefully controlled studies, and their knowledge of the empirical literature allows them to see what philosophical theories have special promise (or lack promise). So philosophers and psychologists can do work that is indistinguishable at one level while still benefiting from their distinctive training. The value of this background also suggests that it would be good if some people continued doing traditional philosophy and some people continued collecting data without much interest in how those data bear on broad theoretical issues.

One can think of traditional philosophy and atheoretical data collection as two ends of a continuum, with every gradation in between. When researchers trained at each pole convene in the middle, that can be highly fruitful. Those who dwell in the middle will also report the results of their work to people who remain more methodologically pure, and that allows theory to trickle down and data to trickle up.

Will the fields of philosophy and psychology ever collapse into each other? I hope not, if that means no one reads Hume or studies rats. I think it would be bad if philosophers had to apply psychologists' standards for tenure and conversely. We need people who are rewarded for collecting data and people who are rewarded for reflecting, sometimes quite speculatively, on what it all means. I also think that the work being done just adjacent to the borders is just as interesting as the work that falls in the unclassifiable middle. Most experimental and empirical philosophy is still recognizable as philosophy, and thus both trends constitute novel approaches that extend beyond both traditional philosophy and traditional psychology. Moreover, some philosophical subfields, such as metaphysics, have less to gain from psychology than they do from other areas, such as physics. So philosophy cannot merge with psychology alone; it would have to splinter off into different sciences. That would be unfortunate, because, despite different interests, philosophy is also united by a shared history and a common stock of issues (realism vs. anti-realism; naturalism vs. anti-naturalism; empiricism vs. rationalism; holism vs. atomism; and so on). I think philosophy departments should remain intact and are not threatened by recent trend toward methodological pluralism.

That does not mean I think things should stay exactly as they are. I think philosophers would benefit from getting some training in other fields. Philosophers interested in mind (and perhaps other areas) should learn how to read social science papers and perhaps even rudimentary experimental design and statistics. Those who balk at the suggestion should bear in mind that most philosophy programs require logic training, and much twentieth-century philosophy borrowed tools from logic. Having philosophers take an empirical methods course would not be so different. I don't think philosophers should abandon their traditional training; the best empirical and experimental philosophers have had traditional training and benefit from it. Empirical methods should be added. Such training would help to make the boundaries between fields more permeable, so that people in different departments could better understand each other, learn from each other, and collaborate. The academy should not be seen as a collection of isolated intellectual fiefdoms but as a constellation of research methods and traditions that can collectively contribute to understanding the world and our place in it.

In the first part of this chapter, I tried to suggest that philosophers should welcome the introduction of laboratory results. Ignoring such results is like walking across the room with a blindfold on. Philosophers can debate which results are relevant, but if I am right that philosophy itself is an observational field, then exclusion of laboratory observation is indefensible. There is a continuum connecting philosophy to other observational fields. Experimental and empirical philosophers have made some steps closer to the middle, and, in so doing, they have enriched philosophy without losing sight of the problems and theories that have driven philosophical inquiry for the last two thousand years.

NOTE

This chapter benefited from discussions with the editors, and from many conversations, over the years, with philosophers who use empirical methods in their work.

REFERENCES

Block, N. (1995). On a confusion about a function of consciousness. *Behavioral and Brain Sciences* 18: 227–247.

Doris, J. M. (2002). *Lack of character*. Cambridge: Cambridge University Press.

Harman, G. (1999). Moral philosophy meets social psychology: Virtue ethics and the fundamental attribution error. *Proceedings of the Aristotelian Society* 99: 315–331.

Knobe, J., and Prinz, J. (2008). Intuitions about consciousness: Experimental studies. *Phenomenology and Cognitive Science.*

Nisbett, R., and Wilson, T. (1977). Telling more than we can know: Verbal reports on mental processes. *Psychological Review* 84: 231–259.

Prinz, J. J. (2002). *Furnishing the mind: Concepts and their perceptual basis*. Cambridge, MA: MIT Press.

Prinz, J. J. (2004). *Gut reactions: A perceptual theory of emotion*. New York: Oxford University Press.

Prinz, J. J. (2007a). Can moral obligations be empirically discovered? In H. Wettstein (ed.), *Midwest Studies in Philosophy* 31.

Prinz, J. J. (2007b). *The emotional construction of morals*. Oxford: Oxford University Press.

Stich, S., and Nichols, S. (1992). Folk psychology: Simulation or tacit theory? *Mind and Language* 7: 35–71.

Swain, S., Alexander, J., and Weinberg J. (2008). The instability of philosophical intuitions: Running hot and cold on truetemp. *Philosophy and Phenomenological Research.*

11

Abstract + Concrete = Paradox

Walter Sinnott-Armstrong

Every area of philosophy is beset, bemused, and beguiled by paradoxes, which are riddles with good reasons for contrary answers and no expert or rational consensus on which answer is best (Sorensen 2003). Some paradoxes depend on curious examples, such as in the liar paradox. Others arise out of ordinary life. The former bother only philosophers, but the latter bother both philosophers and common folk. The latter, ordinary kind of paradox will be my topic here.

Some such paradoxes have persisted for centuries and arise from questions like these: Can we be free or responsible when our acts and wills are determined? Can we know anything despite skeptical scenarios and regresses? Can minds fit into the physical world? Is it morally wrong to violate individual rights in order to prevent greater suffering?

To resolve paradoxes like these, philosophers often appeal to intuitions. Here an intuition is roughly a felt attraction to, or an inclination to believe, a certain claim whose attractiveness does not depend on any conscious inference. Such an attraction or inclination need not issue in a full belief but can remain merely an appearance that is not completely endorsed. A claim that is attractive to someone independently of inference can also be supported by inferences in other people or even in that person.

Unfortunately, intuitions conflict in many paradoxes of ordinary life. While one philosopher appeals to an intuition that favors one side of such a paradox, other philosophers can appeal to intuitions on the other side. That's what makes it a paradox. Each side then needs to discount or explain away at least some intuitions. We usually do not like it when our own intuitions are explained away as illusions or confusions, and no solution captures all of our intuitions, so no solution pleases everyone.

How can experimental philosophy help? One project uses empirical research to undermine the intuitions on one side of a paradox and, thereby, to support the other side. For example, Nichols, Stich, and Weinberg (2003) take sides against skeptical arguments. Another project within experimental philosophy is doubly negative insofar as it uses experiments to undermine the intuitions on both sides of a paradox. For example, Weinberg, Nichols, and Stich (2001) present evidence for hypotheses that are said to undermine "much of what has been done in epistemology in the analytic tradition" (2001, 1). If so, not only skeptics but also their opponents, at least in analytic epistemology, are in trouble.

Both of these projects differ from mine. My purpose is not to resolve philosophical paradoxes or to undermine philosophical intuitions. I just want to understand such paradoxes and intuitions. Why are these paradoxes so puzzling? Why are they so intractable? How do they arise? Those are the questions I will address here.

An answer is provided by an emerging pattern in some studies by experimental philosophers. These studies suggest that humans have two kinds of intuitions: abstract and concrete.[1] Conflicts between intuitions of these kinds give rise to many philosophical paradoxes. Most people have both kinds of intuitions to some extent, although some philosophers emphasize one kind of intuition, and others emphasize the other.[2] Each of these kinds of intuitions can provide the basis for a coherent philosophical position with its own attractions. No coherent theory can capture them all, since they conflict.

This account of paradoxes is openly speculative. Experimental philosophy is way too young to know where it is leading. Many studies in experimental philosophy have flaws (Bernstein, in progress). My account is also incomplete. Several factors other than abstraction, such as emotion and culture, surely affect philosophical intuitions. In addition, my account is limited. I would never claim to cover all philosophical paradoxes, or even all philosophical paradoxes that arise in everyday life. Still, I offer these limited and incomplete speculations in the hope that they might stimulate non-experimental philosophers to look at experimental philosophy in a new light and also in the hope that they might lead experimental philosophers to discuss and test whether their results really do fit this pattern.

To illustrate the pattern, I will focus on two examples from different areas of philosophy: Nichols and Knobe (this volume) on responsibility, and Nichols, Stich, and Weinberg (2003) on skepticism. The former concerns a paradox in metaphysics, whereas the latter lies inside epistemology. I will briefly mention a few additional examples from other areas of philosophy, including ethics. Since the abstract versus concrete pattern recurs in such disparate areas of philosophy, maybe there is something to it.

After showing how these examples fit the pattern, I will add even more speculations about why this pattern recurs in popular thinking. Here I will invoke psychological studies that find analogous patterns in how we represent ourselves and other people. There are good reasons why we evolved with both abstract and concrete representations of people and also why they conflict. Based on this empirical research, I will suggest that humans have two representational systems that generate two kinds of intuitions and that also make conflicts likely.

This explanation is neutral on philosophical truth. Nothing here attempts to resolve or dissolve the philosophical paradoxes. Indeed, my account might give some reason to doubt that these puzzles can ever be resolved or dissolved. Nonetheless, these speculations might help us understand part of how we got trapped into these paradoxes.

1. RESPONSIBILITY

One of the most popular philosophical paradoxes concerns free will and moral responsibility. It can be presented as an inconsistent set of claims:

(1) Every action is caused.
(2) If any act is caused, then it is completely determined.
(3) If any act is completely determined, then it is not done from free will.
(4) If any act is not done from free will, then its agent is not fully morally responsible for doing that act.
(5) If any agent is not fully morally responsible for doing an act, then that agent should not be punished for doing that act.
(6) Yet, some agents should be punished for some acts.

Logicians would agree that (1)–(6) cannot all be true (as long as "should" in [6] implies "not should not").

Much of the debate about this paradox occurs between incompatibilists and compatibilists. Each view comes in many versions, but the thesis that will concern us here is this implication of (3)–(4):

> *Incompatibilism* (about moral responsibility) = If any act is completely determined, then its agent is not fully morally responsible for doing that act.

Incompatibilists accept this claim, and compatibilists deny it. The denial of incompatibilism is then compatibilism.

The most common way to support incompatibilism is simply to claim that it is intuitively obvious. Another move is to ask a rhetorical question, "How could an agent be fully morally responsible for an act that was completely determined?" Some philosophers, including van Inwagen (1983) and Pereboom (2001) do present arguments for incompatibilism, but their arguments inevitably rely on additional intuitions. Hence, the debate comes down to whether incompatibilism really is supported by intuitions.

Whose intuitions? Most philosophers do not answer this question. They express their own intuitions and hope that their audience will share those intuitions or at least play along. Sometimes they claim that their intuitions are privileged because their intuitions result from superior reflection and that other people would agree with them if they reflected adequately. Still, these philosophers' insights are usually supposed to be insights into concepts of responsibility and freedom that common folk share.[3] To assess such claims by philosophers, we need to explore common intuitions of normal folk. Moreover, my goal here is to understand how this paradox of responsibility arises and why it persists not only among professional philosophers but also among common folk. If the conflicting intuitions regarding responsibility were held only by a few special philosophers, then the paradox would not be so popular or so old. In order to understand the paradox, then, we need to look at common intuitions of normal folk.

By *intuitions,* I mean inclinations to believe claims whose attractiveness does not depend on any conscious inference. By *common* intuitions, I mean intuitions that are not especially reflective, though they might be reflective to some degree.[4] By *normal* folk, I mean people who suffer from no special mental condition and are not officially committed to any theory or trained to any unusual degree, although they might have taken a few philosophy courses. Common intuitions of normal folk are the topic of most studies in experimental philosophy.

Incompatibilists often claim that normal folk have an intuition that incompatibilism is true. This claim was empirically tested by Nahmias, Morris, Nadelhoffer, and Turner (this volume), whose results suggest that common intuitions of normal folk run against incompatibilism and toward compatibilism insofar as their subjects call people morally responsible for certain acts that were said to be determined. If this were the whole story, then incompatibilism could not be supported by such intuitions.

A more complicated story emerges in recent work by Nichols and Knobe (this volume). They first gave subjects the following scenario:

> Imagine a universe (Universe A) in which everything that happens is completely caused by whatever happened before it. This is true from the very beginning of the universe, so whatever happened at the beginning of the universe caused what happened next, and so on right up until the present. For example, one day John decided to have French fries at lunch. Like everything else, this decision was completely caused by what happened before it. So, if everything in this universe was exactly the same up until John made his decision, then it *had to happen* that John would decide to have French fries. (10)

Over 90% of the subjects denied that their own universe is determined in this way. Then half of the subjects were asked:

> *Question 1:* In Universe A, is it possible for a person to be fully morally responsible for their actions?

The other half of the subjects were instead asked:

> *Question 2:* In Universe A, a man named Bill has become attracted to his secretary, and he decides that the only way to be with her is to kill his wife and 3 children. He knows that it is impossible to escape from his house in the event of a fire. Before he leaves on a business trip, he sets up a device in his basement that burns down the house and kills his family. Is Bill fully responsible for killing his wife and children?

Of those who were asked Question 1, 86% responded that it is *not* possible for a person to be fully morally responsible for any act in Universe A. In contrast, of those who were asked Question 2, 72% said that Bill *is* fully responsible for his act in Universe A. Since the groups were chosen arbitrarily, if the subjects who answered Question 2 had been given Question 1 instead, then they probably would also have overwhelmingly answered Question 1 in the negative.

The problem, of course, is that these two responses—"No" to Question 1 and "Yes" to Question 2—are logically incompatible. How could subjects give both answers? There seem to be three main possibilities:

(i) Normal folk really have only one intuition in favor of compatibilism, and their negative responses to Question 1 do not reflect real intuitions because those responses were based on some kind of confusion or performance error.

(ii) Normal folk really have only one intuition in favor of incompatibilism, and their positive responses to Question 2 do not reflect real intuitions because those responses were based on some kind of confusion or performance error.

(iii) Normal folk have both intuitions (one in favor of compatibilism and the other in favor of incompatibilism), so their intuitions are inconsistent.

Of course, it could also be true that some folks have one intuition, others have another, and some have both. Still, we can ask whether (i), (ii), or (iii) is the dominant pattern.

Consider (i). Defenders of compatibilism might try to explain away the negative responses to Question 1 as due to some confusion.[5] But why would subjects be confused by Question 1? It is simple enough, and not many subjects reported confusion with this question (personal communication with Nichols). Defenders of compatibilism might argue that subjects need concrete, emotional cases to trigger a proper understanding of responsibility, but that cannot explain the high level of consistency in negative answers to Question 1. Defenders of compatibilism might instead claim that subjects were misled by a prior commitment to a theory of incompatibilism. But why would 86% of these subjects be committed to incompatibilism? Such a high rate of negative responses cannot plausibly be ascribed to commitment to a theory unless that theory has some basis in intuition.[6] Hence, (i) seems implausible.

Next, consider (ii). Defenders of incompatibilism need to explain away the positive answers to Question 2. Question 2 is more complex than Question 1, so maybe it confused subjects. However, there is again no evidence in their reports or elsewhere that these subjects were confused. Moreover, their responses to Question 2 resemble responses by other subjects when asked about concrete actions in experiments by Nahmias et al. (this volume) and by Woolfolk, Doris, and Darley (this volume). It is hard to believe that these subjects were merely confused about so many clearly explained cases.

Defenders of incompatibilism still might try to explain away the positive responses to Question 2 as performance errors due to emotion or affect. Perhaps subjects' anger at Bill made them ascribe responsibility when they didn't really believe that Bill is responsible. It is not clear, however, why emotions should be associated with errors or contrasted with belief. Some philosophers and psychologists suggest that our emotions reflect beliefs and support cognition. Moreover, when performance errors are revealed (such as when someone points out a subject/verb disagreement), subjects usually admit their error, at least in simple recurring cases. In this relatively simple case, however, people do not give up their belief that Bill is responsible even when they admit that Bill's act made them angry. It seems, therefore, that subjects really do have intuitions behind their positive answers to Question 2.

This leaves (iii).[7] It looks as if common folk have one intuition (or group of intuitions) that pushes them toward incompatibilism and also another intuition (or group of intuitions) that pulls them away from incompatibilism. This is not to say that people intuit the truth of incompatibilism and also intuit the falsehood of incompatibilism at the same time. The intuitions are triggered in different circumstances. Moreover, the two intuitions work on different levels. Their intuition in favor of incompatibilism is abstract insofar as it answers Question 1, which does not mention any particular person or act or victim or time or place.[8] It is an intuition about a possibility and a universal conceptual connection between determinism and responsibility. In contrast, Question 2 does mention particular agent, victims, and act. In that way, it is concrete.[9] Nonetheless, despite their differences, these intuitions do conflict in the sense that the propositions that are intuited cannot both be true.[10]

How could we hold both intuitions despite their incompatibility? One possibility is that one intuition results from affect or emotion, while the other intuition results from something else (either another affect or some unemotional cognition). Another possibility is that one intuition reflects an abstract way of thinking, whereas the other reflects a concrete way of thinking. I will call these the affect account and the abstraction account, respectively.

To decide between these accounts, Nichols and Knobe performed a second experiment. They tried to construct cases that do and do not engage emotion or affect but are equally concrete rather than abstract. Here they are:

> As he has done many times in the past, Bill stalks and rapes a stranger. Is it possible that Bill is fully morally responsible for raping the stranger?

> As he has done many times in the past, Mark arranges to cheat on his taxes. Is it possible that Mark is fully morally responsible for cheating on his taxes?

Half of the subjects were instructed to imagine that the agent is in a deterministic universe, like Universe A above. The other half were instructed to imagine that the agent is in an indeterministic universe. This table gives the results:

Is the agent fully morally responsible?	Indeterministic universe	Deterministic universe
High affect case (Bill the rapist)	95%	64%
Low affect case (Mark the tax cheater)	89%	23%

Nichols and Knobe conclude, "The overall pattern of results…suggests that affect is playing an important role in the process that generates people's compatibilist intuitions" (this volume).

Unfortunately, Nichols and Knobe did not control completely for concreteness.[11] Their story of Mark never says that Mark does cheat on his taxes. He only "arranges to cheat on his taxes." I am not sure exactly what this means, but it seems less concrete than actually cheating on taxes. Moreover, cheating on taxes is not terribly concrete itself, because there are many very different ways to cheat on taxes, and many subjects might not have any concrete ideas about how to cheat on taxes (especially among college students who often do not file their own tax forms, and their subjects were college students). In contrast, when the story says, "Bill stalks and rapes a stranger," stalking rules out date rape, marital rape, and so on. Hence, this description conjures up more concrete images. Thus, at least some of the difference between the cases of Mark the tax cheater and Bill the rapist might be due to concreteness instead of affect. Only more experiments will show.

In any case, Nichols and Knobe's conclusion is, properly, only that "affect is playing an important role" (this volume). This conclusion is compatible with the claim that concreteness also plays an important role.[12] I would never claim that the difference between abstraction and concreteness explains all that is going on in these complex issues. Still, it does seem to be playing some role, so it explains some of the variance in the reported results.

The abstraction account would also explain some recent results of Roskies and Nichols (in progress). They tested whether intuitions of moral responsibility are affected by whether questions are asked about this actual world or, instead, about an alternate possible world. Subjects in the alternate condition read this scenario:

> Imagine an alternate universe, Universe A, that is much like earth. But in Universe A, many eminent scientists have become convinced that in their universe, every decision a person makes is completely caused by what happened before the decision—given the past, each decision *has to happen* the way that it does. These scientists think that a person's decision is always an inevitable result of their genetic makeup combined with environmental influences. So if a person decides to commit a crime, this can always be explained as a result of past influences. Any individual who had the same genetic makeup and the same environmental influences would have decided exactly the same thing. This is because a person's decision is always completely caused by what happened in the past.

Subjects in the actual condition read the same scenario except that the first two sentences were replaced by this one:

> Many eminent scientists have become convinced that every decision a person makes is completely caused by what happened before the decision—given the past, each decision *has to happen* the way that it does.

Subjects were then asked how much they agree with this statement:

> If these scientists are right, then it is impossible for a person [in Universe A] to be fully morally responsible for their actions.

(The bracketed words occurred only for those in the alternate condition.) Responses were given on a 7-point scale from 1 = disagree completely to 7 = agree completely, with 4 as the midline.

The only difference between these conditions is that subjects in the actual condition are asked about the actual world, whereas subjects in the alternate condition are asked about the alternate world. This one change affected responses. The mean response in the actual condition was 3.58, but the mean response in the alternate condition was 5.06. This difference is very significant, and it crosses the midline, so the mean response in the actual condition was disagreement, but the mean response in the alternate condition was agreement.

Why should it make any difference whether subjects are asked about the actual world or an alternate world? That's not clear. Roskies and Nichols discuss two possibilities. One is parallel to complex two-dimensional semantics. The other invokes a combination of depth of processing, motivation, and affect.

Another possible factor is abstraction as opposed to concreteness. When we think about the actual world, we know much more about it. The point is not that we could ever produce anywhere near a complete description of the actual world. We can't. The point is only that we gain and retain a tremendous amount of information from our lifetimes of experiences, so we form a vast array of beliefs, images, and other cognitive attitudes about the actual world. I can also remember or imagine many particular events in the actual world. In contrast, the alternate universe is described as "much like earth," which does not give us any concrete detail. Does my family live there? Which environmental influences affect actions in that world? How much immorality is there? Which laws are enforced? What happened in its history? In this respect, the alternate condition is much less concrete than the actual condition. If concreteness tends to stimulate compatibilist intuitions but abstraction tends to stimulate incompatibilist intuitions, then the relative concreteness of the actual condition might explain why subjects in that actual condition agreed less with the claim that people in the actual world cannot be morally responsible for their actions.

This explanation is compatible with and even complements the affect account if emotions are engaged more by concrete cases than by abstractions, as seems likely. However, we will see that the abstraction account extends further into realms where affect is lacking. The abstraction account, if it works, is then more general and basic.

2. SKEPTICISM

To see how the abstraction account extends into unemotional areas, consider epistemology. A traditional epistemological paradox arises from the brain-in-a-vat hypothesis, which postulates that I am no more than a brain in a vat stimulated by a super-intelligent scientist so as to produce all of my actual experiences. The paradox can be represented by this inconsistent set.

(1) For any belief and any hypothesis, if the hypothesis is inconsistent with the belief, and if I do not know that the hypothesis is false, then I do not know that the belief is true.
(2) The brain-in-a-vat hypothesis is inconsistent with my belief that I have legs.
(3) I do not know that the brain-in-a-vat hypothesis is false.
(4) Yet, I do know that I have legs.

As before, different philosophers reject different claims in this inconsistent set. Roughly, Unger (1975) denies (4), Moore (1959) denies (3), Putnam (1981) denies (2), and Nozick (1981) denies (1).

Let's focus on (3). How could I rule out the hypothesis that I am a brain in a vat? I could not appeal to any experience, because all of my actual experiences are predicted and explained by the hypothesis that I am a brain in a vat. The hypothesis seems internally consistent, so it cannot be ruled out by logic or semantics (pace Putnam 1981). Another move claims that I know that I am not just a brain in a vat, because I know that I have legs, but mere brains do not have legs. Dogmatic skeptics[13] respond that these knowledge claims beg the question, so I do not know that I am not a brain in a vat, just as (3) says.

This part of the debate comes down to whether (3) is true (or plausible or justified). Dogmatic skeptics accept (3). Common sense philosophers reject (3). What do normal folk say about (3)? To answer this question, Nichols, Stich, and Weinberg (2003) presented subjects with this scenario:

> George and Omar are roommates and enjoy having late-night 'philosophical' discussions. One such night Omar argues, "At some point in time, by, like, the year 2300, the medical and computer sciences will be able to simulate the real world very convincingly. They will be able to grow a brain without a body, and hook it up to a supercomputer in just the right way so that the brain has experiences exactly as if it were a real person walking around in a real world, talking to other people, and so on. And so the brain would believe it was a real person walking around in a real world, etc., except that it would be wrong—it's just stuck in a virtual world, with no actual legs to walk and with no other actual people to talk to. And here's the thing: how could you ever tell that it isn't really the year 2300 now, and that you're not really a virtual-reality brain? If you were a virtual-reality brain, after all, everything would look and feel exactly the same to you as it does now!"
>
> George thinks for a minute, and then replies: "But, look, here are my legs." He points down to his legs. "If I were a virtual-reality brain, I wouldn't have any legs really—I'd only really be just a disembodied brain. But I know I have legs—just look at them!—so I must be a real person, and not a virtual-reality brain, because only real people have real legs. So I'll continue to believe that I'm not a virtual-reality brain."

George and Omar are actually real humans in the actual real world
today, and so neither of them are [sic] virtual-reality brains, which means
that George's belief is true. But does George know that he is not a virtual-
reality brain, or does he only believe it? (241–242)

Among 15 subjects who had taken three or more philosophy courses, only 20%
claimed that George really knows. In contrast, among 48 subjects who had
taken two or fewer philosophy courses, 55% claimed that George really knows.

Nichols, Stich, and Weinberg (2003) take these empirical results to support
a normative conclusion: the "skeptical intuition" (228)—that is, the belief that
(3)—is "not to be trusted" (228). This conclusion is supposed to be "bad news
for the skeptical arguments that rely on those intuitions" (227).

Skeptics can respond in several ways. First, skeptics need not rely on any
intuition that (3). Indeed, I do not know any skeptics who claim to intuit (3),
that is, to be attracted to it or inclined to believe it independently of any inference. Even if (3) is not intuitive because it seems incorrect at first, skeptics can
still base (3) on an inference from further claims about what is necessary for
knowledge. These additional claims might or might not be based on intuition,
but at least the belief in (3) need not be an intuition.

Second, even if (3) is accepted by more subjects who have taken more philosophy courses, that finding might show that these students learned something in
their philosophy courses. They might have learned to question common sense
and to draw out unforeseen implications of their assumptions. They might
even have learned that they do not really know some of the things they thought
they knew before they studied philosophy.

Of course, these replies might strike some as implausible. Still, I doubt that
the empirical results in Nichols, Stich, and Weinberg (2003) by themselves can
undermine dogmatic skepticism. But I will not enter that fray here.

Instead, I want to distinguish this normative issue about skepticism from the
descriptive issue that interests me here. Regardless of what is justified, I want to
ask which intuitions people in fact have. As in the case of responsibility, there
are three main possibilities:

  (i)   Normal folk have only one intuition, and it is in favor of (3)
        and, hence, in favor of dogmatic skepticism.
  (ii) Normal folk have only one intuition, and it is against (3)
        and, hence, against dogmatic skepticism.
  (iii) Normal folk have both intuitions (one in favor of skepticism and
        the other against skepticism), so their intuitions are inconsistent.

Position i seems unlikely from the start, but it is also refuted by the results of
Nichols, Stich, and Weinberg (2003). It would be hard to explain why 55% of
their non-philosophical subjects reject (3) if normal folk had only one intuition in favor of (3) and no intuition at all against (3).

Position (ii) is also too simple. After all, 45% of their non-philosophical
subjects accept (3). Why would so many normal folk say this if they had only

one intuition against (3) and no intuition at all in favor of (3)? Moreover, when the two groups of subjects are combined, only 29 of 63 or 46% of their subjects said that George really knows, so the majority agreed with (3). Finally, in my experience (which is admittedly unsystematic but reiterated by other teachers), most students feel the force of (3) even if they finally reject it.

This leaves position (iii).[14] When people have conflicting intuitions, as (iii) claims, they can go either way, depending on which intuition is stronger for them. Thus, position (iii) can explain why 45% of non-philosophers accept (3), namely, because their intuition in favor of (3) is stronger at the time than their intuition against (3). Position (iii) can also explain why 55% of non-philosophers reject (3), namely, because their intuition against (3) is stronger at the time than their intuition in favor of (3).

These explanations might seem too good to be true, or too flexible to have definite content, but they do suggest predictions. They predict that subjects who reject (3) and also those who accept (3) will both show signs of internal conflict, such as longer reaction times and brain activity in areas associated with cognitive conflict. Moreover, position (iii) suggests that many subjects will accept (3) in some circumstances and reject (3) in other circumstances, depending on which intuition is primed (although individual subjects and groups of subjects will vary in their tendencies). It would be interesting to run these experiments, but they show in advance how position (iii) is falsifiable.

The conflicting intuitions postulated in position (iii) seem abstract and concrete in much the same way as the conflicting intuitions about responsibility in the preceding section. This might not be obvious, because the George and Omar story is partly abstract and partly concrete. It is concrete insofar as it refers to a particular incident, particular people, and a particular claim: that George has legs. At the end, however, the question is not about George's legs but instead about whether George knows that he is not a virtual-reality brain. That question is abstract insofar as it affects almost all of George's beliefs indiscriminately. The brain-in-a-vat scenario is also abstract in that many details are not spelled out. Who is the super-intelligent scientist? Is she alone? Why does she bother to create our experiences? Since this scenario mixes abstract and concrete elements, this scenario could trigger abstract intuitions in some people and concrete intuitions in others. That is just what happened.

Which people? Position (iii) can also explain why subjects with more philosophy courses are more likely to accept (3). Some smart students find it difficult or silly to think abstractly about brains in vats. Others find it natural and interesting. The latter group tends to come back for more philosophy. That is no surprise, and it would explain why people who take more philosophy courses base their answers more on abstract intuitions. The philosophy courses might strengthen their tendency to think abstractly, but they probably had some inclination toward abstraction from the start or they would never have taken philosophy or come back for more.[15]

These stories do not, of course, provide any positive support for position (iii) until they are confirmed, but they can be tested empirically. Just test first-year college students for degrees of abstract thought before they take any philosophy courses, then retest them after four years of college, and check for correlations between amount and kind of philosophical training and changes in abstract thinking. With appropriately sophisticated methods, we might be able to tease apart the influences of training and of prior inclinations in order to determine whether position (iii) really does explain why subjects who take more philosophy are more likely to accept (3).

In addition, Nichols, Stich, and Weinberg (2003) report that lower socioeconomic status (SES) subjects were less likely to go along with skeptical arguments. This tendency might reflect less inclination to abstract thought and more desire to stay firmly rooted in the real concrete world.[16] Of course, this is not proven. Nor is it a criticism. Nor am I claiming that low SES people cannot think abstractly or that they cannot follow instructions in thought experiments. The point is only that groups with less inclination to abstract thought will be less inclined to accept (3). That could explain why low SES subjects accepted (3) less often than did higher SES subjects.[17] Thus, the abstraction account can explain many of the findings in Nichols, Stich, and Weinberg (2003).

Finally, let me report a very small study of my own (with help from David Lamb). Although Nichols, Stich, and Weinberg (2003) focus on arguments from skeptical scenarios, traditional skeptics more often use a regress argument. They claim that you cannot know that a claim is true if you do not have or cannot give any reason for believing that it is true. This reason can be presented in an argument, but that argument cannot help you know that its conclusion is true unless you know that its premises are true. So you need a reason to believe those premises, and then the same requirements apply over and over again. This regress of reasons must either (a) stop at a claim with no reason to believe it or (b) circle back on itself or (c) go on infinitely. Dogmatic skeptics argue that none of these alternatives is acceptable, so nobody knows anything.

Of course, this skeptical argument cannot get off the ground without its premise that you cannot know that a claim is true if you do not have or cannot give any reason for believing that it is true. Some dogmatic skeptics might claim that this premise is immediately obvious and, hence, the content of an intuition. Opponents, however, often deny this premise.

What do normal folk think? To find out, we presented subjects with the following abstract question:

> People sometimes believe things for no good reason. For example, people sometimes believe what a politician says about the economy when they have no good reason to trust what the politician says. Our question is about knowledge: If a person cannot give any good reason to believe a claim, is it possible that the person *knows* that the claim is correct?

For a second group of subjects, we used the same opening (up to the colon), but we replaced the question with a more concrete version:

> If you cannot give any good reason to believe that the person whom you believe to be your mother really is your mother, is it possible that you *know* that she is your mother?

Of the 25 subjects who received the abstract question, 13 (52%) replied, "Yes." In contrast, of the 25 subjects who received the concrete question, 22 (88%) replied, "Yes." Although these results need to be replicated, these initial findings suggest, again, that abstraction and concreteness affect philosophical intuitions.

Of course, this one dichotomy is not the whole story. Emotion or affect also makes a difference at least in some cases, such as responsibility. However, the affect account cannot explain intuitions about knowledge when emotion is not involved. In that sense, at least, the abstraction account provides a more powerful explanation of our philosophical intuitions.

3. ETHICS AND OTHER AREAS OF PHILOSOPHY

Abstract and concrete intuitions conflict again in ethics. One striking example is Study 3 in Carlsmith, Darley, and Robinson (2002).[18] They told 351 Princeton undergraduates about a crime and then asked whether they were most interested in punishing the perpetrator or in preventing similar crimes in the future. Participants generally supported both the just deserts perspective with its emphasis on punishing the perpetrator and also the deterrence perspective with its emphasis on preventing future crime. Next, participants were asked whether the company (which was the punisher in this case) should expend the minimal, normal, or maximal available resources for catching the perpetrator and for preventing similar crimes in the future. Participants allocated significantly more resources toward preventing similar future crimes than toward catching the perpetrator (Carlsmith et al. 2002, 293–294). These responses showed that these participants endorsed deterrence as at least part of the general purpose of punishment.

Nonetheless, when subjects were asked to choose a sentence in a particular case, their choices were not affected at all by factors that they recognized as affecting deterrence. For example, according to deterrence theory, when crimes are hard to detect or criminals are hard to catch and convict, punishments need to go up in order to achieve the same level of deterrence. Also, when certain crimes are very common, more punishment is needed in order to reduce the level of crime to an acceptable level. Publicity also affects the amount of deterrence achieved by a certain punishment. However, subjects did not change their favored punishments when apprehension rates, conviction rates, crime rates, and publicity were varied. Instead, they changed their favored punishments only in response to changes in the harm done by the crime and other factors that affect just deserts.

These results suggest another clash between abstract and concrete intuitions. As Carlsmith et al. (2002) put it,

> Although participants expressed support for deterrence as a goal of punishment at an abstract level, they failed to assign punishment in a way that was consistent with this stated goal....Their punishment assignments were instead consistent with a theory of punishment based on the moral deservingness of the perpetrator. (295)

These intuitions, thus, follow a pattern similar to the one we saw in studies of responsibility and knowledge. Subjects have conflicting intuitions at different levels of abstraction. When the question is posed abstractly, people tend to endorse deterrence theory, at least as a major consideration. However, when the question is posed concretely, their views do not follow deterrence theory, and even conflict with it.

Examples could be multiplied. When Singer (1972) argues that the affluent have strong moral obligations to help the needy, many people seem to go along with his abstract moral principles but balk at his concrete applications to their own luxuries.[19] When Knobe (2003) finds that ascriptions of intentionality depend on whether effects are good or bad, this result can be seen as a conflict between an abstract intuition (that to call something intentional is purely psychological and descriptive rather than normative) and a concrete intuition (that, in Knobe's cases, the bad CEO acted intentionally but the good CEO did not). This conflict occurs not in ethics or epistemology but, rather, in philosophy of mind or action theory. And don't forget Zeno, whose metaphysical paradoxes show how concrete intuitions about motion conflict with abstract arguments concerning infinity (Sorensen 2003, ch. 4). Thus, the abstraction account has the potential to explain many paradoxes in diverse areas within philosophy.

4. FOUR DUAL SYSTEMS

As I said, my goal is not to resolve these paradoxes but only to understand their nature and sources. My explanation is bound to be speculative, since so little work has been done in this area. Nonetheless, I want to tie philosophical paradoxes to some seemingly unrelated research in psychology.

Psychologists have done lots of fascinating work on memory and how it affects knowledge of oneself and of other people. The emerging picture postulates multiple independent memory systems. Among others are episodic and semantic memory. Episodic memory represents particular or specific events, including actions by a person. Semantic memory represents more abstract properties or general traits of a person. The independence of these systems is shown most dramatically by patients with brain damage who lose one system but retain the other (including K. C. as reported by Tulving 1989 and W. J. as reported by Klein, Loftus, and Kihlstrom 1996).

These distinct systems seem to become engaged in a certain order as we get to know people, according to Klein, Cosmides, Tooby, and Chance (2002).

When we first meet a person (possibly absent some stereotype or report), we tend to use episodic memory to represent particular actions or incidents that illustrate that person's character. Later, when we have had too many experiences with that person for us to store them all in readily accessible episodic memory, if those experiences fit a stable enough pattern, then we abstract from multiple experiences to form a general trait summary (such as "polite") that is stored in semantic memory. At that time, to make room for new episodic memories, we suppress representations of the particular events that instantiate the stored trait summary. We do still represent episodes that are inconsistent with the trait summary (such as episodes when this person was impolite), and we retrieve these trait-inconsistent episodes along with the trait summary when we think about the person.[20] The explanation for this tendency might be that the inconsistent episodic memories serve to bound or restrict overextension of the trait summaries into areas where they would lead to inaccurate predictions of behavior. The dual system, thus, balances speed and efficiency (by using trait summaries in semantic memory) with accuracy (by retaining inconsistent experiences in episodic memory).

This theory is far from proven, but it does explain many otherwise surprising observations. For example, trait-inconsistent episodes were primed and recalled faster than trait-consistent episodes, which were not primed. Moreover, this effect was larger for traits that better describe people who are known more intimately. (For details and references, see Klein et al. 2002.) It is hard to see how to explain such results without something like the story above.[21]

The studies done and discussed by Klein et al. thus suggest that, at least in one area of cognition, humans have two representational systems: one abstract and the other concrete. They also suggest that these systems naturally conflict with each other, because the concrete system stores counter-instances to the generalizations in the abstract system.

This dual system parallels what we saw in philosophical intuitions. As with trait summaries and episodes, on many philosophical issues people tend to have both abstract and concrete intuitions that naturally conflict. Trait summaries are not universal in the exactly same way as abstract philosophical intuitions, and concrete examples in philosophy are not as detailed as real life episodes in memory. (See notes 1 and 9.) Still, the analogy is suggestive. Perhaps the intuitions that conflict in philosophical paradoxes arise from different systems in our brains and minds that resemble the systems that Klein et al. found behind memory and knowledge of self and other.

If so, this proposal would explain a lot. First, it would explain why philosophical intuitions are so persistent. Philosophers who deny responsibility often admit that they have to fight the appearance of responsibility in horrible criminals. Compatibilists often admit a tendency to think that determinism rules out full moral responsibility, even though they explain away that tendency as a confusion. The same pattern recurs for paradoxes in epistemology and ethics. Both sides of the debate usually feel the force of intuitions on the other side. These appearances, even if illusory, are just what one would expect if the philosophical intuitions come from distinct representational systems that are inherent in all or almost all human minds, though to differing degrees.[22]

Moreover, we can also understand why humans have both systems. The abstract intuition of incompatibilism enables us to identify excuses quickly. If someone pushes me into you, then I can say that I was caused to bump you, and you immediately see the relevance of what I say. If someone threatens to kill me if I do not hand over our money, then I can say that he made me hand it over, and you immediately recognize my excuse. The abstract principle "if determined, then not responsible" provides a fast and frugal heuristic for identifying excuses. (Cf. Gigerenzer et al. 1999.) However, this principle can carry us too far. When childhood experiences are seen as causing brain states that make someone want to rape or murder, we do not want to apply the incompatibilist generalization. This overextension of the incompatibilist principle can be prevented by storing representations of particular instances where agents are fully morally responsible despite having been caused by external forces. Thus, just as in the case of knowing oneself and others, the abstract representations provide speed, but the concrete representations are needed to restrict applications. The two systems work well together, even though they often produce philosophical paradoxes.

Of course, the full story cannot be so simple or neat. Abstract cases and questions do not always stimulate only abstract representations. Nor do concrete cases stimulate only concrete representations. Almost any case will stimulate some intuitions of both kinds, and these intuitions will intermingle in complex ways. Moreover, contextual framing and priming will affect intuitions. Emotion or affect is also relevant and interacts with concreteness, since emotion arouses concrete representations, and abstract descriptions tend to dampen emotion. And different individuals and groups will emphasize different kinds of intuitions, depending on temperament, training, and culture. For all of these reasons and more, survey responses will vary a lot, and only some of this variance will be explained by the dichotomy between abstract and concrete. Far from undermining the abstraction account, however, these variations enable the abstraction account to be part of a larger explanation of observed patterns of responses. Much more work needs to be done in order to understand how people react to philosophical paradoxes, but it looks as if conflicts between concrete and abstract representations are likely to play a significant role in that larger theory.

5. WHAT'S LEFT FOR PHILOSOPHERS?

Even if it is not exactly abstract and concrete intuitions that conflict in philosophical paradoxes, it still seems plausible, I hope, that many philosophical paradoxes arise from psychological tendencies deep in human nature. Of course, culture can affect these tendencies and also give rise to paradoxes, but paradoxes are unlikely to last long or spread far unless their sources are profound. Such is the case with popular philosophical paradoxes. Somehow many people have intuitions that we have some knowledge, even though they also have other intuitions that lead to skepticism. Somehow many people have intuitions that horrific criminals are fully morally responsible, even though they also have other intuitions that point toward hard determinism. And so on.

How can we deal with such conflicts? One strategy is to reinterpret the intuited claims so as to make them consistent. (See note 5, for example.) Then we don't need to choose between them. Unfortunately, such reinterpretations rarely, if ever, fully capture the intuitions behind the paradox. If they did, the paradox would not last long.

A second method is to look inside ourselves and ask which intuition is more forceful psychologically. The problem here is stability. While working in my study, my abstract intuitions often lead me toward skepticism, as Hume said, and toward hard determinism and consequentialism, I claim. But when I leave my study and enter the "real" world, or when a burglar breaks into my study, then my concrete intuitions gain prominence. Thus, if my view depends on the psychological force of my intuitions, I will change my view at least twice each workday.

A third tactic seeks an argument for one intuition over the other. The refuted intuition might persist despite the argument against it, but it retains no more philosophical force than the fact that one line still appears longer in the Müller-Lyer illusion. This tactic can't work, however, without some way to argue for one intuition over the other.

We might hope to show that either abstract or concrete intuitions are more reliable or better justified in general. But why? It is hard to see any general reason to prefer abstract intuitions to concrete intuitions or vice versa.[23]

Another possibility is to reveal an internal inconsistency in the intuitions on one side of each paradox. Dogmatic skeptics sometimes try to show that common sense is inconsistent, but their opponents retort that such skepticism is inconsistent. Similarly, hard determinists try to refute moral responsibility or free will with slippery slopes, and then defenders of moral responsibility start at the other end of the same slippery slope and argue for the opposite conclusion. In any case, I do not see why either skepticism or anti-skepticism or either an assertion or denial of moral responsibility must be internally inconsistent. Each view does conflict with intuitions on the other side, but internal inconsistency can always be avoided by denying premises that reflect opposing intuitions.

We still might hope to give some positive argument for one side of the paradox. But how can you argue that some people really do know something without begging the question against skeptics? And how can dogmatic skeptics argue that nobody knows anything without using any premise that their opponents deny? Similarly, any argument against moral responsibility will have premises that defenders of moral responsibility can give up at some cost, but they might be willing to pay that price in order to keep moral responsibility. Any argument for moral responsibility will appeal to intuitions that opponents will be able to explain away as illusions or confusions. Maybe each side thinks that the other side cannot refute or match its knockdown arguments. But that is not how the situation appears to most neutral observers. Most neutral observers on such philosophical issues can see that neither argument is beyond question.

A final move is to shift the burden of proof to opponents and insist that the preferred side needs no argument. Each side can build up the intuitions in its favor and argue that anyone who denies those intuitions has the burden of proof. Unfortunately, the other side can say exactly the same thing. In the end, there is no accepted standard for burden of proof that helps to resolve philosophical paradoxes. Besides, both sides seem to have some burden of proof, since each side makes a claim when they could suspend belief.

So, we are back to intuitions. Maybe we just need to learn to live with conflicting intuitions. We can still look for arguments to back up certain intuitions. Perhaps sometimes we will succeed. But, when we fail to find arguments that pass muster, or when we find equally good arguments on both sides, then we are left with a paradox.

This is where Pyrrhonians find themselves (Sextus Empiricus 2000). They feel the pull of both sides and recognize that they cannot have it both ways. They cannot prove that no resolution is possible, but they cannot imagine how any resolution would succeed or even proceed. Pyrrhonians sometimes seek this state as a source of their cherished *ataraxia* or tranquillity, but many other people do not find it so tranquil or attractive. Whether we like it or not, however, this situation might be part of the human condition, and experimental philosophy can help us understand how we ended up in it.[24]

NOTES

Thanks to Robert Audi, Bob Fogelin, Joshua Knobe, Don Loeb, Mark Moyer, Shaun Nichols, and Roy Sorensen for helpful comments on drafts.

1. The slippery terms "abstract" and "concrete" can refer either to the dichotomy between universal and particular or to the separate dichotomy between general and specific (as well as to other dichotomies). My account in Section 4 will use a distinction between one kind of representation that is both universal and general and another kind of representation that is both particular and specific. It is not clear which distinction is essential. It is also not clear exactly which features of stimuli trigger the different kinds of representations. These details must be left to future work. For now, the dichotomy between abstract and concrete will have to remain inspecific, but I hope we can make some progress anyway.

2. Compare the distinction between "tough-minded" and "tender-minded" philosophers in William James (1907, first lecture).

3. Instead of analyzing common concepts, some philosophers recommend new concepts that are supposed to avoid paradoxes. My remarks do not apply to such revisionists, but we can ignore them here, because they cannot help to explain common intuitions and paradoxes, which is my goal.

4. Audi (2001) explains how intuitions can be based on reflection without being based on any conscious inference.

5. For example, Robert Audi (1993) claims that incompatibilists conflate "If laws and prior conditions hold, then the agent must do the act" with "It must be the case that, if laws and prior conditions hold, then the agent does the act." The latter is true, but the former is not (if it is read so that its modal operator is in its consequent). It is hard to see, however, where van Inwagen, Pereboom, and other incompatibilists commit this simple fallacy.

6. Recall that over 90% of the subjects denied that their own universe is like one where human acts are completely determined. Vargas argues, "It is difficult to see what could be driving those responses if there were not incompatibilist (specifically, libertarian) self-conceptions at work at some level" (2006, 241).

7. Views like (iii) have been proposed by Smilansky (2000) and Vargas (2006). Another possibility is (iv), that normal folk have no intuitions on either side of the paradox, but that conflicts with the evidence given my broad notion of intuition, and it would not help to explain how paradoxes arise.

8. The abstractness or concreteness of a question is distinct from the abstractness or concreteness of an intuition, even when the intuition is an inclination to believe an answer to the question. An abstract question can stimulate concrete intuitions, and a concrete question can give rise to abstract intuitions. Which kinds of questions stimulate which kinds of intuitions is an empirical question worth investigating. In the cases under discussion, however, whether the question is abstract or concrete seems to affect how many of the resulting intuitions are abstract or concrete.

9. Of course, Question 2 is not completely concrete, since it leaves many details unspecified. Still, Question 2 is relatively concrete compared with Question 1. In any case, what matters is not whether the question really is abstract but only whether subjects see it as abstract and whether that affects how they answer it.

10. Formally, the content of this concrete intuition uses a constant (D&Ra), whereas the content of the abstract intuition uses a variable $(D->\sim(x)Rx)$. These contents are inconsistent.

11. Other differences also need to be considered: Tax cheating is more common than rape. Some subjects might think it is not their job to blame people for tax cheating, but they would blame people for rape. It would be an outrage not to punish for rape, but legal systems may legitimately choose not to punish for tax cheating or, at least, for acts that currently count as tax cheating. And so on. All of these differences might affect the reported results.

12. In their earlier study, 86% said it is *not* possible to be fully morally responsible in a deterministic universe. Here 23% hold Mark responsible. Why? Maybe concreteness? It is not clear whether this difference is statistically significant.

13. Dogmatic skeptics claim that nobody knows anything. I call them "dogmatic" to distinguish them from Pyrrhonian skeptics who suspend belief about the claim by dogmatic skeptics that nobody knows anything.

14. As before, the possibility that normal folk have no intuitions on either side of the paradox conflicts with the evidence given my broad notion of intuition and would not help to explain how paradoxes arise and persist.

15. As we will see below in our discussion of Klein et al. (2002), people tend to switch from concrete representations of episodes to abstract representations of general traits as they get to know people better. This tendency might help to explain why people who are more familiar with philosophy also tend more toward abstract thought instead of concrete examples.

16. Nichols, Stich, and Weinberg (2003) instead conclude, "Low SES Westerners regard knowledge as less demanding than do high SES Westerners" (14). My suggestion is that they regard knowledge as equally demanding, but low SES Westerners think the demands are met. To see why, consider the Zebra case in Nichols, Stich, and Weinberg. Maybe high SES college students play along with the scenario, but low SES subjects think the example is easy, because real zoos don't actually paint mules. These low SES subjects are thinking about the real world, because they need to live there and don't

see the point of ignoring real limits. That is a sense in which they are more concrete. Similarly, in the conspiracy case in Nichols, Stich, and Weinberg (2003), maybe low SES subjects discount the claim that "it is possible that...," because they know it is unlikely. They think about a concrete case in the real world, because they see no point in reasoning abstractly. This tendency might explain the experimental results without claiming that low and high SES subjects have different standards of knowledge.

17. A similar explanation might apply to differences between East Asians and Europeans. Nichols, Stich, and Weinberg (2003) found East Asians to be less likely than Westerners to go along with skeptical claims and arguments. These findings can be explained by the abstraction account plus some generalizations from Nisbett et al. (2001). Nisbett characterizes the dominant Western style of thought as "involving detachment of the object from its context, a tendency to focus on attributes of the object in order to assign it to categories, and a preference for using rules about the categories to explain and predict the object's behavior" (Nisbett et al. 2001, 239). In contrast, Nisbett characterizes the dominant style of thought among East Asians as "involving an orientation to the context or field as a whole, including attention to relationships between a focal object and the field, and a preference for explaining and predicting events on the basis of such relationships" (Nisbett et al. 2001, 239). In other words, Westerners think in terms of abstract categories and rules that detach individual objects from their concrete contexts, whereas East Asians think more about relationships to concrete objects in the concrete context. If this is correct, and if a tendency toward abstract thinking inclines people more toward accepting (3), whereas a tendency toward concrete thinking inclines people more toward rejecting (3), then this might explain why East Asians are less likely than Westerners to go along with skeptical claims.

18. These authors are psychologists rather than philosophers, but many psychology experiments count as experimental philosophy.

19. Greene (2008) describes additional studies where people's moral intuitions are affected by whether cases are described abstractly or concretely.

20. The notion of inconsistency here is not logical, since, for example, the fact that someone is polite (or impolite) on one particular occasion is logically compatible with the claim that this person has the general character trait of being impolite (or polite). Particular episodes can still be called "trait-inconsistent" insofar as these episodes are evidence against the person having the trait, and the episodes and traits support conflicting predictions of the person's future behavior.

21. Many details in Klein's account are unnecessary for my purposes here. I could even just refer to multiple heuristics (the toolbox of Gigerenzer et al. 1999). Still, Klein's story does seem to match patterns in philosophical intuitions.

22. Klein's story about how abstract representations get invoked over time suggests that those who have worked on punishment for long enough might find it easier to recall or imagine concrete examples where punishment is undeserved but prevents crime than to think of examples where punishment is deserved and also prevents crime. Yet common people with less experience with punishment might display the reverse tendency. Similarly for responsibility and knowledge. It would be interesting to test these predictions.

23. Compare the problem of the criterion in Chisholm (1989, 6–7). Generalists or methodists start with abstract criteria (for example, of knowledge) and reject any cases that violate those criteria. Particularists start with concrete cases (for example, of what we know) and reject any criteria that conflict with those cases. Chisholm does not give, and I do not know, any good argument for either generalism or particularism as opposed to the other.

REFERENCES

Audi, R. 1993. "Modalities of Knowledge and Freedom." In *Action, Intention, and Reason*, 253–280. Ithaca: Cornell University Press.

Audi, R. 2001. *The Architecture of Reason*. New York: Oxford University Press.

Bernstein, M. In progress. "Experimental Philosophy Meets Experimental Design: 23 Questions."

Carlsmith, K. M., Darley, J. M., and Robinson, P. H. 2002. "Why Do We Punish? Deterrence and Just Deserts as Motives for Punishment." *Journal of Personality and Social Psychology* 83: 284–299.

Gigerenzer, G., Todd, P., and the ABC Research Group. 1999. *Simple Heuristics That Make Us Smart*. New York: Oxford University Press.

Greene, J. 2008. "The Secret Joke of Kant's Soul." In W. Sinnott-Armstrong (ed.), *Moral Psychology, Volume 3: The Neuroscience of Morality: Emotion, Brain Disorders, and Development*. Cambridge, Mass.: MIT Press.

James, W. 1907. *Pragmatism*. Indianapolis: Hackett, 1981.

Klein, S., Cosmides, L., Tooby, J., and Chance, S. 2002. "Decisions and the Evolution of Memory: Multiple Systems, Multiple Functions." *Psychological Review* 109: 306–329.

Klein, S. B., Loftus, J., and Kihlstrom, J. F. 1996. "Self-Knowledge of an Amnesic Patient: Toward a Neuropsychology of Personality and Social Psychology. *Journal of Experimental Psychology* 125: 250–260.

Knobe, J. 2003. "Intentional Action and Side Effects in Ordinary Language." *Analysis* 63: 190–193.

Moore, G. E. 1959. *Philosophical Papers*. London: George, Allen and Unwin.

Nahmias, E., Morris, S., Nadelhoffer, T., and Turner, J. 2005. "Surveying Freedom: Folk Intuitions about Free Will and Moral Responsibility." *Philosophical Psychology* 18: 561–584.

Nahmias, E., Morris, S., Nadelhoffer, T., and Turner, J. Forthcoming. "Is Incompatibilism Intuitive?" *Philosophy and Phenomenological Research*.

Nichols, S., and Knobe, J. 2007. "Moral Responsibility and Determinism: The Cognitive Science of Folk Intuitions." *Noûs*.

Nichols, S., Stich, S., and Weinberg, J. 2003. "Meta-Skepticism: Meditations in Ethno-Methodology." In S. Luper (ed.), *The Skeptics*, 227–247. Aldershot, England: Ashgate Publishing.

Nozick, R. 1981. *Philosophical Explanations*. Cambridge: Belknap Press.

Pereboom, D. 2001. *Living without Free Will*. New York: Cambridge University Press.

Putnam, H. 1981. *Reason, Truth, and History*. Cambridge: Cambridge University Press.

Roskies, A., and Nichols, S. In progress. "Bringing Moral Responsibility Down to Earth."

Sextus Empiricus. 2000. *Outlines of Scepticism*, trans. Julia Annas and Jonathan Barnes. Cambridge: Cambridge University Press.

Singer, P. 1972. "Famine, Affluence, and Morality." *Philosophy and Public Affairs* 1: 229–243.

Smilansky, S. 2000. *Free Will and Illusion*. Oxford: Clarendon Press.

Sorensen, R. 2003. *A Brief History of the Paradox: Philosophy and the Labyrinths of the Mind*. New York: Oxford University Press.

Tulving, E., Schachter, D. L., McLachlan, D. R., and Muscovitch, M. 1988. "Priming of Semantic Autobiographical Knowledge: A Case Study of Retrograde Amnesia." *Brain and Cognition* 8: 3–20.

Unger, P. 1975. *Ignorance: A Case for Skepticism*. New York: Oxford University Press.

van Inwagen, P. 1983. *An Essay on Free Will.* New York: Oxford University Press.

Vargas, M. 2006. "Philosophy and the Folk: On Some Implications of Experimental Work for Philosophical Debates on Free Will." *Journal of Cognition and Culture* 6: 239–254.

Weinberg, J., Nichols, S., and Stich, S. 2001. "Normativity and Epistemic Intuitions." *Philosophical Topics* 29: 429–460.

12

Experimental Philosophy
and Philosophical Intuition

Ernest Sosa

Our topic is experimental philosophy as a naturalistic movement and its bearing on the value of intuitions in philosophy. I explore first how the movement might bear on philosophy more generally and how it might amount to something novel and promising. Then I turn to one accomplishment repeatedly claimed for it already: namely, the discrediting of armchair intuitions as used in philosophy.[1]

Experimental philosophy bears on traditional philosophy in at least two ways. It puts in question what is or is not believed *intuitively* by people generally. And it challenges the *truth* of beliefs that *are* generally held, ones traditionally important in philosophy. Each challenge is based on certain experimental results.

How might such experimental results bear on philosophical issues? Here's an example. Traditional skepticism relies crucially on the idea that for all we can really tell, life is but a dream. Whether one enjoys waking life or an extended dream, one has the very same stream of consciousness regardless, so how can one possibly tell the difference? This depends on a conception of dreams as something like hallucinations, however, and we might discover that dreams are not quite like that. Perhaps to dream is much more like imagining than like hallucinating. If so, how might this bear on the traditional skeptical problematic?

Even if it *is* part of common sense that in dreams we have conscious experiences intrinsically just like those of waking life, an experimentally based approach might show that common sense is just wrong, in a way that bears crucially on a perennial problematic of philosophy, that of radical skepticism.

Mining the sciences is not in itself novel, of course. Philosophers have been doing that for a very long time, with striking results. Just think of how twentieth-century physics bears on the philosophy of space and time, or split-brain phenomena on issues of personal identity, to take just two examples. Perhaps the novelty is rather that experimental philosophers do not so much *borrow* from the scientists as that they *become* scientists. This they do by designing and running experiments aimed to throw light on philosophically interesting issues. And if philosophers are ill equipped to probe the brain in the ways of neuroscientists, it is easy enough to broaden the movement's self-conception to include interdisciplinary work, provided neuroscientists care enough about such issues with philosophical import, as no doubt some already do. Indeed, many experimental philosophers would already define the movement in this interdisciplinary way.

In any case, most of the actual work so far done in experimental philosophy has involved social psychology. Some of the best-known work has involved surveys designed to probe, and to question, people's intuitions on various philosophical issues. So the novelty might involve the methodologically self-conscious pursuit of such an approach. This anyhow is the side of experimental philosophy that I will be discussing. If the movement is to substantiate a claim to novel results of striking interest to philosophy, this work on intuitions, and other work similarly dependent on surveys, would seem to be particularly important.[2]

My defense against experimentalist objections to armchair intuitions is anchored in the fact that verbal disagreement need not be substantive. This defense will be developed presently, but first: How should we conceive of intuitions?

It is often claimed that analytic philosophy appeals to armchair intuitions in the service of "conceptual analysis." But this is deplorably misleading. The use of intuitions in philosophy should not be tied exclusively to conceptual analysis. Consider some main subjects of prominent debate: utilitarian versus deontological theories in ethics, for example, or Rawls's theory of justice in social and political philosophy, or the externalism/internalism debate in epistemology; and many others could be cited to similar effect. These are not controversies about the conceptual analysis of some concept. They seem moreover to be disputes about something more objective than just a description or analysis of our individual or shared concepts of the relevant phenomena. Yet they have been properly conducted in terms of hypothetical examples and intuitions about these examples. The questions involved are about rightness or justice or epistemic justification. Some such questions concern an ethical or epistemic subject matter, and not just our corresponding concepts.

There can be such a subject matter, beyond our concepts of it, moreover, even if rightness, justice, and epistemic justification are not *natural kinds*. Nor need they be socially constructed kinds, either. Indeed, we can regard philosophical controversies as objective without ever going into the ontological status of the entities involved, if any. Mostly we can conduct our controversies, for example, just in terms of where the *truth* lies with regard to them, leaving aside questions of objectual ontology.

Prima facie there is a role for intuition in simple arithmetic and geometry, moreover, but *not only* there. Just consider how extensively we rely on intuition. Take, for example, any two sufficiently different shapes that you perceive on a surface, say the shapes of any two words. If they are words in a foreign language, you may not even have a good *recognitional* grasp, a good concept of any of those shapes. Still you may know perfectly well that they are different. And what you know is not just that the actual *tokens* are different: you also know that any word token *so* shaped *would* be differently shaped from any *thus* shaped (as you demonstrate the two shapes in turn). Or take any shape and any color, or any shape and any sound. And so on, and so forth. Why deny ourselves a similar intuitive access to the simple facts involved in our hypothetical philosophical examples? That we enjoy such access would seem to be the default position, absent some specific objection.

I apply virtue epistemology to the specific case of a priori knowledge, and more specifically to foundational a priori knowledge, to *intuitive* justification and knowledge. Traditionally such intuitions have been understood in accordance with two prominent models: (a) the perceptual, eye-of-the-mind model, and (b) the Cartesian introspective model. Each of these models is subject to fatal objections, however, which prepares the way for my proposed competence-based account.

On my proposal, to intuit that p is to be attracted to assent simply through entertaining that representational content. The intuition is *rational* if and only if it derives from a *competence* and the content is explicitly or implicitly modal (i.e., attributes necessity or possibility). This first approximation is then defended against the two main published lines of attack on intuitions: the calibration objection and the cultural divergence objection.[3]

One might quite properly wonder why we should restrict ourselves to modal propositions. And there is no very deep reason. It's just that this seems the proper domain for philosophical uses of intuition. True, contingent intuitions might also derive from a competence. For example, there is a "taking experience at face value" competence, whose resulting intuitions would be *of the form* "if things appear thus and so, then they *are* thus and so." These I would call "empirical" intuitions, however, to be distinguished from the "rational" intuitions involved in abstract, a priori, armchair thought of the kind we do in philosophy.

It might be objected that the proposed account is *too externalist*. But two sources of such worry need to be distinguished. One is the *access* worry, the other the *control* worry, and the two are largely independent. These raise large and fascinating issues of internalism versus externalism. Here I can only gesture, inadequately, at my preferred stance.

First, regarding access, we cannot well insist on armchair access to the justifying power of our sources, since their justifying power depends crucially on their reliability, and this is not knowable from the armchair for our competences generally. (This is not to deny that a source's justifying power is boosted, reaching a special level, when we *do* have access to its reliability; or at least that, when the source operates in combination with such awareness, we attain a higher, reflective level for the resulting beliefs.)

Second, regarding control, we cannot well insist on *total* control. We must depend on favorable circumstances in all sorts of ways, and these are often relevantly beyond our control. We must depend on a kind of epistemic luck.

If we insist that true knowledge requires *armchair* access to the reliability of our competences or *total* control regardless of our situation, the outcome is extreme skepticism, which I do not regard as a *reductio* exactly, though I do think it limits the interest of the notions of *absolute* knowledge thus induced.

When we rely on intuitions in philosophy, then, in my view we manifest a competence that enables us to get it right on a certain subject matter, by basing our beliefs on the sheer understanding of their contents. How might survey results create a problem for us? Suppose a subgroup clashes with another on some supposed truth, and suppose they all ostensibly affirm as they do based on the sheer understanding of the content affirmed. We then have a prima facie problem. Suppose half of them affirm <p> while half deny it, with everyone basing their respective attitudes on the sheer understanding of the representational content <p>. Obviously, half of them are getting it right, and half wrong. Of those who get it right, now, how plausible can it be that their beliefs constitute or derive from rational intuition, from an attraction to assent that manifests a real competence?

Not that it is logically incoherent to maintain exactly that. But how plausible can it be, absent some theory of error that will explain why so many are going wrong when we are getting it right? Unless we can cite something different in the conditions or in the constitution of the misled, doubt will surely cloud the claim to competence by those who ex hypothesi are getting it right.

If there is a large disagreement in color judgments within a certain population, how can we sustain the claim to competence by those whose excellent color vision guides them systematically to the truth? Presumably we need to explain the error of the others by appeal to some defect in their lighting conditions or in their color vision, something wrong with their rods and cones or the like. Even if we reject the perceptual model of intuition, so long as we still appeal to competence, we need something analogous to the error theory that protects our color vision from the disagreement of the color blind and of those misled by bad light. We need an error theory that attributes the error of those who disagree with us to bad constitution (blindness) or to bad situation (bad light).

That would seem to be so, moreover, regardless of whether the subject matter is fully objective (as, perhaps, with shape perception), or quasi-objective and reaction-dependent (as, perhaps, with color perception, or with socially constructed phenomena).

So there will definitely be a prima facie problem for the appeal to intuitions in philosophy if surveys show that there is extensive enough disagreement on the subject matter supposedly open to intuitive access.

The bearing of these surveys on traditional philosophical issues is questionable, however, because the experimental results really concern in the first instance only people's responses to certain words. But verbal disagreement *need* not reveal any substantive, real disagreement, if ambiguity and context might account for the verbal divergence. If today I say, "Mary went to the bank yesterday," and tomorrow you say, "Mary did not go to the bank yesterday," we need not disagree, given ambiguity and contextual variation. The experimentalists have not yet done enough to show that they have crossed the gaps created by such potential differences in meaning and context, so as to show that supposedly commonsense intuitive belief is really not as widely shared as philosophers have assumed it to be. Nor has it been shown beyond reasonable doubt that there really are philosophically important disagreements rooted in cultural or socioeconomic differences (or so I have argued elsewhere in some detail) (see Bishop & Murphy, 2007).

Within the movement itself, one finds a growing recognition that the supposed "intuitive disagreements" may be only verbal. Thus, a recent paper by Shaun Nichols and Joseph Ulatowski contains the following proposal:

> Our hypothesis is that 'intentional' exhibits interpretive diversity, i.e., it admits of different interpretations. Part of the population, when given ... [certain] sorts of cases, interpret 'intentional' one way; and part of the population interpret it in another way. On one interpretation both cases are intentional and on the other interpretation, neither is. In linguistics and philosophy of language, there are several ways that a term can admit of different interpretations: the term might be ambiguous, polysemous, or exhibit certain forms of semantic underspecification. We mean for the interpretive diversity hypothesis to be neutral about which form of interpretive diversity holds for 'intentional.'[4]

To the extent that experimental philosophy adopts this way of accounting for diversity of verbal intuitive responses, it will avoid substantive clashes in favor of merely verbal disagreement. But once such disagreements are seen to be verbal, the supposed problem for philosophical intuition evaporates.

The defense of philosophical intuition by appeal to "merely verbal disagreement" may be rejected because the implied failures of communication would threaten to make intuition reports useless for joint philosophical theorizing. Although this point is sometimes pressed, I can see no real threat in it. The appeal to divergence of interpretation is a *defensive* move, made against those who claim that there *is* serious disagreement in supposed intuitions. It is only against such a claim of disagreement that we must appeal to verbal divergence. But any such claim need be taken seriously only when adequately backed by evidence. And this is surely a matter to be taken up case by case. Among possible sources of such attention-demanding evidence, two stand out. First, the evidence might be gathered empirically, through surveys. Second, the evidence might be internal to our field, owed to dialectic with fellow philosophers, where we seem to disagree persistently, for example, on what to think about various hypothetical cases. One attractive option, once we have reached that stage, having exhausted other options, would be to consider whether we may be "interpreting" our terms somewhat differently.

Consider a further case study of how an apparent clash of intuitions can turn out to be only verbal. We turn to a recent paper by Shaun Nichols and Joshua Knobe about the bearing of intuitions on the problematic of free will and determinism (Nichols & Knobe 2007). In their view intuitions relevant to

this problematic are heavily influenced by affect. Here is a brief description of
the study, its results, and the morals drawn.

First the distinction between a fully determinist universe D and an indeterminist universe I is presented to experimental subjects, 90% of whom report
that our own universe is more like I than like D.

Now for the shocking results: When subjects are asked the abstract question
whether agents in D are fully morally responsible, 86% say that they are not:
no agent can be fully morally responsible for doing what he is fully determined
to do. However, when a dastardly deed is attributed with a wealth of detail to a
particular agent in D, and those same subjects are asked whether that agent is
then fully morally responsible, 72% report that in their view he is!

Nichols and Knobe consider various ways to account for this amazing divergence. In the end, they find it most plausible to think that some performance
error is responsible. Affect, they suggest, degrades intellectual performance in
general, whether the relevant competence be memory, perception, inference, etc.

Of course, that explanation will leave intuition affected as lightly as are perception, memory, and inference, unless some further relevant difference can be
specified.

In any case, there is an alternative explanation that will cast no affect-involving
doubt on the intuitions in play. This other possibility came to mind on reading
their paper and was soon confirmed in the article on moral responsibility in the
Stanford Encyclopedia of Philosophy, where we are told that at least two different
senses of 'moral responsibility' have emerged: the attributability sense, and the
accountability sense.

On the attributability view, to say that S is responsible for action A is to say
that A is attributable to S as his own doing, and, we are told in the article, as an
action that reveals something about S's character.

On the accountability view, to say that S is responsible for action A is to say
that S is properly *held* accountable or responsible for A, in such a way that various good (or bad) things may be visited upon S *for* doing A.

So, here again, quite possibly the striking divergence reported above is expli-
cable mainly if not entirely through verbal divergence.

Indeed, we may plausibly go beyond the explanation suggested in the
Stanford Encyclopedia, by suggesting that in common parlance 'accountability'
need *not* be tied to manifestation of character. Those attracted to 'agent causation,' including philosophers such as Thomas Reid and Roderick Chisholm,
would not make that linkage. So, there is a notion of attributability-responsibility
that is inherently incompatibilist in requiring only that the agent have caused
his action, free of antecedent determinants, *free even of determination by his or
her character*.

If so, we may then find different 'interpretations' at work in the verbal
disagreement between the affect-affected intuiters (who react to the specific
description of the dastardly deed) and the cold theoretical intuiters (who
respond to the abstract question of whether any agent can be responsible in D).
Of course, it remains to be seen why the one concept is more readily engaged

by the affect elicited with the specific case, and the other more readily by cold reasoning about the abstract issue. But pessimism about explaining this would seem premature.

Let us turn next to a further line of experiment-based objection against philosophical intuition, which appears in a recent paper by Stacey Swain, Joshua Alexander, and Jonathan M. Weinberg, as follows:

> We found that intuitions in response to…[Keith Lehrer's Truetemp Case] vary according to whether, and what, other thought experiments are considered first. Our results show that: (1) willingness to attribute knowledge in the Truetemp Case increases after being presented with a clear case of nonknowledge, and (2) willingness to attribute knowledge in the Truetemp Case decreases after being presented with a clear case of knowledge. We contend that this instability undermines the supposed evidential status of these intuitions. (Swain, Alexander, & Weinberg, in preparation)

Well, maybe, to *some* extent. But surely the effects of priming, framing, and other such contextual factors will affect the epistemic status of intuition in general, only in the sort of way that they affect the epistemic status of perceptual observation in general. One would think that the ways of preserving the epistemic importance of perception in the face of such effects on perceptual judgments would be analogously available for the preservation of the epistemic importance of intuition in the face of such effects on intuitive judgments. The upshot is that we have to be *careful* in how we use intuition, not that intuition is useless. It is of course helpful to be shown how intuition can go astray in unfavorable conditions, just as perception can go similarly astray. But the important question is untouched: Can intuition enjoy relative to philosophy an evidential status analogous to that enjoyed by perception relative to empirical science?

We turn, finally, to a recent line of attack on philosophical intuition, one also in line with the experimental philosophy movement.[5] According to a recent book by Michael Bishop and J. D. Trout, epistemology should look beyond its navel and adopt the more worthy project of developing prescriptions that will have some use in the real world. By contrast, the methods of "Standard Analytic Epistemology" (SAE) "are suited to the task of providing an account of the considered epistemic judgments of (mostly) well-off Westerners with Ph.D.'s in Philosophy" (Bishop & Trout, 2005).

Normative disciplines concerned with prescription and evaluation have a theoretical side and a more applied side. The latter we might call 'casuistry' *in a broad sense.* We are familiar with the casuistry of advice columnists, priests, parents, therapists, and friends, tailored to specific individual cases, and we also know the more general, policy-oriented casuistry of applied ethics, a large and thriving sub-discipline. Insofar as there is such a thing as applied epistemology, I suppose it is to be found largely, though not exclusively, in the similarly large and active field of critical reasoning.

It may be objected that even if intuition is defensible abstractly as a possible source of normative knowledge, its role in epistemic casuistry will be small by

238   The Future of Experimental Philosophy

comparison with our knowledge of the relevant scientific facts about our intellectual equipment and its social and physical setting, about its reliability, and about the reliability of various information-gathering methods.

That may or may not be so. I find it difficult to assess such size of role, especially since the prospects for epistemic casuistry are so unclear, and I mean epistemic casuistry *as a discipline*, with generally applicable rules. Of course, we know a lot about reliable methods, for example, about how to determine a huge variety of facts through the use of a corresponding variety of instruments. And we also know how to use library sources, which newspapers to trust, which statistical methods are reliable, et cetera. But there really is no discernible unified discipline there. Such casuistry would encompass all the manuals for all the various instruments and how to read all the various gauges, for one thing. And it would also include the variegated practical lore on how to tell what's what and on what basis: the lore of navigation, jungle guidance, farming tips, and so on and so forth. That is all of course extremely useful, but it is no part of the traditional problematic of epistemology. Nor is there any reason to replace either of epistemic casuistry or traditional epistemology with the other. Each has its own time and place.

Traditional epistemology enjoys the coherence provided by its unified set of central questions concerning the nature, conditions, and extent of knowledge and justification. Some may regard such questions with distaste. But philistinism is not to be feared by a discipline that has attracted unexcelled minds over the course of millennia, and in cultures as diverse as those of Buddhist India and classical Greece, and many others.

In any case, even if the role of intuition in epistemic casuistry is small, I fail to see an objection here. Our question has been whether intuition can be understood clearly and defended adequately as a source of foundational a priori justification. Once that is accomplished, our task is completed, especially if intuition's role in epistemic casuistry is *indispensable*, no matter how large or small.

Nevertheless, Bishop and Trout press their case against the theoretical side of SAE, as follows:

> As we have…argued, when it comes to epistemic judgments, the theories of SAE define what we "*do* do" not what we "*must* or *ought* to do." They…merely tell us how we *do* make epistemic judgments (and by "we," we mean the tiny fraction of the world's population who has studied SAE)….
>
> The proponent of SAE is replacing normative questions about how to evaluate reason and belief with descriptive questions about how proponents of SAE evaluate reason and belief. (Bishop & Trout, 2005, p. 110)

But this misconstrues the way intuition is supposed to function in epistemology and in philosophy more generally, which is by analogy with the way observation is supposed to function in empirical science.

Empirical theories are required to accord well enough with the deliverances of scientific observation. Does empirical inquiry merely tell us how we *do* make empirical observations? (And by 'we' I mean only the tiny fraction of the world's population who has studied empirical science.) Is the proponent of empirical science replacing questions about the tides, the circulation of the blood, the movements of the planets, and so on, with questions about how proponents of empirical science make certain observations?

That implied parody is supposed to bring out the misconstrual that I find in Bishop and Trout. Intuitions are supposed to function like observations. The data for empirical science include not *just* claims *about* the observations of some few specialists. The set of empirical data includes also claims about the subject matter of the specialists' fields of study, about truths concerning the natural phenomena under study. Similarly, philosophical data would include not *just* claims *about* the intuitions shared by some few specialists. Also prominently included would be claims about the subject matter of the philosophers' fields of study, including evaluative or normative truths of epistemology, for example.

Perhaps there is some crucial difference between natural phenomena and evaluative phenomena that rules out any such analogy. Perhaps there are no normative truths, for example, by contrast with the evident availability of empirical truths. But if this is the real issue, then we need to consider whether in principle there could or could not be the truths that there seem intuitively, commonsensically, to be. And how could we possibly approach such a question except philosophically, through the sort of reflection plus dialectic that depends crucially on philosophical intuition?

Even if it turns out that there *is* such a fundamental semantic divergence between empirical and normative subject matter, finally, a relevant analogy between observation and intuition might *still* survive such semantic divergence. This too would need to be debated philosophically. Progress on such issues of metaphilosophy depends thus on progress *within* philosophy.

NOTES

1. This essay was originally a paper presented in the "Experimental Philosophy" symposium at the 2006 Pacific Division meetings of the APA.

2. Of course, even if just doing interdisciplinary work with scientists is not surprisingly distinctive or novel, it is still a time-honored tradition, which contemporary experimental philosophy might admirably extend.

3. I argue for this approach more fully in earlier papers (Beyer & Burri, 2007; DePaul & Ramsey, 1998; Greenough & Lynch, 2006). And I return to it in Sosa (2007).

4. "Intuitions and Individual Differences: the Knobe Effect Revisited," available at http://www.rci.rutgers.edu/~stich/Experimental_Philosophy_Seminar/experimental_philosophy_seminar_readings.htm.

5. Of course, not every advocate of 'experimental philosophy' would endorse everything in the loose conglomerate that falls under that flexible title. Furthermore, there is a recent strain of experimental philosophy with a more positive view of intuitions. Proponents of this strain use experimental evidence to reach a better understanding of those intuitions and of their underlying competence(s). Compare, for examples, the following: Knobe, forthcoming; Nahmias, Morris, Nadelhoffer, & Turner, forthcoming; Nichols, 2002 (my thanks here to Joshua Knobe).

REFERENCES

Beyer, C., & Burri, A. (2007). Intuitions: Their nature and epistemic efficacy. *Grazer Philosophische Studien. Philosophical Knowledge—Its Possibility and Scope* [Special issue].

Bishop, M., & Murphy, D. (eds.) (2007). A defense of intuitions. In *Stich and his critics*. Oxford: Blackwell Publishers. Available at http://homepage.mac.com/ernestsosa/Menu2.html.

Bishop, M. A., & Trout, J. D. (2005). *Epistemology and the psychology of human judgment* (p. 107). New York: Oxford University Press.

DePaul, M., & Ramsey, W. (eds.) (1998). Minimal intuition. In *Rethinking intuition*. New Jersey: Rowman & Littlefield.

Greenough, P., & Lynch, M. (eds.) (2006). Intuitions and truth. In *Truth and realism*. New York: Oxford University Press.

Knobe, J. (Forthcoming). The concept of intentional action: A case study in the uses of folk psychology. *Philosophical Studies*.

Nahmias, E., Morris, S., Nadelhoffer, T., & Turner, J. (Forthcoming). Is incompatibilism intuitive? *Philosophy and Phenomenological Research*.

Nichols, S. (2002). Norms with feeling: Towards a psychological account of moral judgment. *Cognition, 84*, 221–236.

Nichols, S., & Knobe, J. 2007. Moral responsibility and determinism: The cognitive science of folk intuitions. *Noûs*.

Sosa, E. (2007). *A virtue epistemology: Apt belief and reflective knowledge*, Vol. 1. New York: Oxford University Press.

Swain, S., Alexander, J., & Weinberg, J. M. The instability of philosophical intuitions: Running hot and cold on Truetemp. (In preparation). Available at http://www.indiana.edu/~eel/.

Index

241